*"Here I am! I stand at the door and knock. If anyone hears
My voice and opens the door, I will come in and eat with him,
and he with Me."* —REVELATION 3:20

Mississippi
Church Suppers

Great American Publishers
www.GreatAmericanPublishers.com
TOLL-FREE 1-888-854-5954

Great American Publishers

171 Lone Pine Church Road • Lena, MS 39094
TOLL-FREE 1-888-854-5954 • www.GreatAmericanPublishers.com

ISBN 978-1-934817-24-7

First Edition

Bible verses referenced throughout the book are from the New International Version (NIV) Bible.

Every effort has been made to ensure the accuracy of the information provided in this book.
However, dates, times, and locations are subject to change.
Please call or visit websites for up-to-date information before traveling.

To purchase books in quantity for corporate use, incentives, or fundraising,
please call Great American Publishers at 888-854-5954.

Contents

God's Plan of Salvation 7

Why Should I Attend Church? 8

Preface 10

Appetizers 13

Soups & Salads 45

Vegetables & Side Dishes 85

Main Dishes 119

Desserts & Sweets 167

Catalog of Churches 235

Index of Churches 254

Index of Recipes 264

Your Favorite Recipes 279

Jesus said to them, "I am the way, the truth, and the life. No one comes to the Father except through Me." —JOHN 14:6

God's Plan of Salvation

God's plan of salvation is as easy as A-B-C.

ADMIT you are a sinner.

Admit that you are a sinner, and in need of salvation from sin. All persons need salvation. Each of us has a problem the Bible calls sin. Sin is a refusal to acknowledge God's authority over our lives.

> *For all have sinned, and fall short of the glory of God.* —ROMANS 3:23

> *For the wages of sin is death.* —ROMANS 6:23

BELIEVE that Jesus is God's Son.

Believe that Jesus Christ is the Son of God and that He is the only way to obtain salvation...to get to heaven. Although we have done nothing to deserve His love and salvation, God wants to save us. When our Lord Jesus Christ died on the Cross, He paid the penalty for all our sins and bridged the gap from God to man.

> *For God so loved the world, that he gave his one and only Son, that whoever believes in him shall not perish, but have eternal life.* —JOHN 3:16

> *Jesus answered, I am the way and the truth and the life. No one comes to the Father except through me.* — JOHN 14:6

This does not mean believing merely that Jesus was a good man, one of the great prophets. It means believing that "Christ Jesus who died—more than that, who was raised to life—is at the right hand of God and is also interceding for us." (Romans 8:34) This faith is the second essential step anyone must take in order to be saved.

CONFESS your sins and ask Jesus into your heart.

Confess your sins to God. Confess your faith in Jesus Christ as Savior and Lord.

> *If we confess our sins, he is faithful and just and will forgive us our sins and purify us from all unrighteousness.* —1 JOHN 1:9

> *If you confess with your mouth, 'Jesus is Lord,' and believe in your heart that God raised him from the dead, you will be saved. For it is with your heart that you believe and are justified, and it is with your mouth that you confess and are saved.* —ROMANS 10:9-10

Will you ask Jesus into your heart today? Are you ready? Say this prayer from your heart and you will be saved:

Dear God: I realize that I'm a sinner and I can't save myself. I believe you sent your Son Jesus to die on the cross to take the penalty of my sins. I ask Jesus now to come into my life and save my soul, and guide and direct my life from this point on as my Lord. In Jesus' name I pray, Amen.

Why Should I Attend Church?

Going to Church Builds our Spiritual Strength

*"Finally, be strong in the Lord and in his mighty power. Put on the full armor of God so that you can take your stand against the devil's schemes. For our struggle is not against flesh and blood but against the rulers, against the authorities, against the powers of this dark world and against the spiritual forces of evil in the heavenly realms." —*Ephesians 6:10-11

Consequently, faith comes from hearing the message, and the message is heard through the word of Christ. —Romans 10:17

Believers are the Body of Christ

The body is the unit, though it is made up of many parts; and though all its parts are many, they form one body, so it is with Christ. —1 Corinthians 12:12

God's Word says Go to Church

Let us not give up meeting together, as some are in the habit of doing, but let us encourage one another—and all the more as you see the Day approaching. —Hebrews 10:25

Let the word of Christ dwell in you richly as you teach and admonish one another with all wisdom, and as you sing psalms, hymns and spiritual songs with gratitude in your hearts to God. —Colossians 3:16

God is There

For where two or three come together in my name, there I am with them. —Matthew 18:20

Church Provides Fellowship with Other Christians

But if we walk in the light, as He is in the light, we have fellowship with one another, and the blood of Jesus, His Son, purifies us of all sin. —1 John 1:7

Be devoted to one another in brotherly love. Honor one another above yourselves. —Romans 12:10

As iron sharpens iron, so one man sharpens another. —Proverbs 27:27

Christ Loves the Church

Husbands, love your wives, just as Christ loved the church and gave himself up for her to make her holy, cleansing her with the washing of the word, and to present her to Himself as a radiant church, without stain or wrinkly or any other blemish but holy and blameless. —Ephesians 5:26

We Gain Spiritual Strength in Prayer

Again, I tell you that if two of you on earth agree about anything you ask for, it will be done for you by my Father in heaven. For where two or three come together in My name, there I am with them. —Matthew 18:19-20

A good thing to remember:
Sheep die individually but live as a flock, fed and protected by a shepherd.

Preface

Welcome to *Mississippi Church Suppers* where churches of all sizes have shared their favorite recipes creating what I like to call "The Ultimate Church Cookbook." These are cherished family recipes made "by hand" and "by love" and handed down through generations of great cooks. It is an honor to share them in this cookbook.

In addition to sharing recipes, these Mississippi Baptist Churches have shared their heart. As you read through the cookbook, you will find a profile for each church letting you know what makes that church special. It is entertaining and inspiring to read about each unique place of worship to our awesome God.

Do you remember the first time you went to church? Maybe you felt awe as you walked up the steps and through beautiful double doors for the first time. Was there a pulpit raised above the sanctuary? Did your church have a special section for the choir? At our church, the choir loft was filled with normal everyday people, but when I heard them sing, it made me think of angels in heaven singing praises to our God.

As a child, my least favorite part of church was sitting still. Mother made sure I sat very still or I could expect to endure a little pinch on the leg to make sure I was behaving. As the pastor began to preach, I would sometimes nod off for a few seconds because I was not used to sitting still for a full hour. I can remember being jerked awake when the pastor decided to get a little louder or slap his hand down on the pulpit for emphasis. I still think he did that when he would see the eyes of the members growing heavy and that he would have a secret chuckle all to himself.

I was blessed because I was raised in a family that believed in going to church every Sunday. I loved that special feeling I had seeing my Father dressed in his suits and ties and not the normal work clothes he wore other days. He was a handsome man beside my Mother dressed in what she called her Sunday Best—high heels with her hair just so (never a hair out of place when Mrs. Virginia went to church).

As the youngest of three children, it was my duty to get all the dirt and grime from my knees so I would not be an embarrassment to the family. This was not always so easy after six days of doing what kids in my day enjoyed...playing outdoors and seeing just how far we could get away from the house before Mother called us back. But, come Sunday, there I would be in a dress sewn by my Mother wearing little white socks and my black "Sunday" shoes.

When you are young, it is so easy to appreciate what God made. My favorite times of day have always been the beginning and the end. I was fascinated with the sunrise as a child and still enjoy sunrises today. It's that special quiet time at the beginning of the day when you can step outside and hear the rest of the world wake up...the chirping of the birds...the smells of breakfast cooking...the noise of people going to work. These days, this is my favorite time of day to talk to God. Reading the Bible is my first priority, then letting Him know how much I am thankful for the prayers he answers and beginning the first of many prayers that will be sent up throughout the day.

Then comes sunsets...How mighty is our God! There is no doubt how mighty when you watch the light display He produces for us each and every day. It reminds me of Genesis 1:16:

> And God made two great lights. The greater light to rule the day and the lesser light to rule the night, he made the stars also.

It's so relaxing to grab a blanket and go sit on a hill to watch the stars. And you might think I would be watching for God's wonders to go to sleep. That is not the case at all. This is when tree frogs begin their night songs along with the crickets issuing their calls to each other, the hooting of owls as they begin their hunting trips in the night. Even watching bats on their nightly journeys reminds me that God is always there for us no matter the time or place.

Do you remember the first Bible verse you learned? I do. It was John 3:16:

> For God so loved the word that he gave his only begotten son that whosoever believed in him should not perish but have everlasting life.

It seems like such a long time ago (probably because it was!). Now, the verse that carries me along life's highway is Philippians 4:13:

> I can do all things through Christ which strengthens me.

And because life has brought its share of trouble—as I'm sure it has for you, also—I always have 2 Corinthians 1: 3-4 to bring me peace:

> Praise be to the God and Father of our Lord Jesus Christ, the Father of compassion and the God of all comfort, who comforts us in all our troubles, so that we can comfort those in any trouble with the comfort we ourselves have received from God.

One thing I can tell you for certain is I am thankful for the life God has given me. He is the one responsible for me and the one true friend all of us can count on. He is always near and ready to listen when you need a friend to confide in. What joy it is to know we speak to the Ultimate One that will lead, guide and direct us on the path we need to take. We need only to listen to Him. Turn around in your mind and look behind you. Do you see one set of footprints or two in the sands of your life? How many steps do you see where God is walking beside you? Are there other times when he is the one carrying you through the hard times, the sad times and times you may have thought life was just not worth it anymore? I pray that it be so for you.

To say I am thankful is such a small thing when there is so much in this world for which to be thankful. I am thankful for this book to come together and my heartfelt appreciation goes to the people of the churches in the book. Each of them spent their time sharing the recipes and stories that make this book special. This gratitude especially includes my home church—Robinhood Baptist Church (Brandon).

I appreciate, too, the people of Great American Publishers who helped make this book a reality. Roger and Sheila Simmons (Mt. Pisgah Baptist Church; Brandon) deserve the best that God can give them for inspiring this book and helping to ensure it gets in the hands of people who need it. Roger and Sheila allow us and encourage us to have a prayer meeting every morning at the beginning of our work day. (Do you need a prayer warrior? We are here. Call us toll-free 888.854.5954 and we will add YOUR prayer request to our daily prayer time.) Brooke Craig is our rock and our leader, and other people have helped along the way too: Christy Kent Campbell, Cyndi Clark, Jayme Coley, Pam Edwards, Amber Feiock, Gennell Goodman, Krista Griffin, Tory Hackett, Pam Larson, Penny Renfroe, Diane Rothery, Sheree Smith, and Nichole Stewart. Thank you all for your generous spirit in helping support his book.

I pray for YOU as I write this. I pray that you will enjoy this special cookbook and accept it in the spirit it was created. *Mississippi Church Suppers* cookbook was created to the Glory of God for your enjoyment. May this book work for Him.

God Bless You,

Anita Musgrove

Project Manager for *Mississippi Church Suppers*

I am the Alpha and the Omega, the First and the Last, the Beginning and the End.
—REVELATION 22:13

Appetizers

"I am the gate; whoever enters through me will be saved. He will come in and go out, and find pasture." —JOHN 10:9

Mother's Hot Dip

Golden Central Baptist Church, Golden ✝ Cherrye Greene

1 large onion, peeled and quartered
8 frozen jalapeño peppers (or 2 from a jar)
1 teaspoon salt
1 teaspoon black pepper

1 teaspoon red pepper
¼ teaspoon oregano
½ teaspoon Worcestershire sauce
2 (14-ounce) cans whole tomatoes

Put all ingredients in blender. Blend 1 minute. Pour into a saucepan and cook over low to medium heat for 20 minutes. Refrigerate about 1 hour before serving with plain tortilla chips.

Golden Central Baptist Church
Golden

13 Red Bay Road
Golden, MS 38847
662-454-7144
www.facebook.com/Central-Baptist-Church

Golden Central Baptist Church is a wonderful place to meet and worship our Lord and Savior Jesus Christ thru beautiful music and the preaching of God's Word. "There's a sweet, sweet Spirit in this place." Here at Golden Central, it is our desire to reach out to our community in every way. Most importantly, we strive to reach them with the Gospel. However, not only do we help them spiritually, but we also try to meet their physical needs, such as providing food and clothes to the families who are struggling. We feel that if we show the community we care about them, it's easier to reach them with the Gospel.

Our mission at Golden Central: "Bring people to Jesus Christ; develop them to Christ-like maturity; equip them for ministry; glorify the name of God."

Mexican Fiesta Dip

First Baptist Church, Brookhaven † *Micah Allen*

3 to 4 Roma tomatoes, chopped
1 bunch green onions, chopped
2 avocados, peeled, pitted and diced
1 bundle cilantro, chopped
2 (4.25-ounce) cans chopped olives
2 (4-ounce) cans chopped green chiles
1 (8-ounce) bottle Wishbone Italian dressing
1 (8-ounce) taco blend shredded cheese

Mix all together and refrigerate. Serve with tortilla chips.

Mexican Dip

Auburn Baptist Church, Tupelo † *Betty Capon*

1 pound ground beef, browned
1 cup cooked rice
1 (16-ounce) package Velveeta cheese
1 (10-ounce) can Rotel tomatoes
1 (10.25-ounce) can tomato soup
1 (1.25-ounce) package taco seasoning

Mix all ingredients together in saucepan over medium heat until smooth. Serve warm with tortilla chips.

Black Bean Dip

Star Baptist Church, Star

1 red onion, chopped
2 tablespoons chopped jalapeños
2 (10-ounce) cans Rotel tomatoes
2 (11-ounce) cans shoepeg corn, drained

2 (15-ounce) cans black beans, drained
½ (16-ounce) bottle zesty Italian salad dressing
2 tablespoons lemon juice

Mix all ingredients together. Refrigerate overnight so all flavors will marry. Serve with Tostitos Scoops.

Corn Dip

Shady Grove Baptist Church, Lucedale ✝ Wanda Watson

2 (15-ounce) cans whole-kernel corn, drained
1 (11-ounce) can white shoepeg corn
1 (11-ounce) can Mexicorn, drained
1 (4-ounce) can diced green chiles, drained
5 green onions, chopped
1 (8-ounce) carton sour cream
1 jalapeño pepper, chopped fine (more or less to your taste)
¾ cup mayonnaise (I use Hellmann's)
2½ cups shredded Cheddar cheese
Tony Chachere's Creole Seasoning, to add a little zing (optional)

Combine all ingredients in a medium bowl; mix well. Cover and store in refrigerator until ready to serve. I recommend serving with Fritos Scoops corn chips, which taste amazing with this dip, but it can also be served with tortilla chips. (Or a spoon.)

A Lotta Guacamole

First Baptist Church of Greenville ✝ Lila Lee McRight

12 avocados
6 lemons
12 tomatoes
6 bunches green onions
1 (8-ounce) bottle Wishbone Italian dressing
6 (4-ounce) cans chopped green chiles
Salt to taste
Pepper to taste
Tabasco to taste
Garlic powder to taste

Peel, pit and dice avocados into a large bowl. Juice lemons and pour over avocados to slow browning. Chop tomatoes and green onions; add to bowl. Add remaining ingredients and mix well. Serve with corn chips.

Buffalo Chicken Dip

Farmington Baptist Church, Corinth

2 (10-ounce) cans chicken, drained
1 (8-ounce) package cream cheese, softened
2 cups shredded sharp Cheddar cheese
½ cup hot sauce
1 cup ranch dressing

Mix all ingredients together and bake 30 minutes at 350°. Serve hot with corn chips.

Buffalo Chicken Dip

Journey Baptist Church, Olive Branch

4 boneless, skinless chicken breasts (about 2 pounds)
1 (12-ounce) bottle Frank's hot sauce (I use mild)
2 (8-ounce) packages cream cheese, softened
1 (16-ounce) bottle ranch dressing
½ cup chopped celery
8 ounces shredded Monterey Jack or sharp Cheddar cheese

Boil, drain and shred chicken (you don't want any remaining chunks). Preheat oven to 350°. In a 9x13-inch baking pan, combine shredded chicken and entire bottle of hot sauce. Spread to an even layer. In large saucepan over medium heat, combine cream cheese and bottle of ranch dressing. Stir until the cheese melts and the mixture is smooth and hot. Pour over chicken and sprinkle with celery. Bake uncovered for 20 minutes. Sprinkle cheese on top and bake 15 to 20 minutes more, until bubbly (do not let the cheese brown, or it will be hard). Let this sit about 10 minutes before serving with Tostitos Scoops.

Chicken Rotel Dip

Toxish Baptist Church, Pontotoc

3 to 4 chicken breasts, boiled and cut into bite-size pieces
1 (10.25-ounce) can cream of chicken soup
1 (8-ounce) carton sour cream
1 (8-ounce) package cream cheese, cubed
1 (10-ounce) can Rotel tomatoes
1 (4-ounce) can sliced mushrooms (optional)

Mix all ingredients and cook over low heat until cream cheese is melted. Serve warm with tortilla chips or Fritos Scoops.

Toxish Baptist Church

Pontotoc

1841 Toxish Road
Pontotoc, MS 38863
662-489-5839

Paul Childress, Pastor

Toxish Baptist Church is located on the original Natchez Trace. The name is said to have derived from a Chickasaw Indian word spelled E TOK SHISH, and translated "root of a tree." The name has also been associated with the word ISH TO KA KA, an Indian word meaning "where greatness abides." Toxish is one of the few places in our state that was developed as a result of British control from the end of the French and Indian War to the close of the Revolutionary War. In 1837, Toxish Baptist Church was organized by Dr. James A. Ware. The church has been housed in four buildings—from a primitive log structure to today's modern brick building. It is the desire of the people who make up Toxish Baptist Church to reach their community for Christ and for the glory of God until His return.

Chicken Dip

Woodland Baptist Church, Columbus

2 (8-ounce) packages cream cheese, softened
1 (12.5-ounce) can chunk chicken
1 (1-ounce) packet dry ranch dressing mix

Combine all ingredients and mix well. Serve with chicken crackers.

Slow Cookery Chili Cheese

Mount Helm Baptist Church, Jackson

1 pound ground beef
1 pound American cheese, cubed
1 (10-ounce) can Rotel tomatoes

½ teaspoon chili powder
2 teaspoons Worcestershire sauce
Corn chips or tortilla chips

Brown ground beef and drain grease. Put beef and remaining ingredients, except chips, in slow cooker. Stir well, cover and cook on high for 1 hour, stirring until cheese is fully melted. Serve immediately or turn to low for serving later. Serve with tortilla or corn chips.

LBJ Dip

Palestine Baptist Church, Nettleton ✝ Pam Williams

1 pound hot ground pork sausage
1 (15-ounce) can Hormel chili without beans

1 (16-ounce) box Velveeta cheese, cubed
Tortilla chips or corn chips for dipping

Cook sausage; drain well and crumble into small pieces. In a microwave-safe dish, mix sausage, chili and cheese. Microwave 2 minutes at a time, stirring each time, until cheese is melted. (If you don't stir frequently, cheese will burn.) Serve hot with tortilla chips or corn chips.

Baked Cheese Dip

Tate Baptist Church, Corinth † *Vicki Shirley*

½ cup mayonnaise
1 (8-ounce) package cream cheese, softened
1 cup shredded Swiss cheese

1 cup shredded mozzarella cheese
10 pieces bacon, cooked and crumbled
Green onions or parsley to taste
1 sleeve Ritz crackers, crumbled

Mix mayonnaise and cream cheese. Add next 4 ingredients and mix well. Pour into a small baking dish and top with crumbled crackers. Bake at 350° for 15 minutes. Serve warm.

Tate Baptist Church

Corinth

1201 North Harper Road
Corinth, MS 38834
662-286-2935

Mickey Trammel, Pastor

At Tate Baptist Church, our mission is to extend the Gospel of Jesus Christ and the love of God to the lost and hurting people of our community. We would like to be viewed by our community as a living, uplifting, and forgiving congregation of believers in Christ, which readily accept everyone.

Starting in 1907 as a mission church, in 1986, having outgrown the building and space located on Tate Street, members voted to relocate to Harper Road. The church moved there in 1992; the name was changed to Tate Baptist Church. In July 2007, the church held a ground-breaking ceremony for a new ministry center and celebrated Tate Baptists' 100th Anniversary.

God continues to grow Tate Baptist Church through various ministries: worship services, Sunday School, prayer services, graded choirs, food bank ministry, and mission groups. The members are committed to serving Him and proclaiming the good news of Jesus Christ.

Boucan Cheese Dip

Magnolia Baptist Church, Hattiesburg ✝ *Vicki Shoemake*

1 (8-ounce) package cream cheese, softened
1 cup shredded sharp Cheddar cheese
½ cup mayonnaise

2 green onions, chopped
6 Ritz Crackers, crushed
8 slices bacon, cooked and crumbled
½ cup Captain Rodney Boucan Glaze

Mix cream cheese, Cheddar cheese, mayonnaise and onions. Place in greased shallow dish. Top with crackers and bake at 350° for 15 minutes. Remove from oven and top with bacon and glaze.

Onion Dip

Pelahatchie Baptist Church, Pelahatchie ✝ *Jewel Carter*

1 (12-ounce) bag frozen chopped onions, thawed
3 (8-ounce) packages cream cheese, softened
2 cups grated Parmesan cheese
½ cup mayonnaise

Squeeze water from onions. Combine cream cheese, Parmesan, mayonnaise and onions in a heat-proof dish. Bake about 15 minutes at 350°.

Pink Dip

Zion Hill Baptist Church, Wesson ✝ *Jacque McCormick*

1 cup mayonnaise
1 cup sour cream
1 cup salsa

1 (1-ounce) package dry Knorr's Vegetable Soup mix

Mix together and chill. Serve with corn chips for dipping.

Spinach Dip

Iuka Baptist Church

1 (10-ounce) package frozen spinach, thawed
1½ cups sour cream
1 (1-ounce) package dry vegetable soup mix (Lipton's)
1 cup mayonnaise
1 cup chopped water chestnuts
3 green onions, chopped
1 loaf Hawaiian bread

Squeeze excess water out of spinach; mix with remaining ingredients. Chill 2 hours. Serve in the center of a hollowed loaf of Hawaiian bread (using bread pieces as dippers) or with crackers.

Iuka Baptist Church

105 West Eastport Street
Iuka, MS 38852
662-423-5246
www.iukabaptist.com

Johnny Hancock, Pastor

The goal of Iuka Baptist Church is to introduce people to Jesus Christ. The Christian faith is all about a personal relationship with Christ. It is not knowing about God. It is about knowing God. We want to help you get to know God and grow in your relationship with Him. Our church has ministries available for every person in the family. Our ministry focus for every age group is small group ministry through our Sunday School. We believe these small groups will connect you with people of your same age and interest. Through these groups you can get to know people personally, develop friendships that can last forever, and learn biblical truths along the way.

Polynesian Dip

Sunrise Baptist Church, Carthage ✝ *Ava Malone*

1 whole fresh pineapple
2 (8-ounce) packages cream cheese, softened
1 (8-ounce) can crushed pineapple, drained
½ cup chopped bell pepper

2 tablespoons finely chopped green onions
2 teaspoons seasoned salt
1 cup chopped pecans
3 tablespoons mayonnaise

Use a knife and slice whole pineapple in half, top to bottom. Remove meat from pineapple leaving outside intact to use as a serving bowl. Chop pineapple meat and combine with remaining ingredients. Fill pineapple with mixture.

Fruit Dip

Bethel Baptist Church, Heidelburg

1 (7-ounce) jar marshmallow crème
1 (8-ounce) package cream cheese, softened

1 teaspoon grated orange rind
1 tablespoon orange juice (or 2 teaspoons orange flavoring)

Mix all ingredients together. Chill at least 4 hours. Use as a dip for various fresh fruits.

(Better make 2 batches; this is a popular dish.)

Shrimp Dip

Bethel Missionary Baptist Church, Seminary † *Verna Mae Rainey*

2 (3-ounce) packages cream cheese, softened
4 teaspoons lemon juice
1½ cups diced cooked shrimp

1 (16-ounce) carton sour cream (2 cups)
2 (1-ounce) packages dry Italian salad dressing mix

Mix all ingredients well. Chill 1 to 2 hours. Serve with chips or crackers.

Shrimp Dip

Ashland Baptist Church † *Stacey Snyder*

1 (4.25-ounce) can shrimp
2 pints sour cream
2 (1-ounce) envelopes dry ranch dressing mix
2 bunches green onions, chopped

Wash and drain shrimp. Mix all ingredients and chill.

Shrimp Dip

Mount Helm Baptist Church, Jackson

¼ cup milk
1 (8-ounce) package cream cheese, softened
1 (4.25-ounce) can deveined shrimp, rinsed, drained and chopped
1 teaspoon lemon juice

1 teaspoon Worcestershire sauce
½ teaspoon garlic salt
1 tablespoon mayonnaise (or Miracle Whip)
1 (5-ounce) jar Kraft Old English cheese spread

Blend milk gradually into cream cheese. Stir in shrimp, lemon juice, Worcestershire sauce, garlic salt, mayonnaise and cheese spread. Cover and refrigerate at least 1 hour. Serve with potato chips and assorted crackers.

Smoked Oyster Dip

Carmel Baptist Church, Monticello ✝ *Mattie Wilson*

1 (8-ounce) package cream cheese, softened
1½ cups mayonnaise
1 teaspoon horseradish
1 tablespoon lemon juice
¼ teaspoon hot sauce
1 (3.75-ounce) can smoked oysters, chopped
1 (4.25-ounce) can chopped black olives

Combine cream cheese, mayonnaise and horseradish well. Add lemon juice and hot sauce; mix well. Stir in chopped oysters and olives. Refrigerate several hours to blend flavors. Remove from refrigerator about 1 hour before serving with crackers. Good and rich.

Hot Seafood Dip

Unity Baptist Church, McHenry

3 (8-ounce) packages cream cheese, softened
6 tablespoons milk
2 tablespoons Worcestershire sauce
1 (6-ounce) can crabmeat

Preheat oven to 350°. Mix all ingredients. Bake 15 minutes. Serve with chips or crackers.

Crab Dip

First Baptist Church, Wiggins

1 (8-ounce) package cream cheese, softened
¼ cup chopped onion
1 garlic clove, minced
1 (6-ounce) can crabmeat
1 teaspoon lemon juice
1 tablespoon milk
½ bell pepper, finely chopped
1 small tomato, chopped

Combine cream cheese, onion, garlic, crabmeat, lemon juice and milk. Mix well and spread in a serving dish. Top with bell pepper and tomato.

First Baptist Church

Wiggins

219 Second Street North
Wiggins, MS 39577
601-928-5226
www.fbcwiggins.org

First Baptist Church of Wiggins was founded in 1896 as Wiggins Baptist Church. Nestled in rural Stone County, First Baptist Church continues to serve the community as a central place of fellowship and worship. Each Sunday, First Baptist Church offers a traditional and contemporary worship service, along with Sunday School classes for all ages. During the week, one can find many opportunities to participate in adult, youth, and children's programs, including Awana, Music and Missions for children, Youth Bible Study, Prayer Meeting, and numerous music programs. All are welcome to come join First Baptist Church of Wiggins in "Reaching Up, Reaching Out, and Reaching In."

Crab Delights

Walnut Grove Baptist Church, Fulton

1 (6-ounce) can crabmeat
1 small onion, chopped
1 cup mayonnaise
1 cup shredded Cheddar cheese
½ teaspoon salt
1 teaspoon curry powder
Sourdough bread, ¼-inch slices

Combine all ingredients, except bread; mix well. Spread on bread slices. Broil until crab mixture is golden and bubbly, being careful not to burn.

Crab Roll Ups

Parkway Baptist Church, Clinton ✝ *Katherine Webster*

¼ cup fat-free mayonnaise
Salt and pepper to taste
3 green onions, chopped
½ cup shredded low-fat
   Swiss Cheese
½ (4-ounce) can chopped
   green chiles, drained
1 cup white crabmeat
6 medium flour tortillas

Combine mayonnaise, salt, pepper, green onions, Swiss cheese and chiles together in a bowl. Fold in crabmeat. Soften tortillas in microwave, covered with a wet paper towel, for 30 seconds. Place filling on one end of tortilla and roll up jellyroll style. Place rolled tortillas, seam side down, in microwave-safe dish and microwave 1 minute. Cut each tortilla into 5 pieces. Serve warm. Makes 30 roll ups.

Mexican Pinwheels

Bethel Baptist Church, Heidelburg

2 (8-ounce) packages cream cheese, softened
1 (4-ounce) can chopped black olives (optional)
1 bunch green onions, chopped
Garlic salt and black pepper to taste
8 to 10 small flour tortillas
1 (15-ounce) container salsa

Mix cream cheese, black olives, green onions and seasonings together. Spread over tortillas and roll up. Place in a container and refrigerate overnight. Before serving, slice tortillas into pinwheels. Serve with salsa for dipping

Chicken Ranch Pinwheel

White Hill Missionary Baptist Church, Tupelo

1 (16-ounce) package large flour tortillas
Shredded lettuce
2 tomatoes, diced
Ranch dressing
1 (22-ounce) package precooked fajita grilled chicken
1 (6-ounce) package cooked hickory bacon
1 (8-ounce) package shredded pepper jack cheese
½ cup butter

For each wrap, lay a tortilla flat. Top with lettuce and tomatoes; pour ranch dressing to taste over tomatoes. Evenly spread chicken over top then top with 2 strips cooked bacon and desired amount of cheese. Firmly wrap tortilla tight (stick a toothpick through to hold together if needed). Repeat until you run out of ingredients. Melt butter in a large skillet; working in batches, heat wraps in skillet until evenly brown. Take the wraps out and evenly slice in half at an angle. Place them on a tray and your appetizer is complete.

Redneck Hors d'oeuvres

Robinhood Baptist Church ✝ *Anita Musgrove*

1 (16-ounce) package sliced ham (rectangle-cut)
1 (8-ounce) package cream cheese, softened
Pinch of salt
1 (16-ounce) jar whole sweet pickles
3 tablespoons mayonnaise

Separate ham slices with a paper towel between each to remove moisture. Mix cream cheese with pinch of salt, 2 tablespoons pickle juice (from jar) and mayonnaise. When ham is dry and working 1 slice at a time, lay ham on cutting board. Spread cream cheese mixture (to taste) on one side lay a whole sweet pickle on the end, make sure pickle goes from one side to the other. Roll up and lay, seam side down, on plate. Repeat until you run out of an ingredient. Refrigerate rolls for at least 1 hour or until just before you are ready to serve. When ready to serve, slice about ¼ inch thick and place on a serving tray.

Pineapple Cheese Ball

Golden Central Baptist Church, Golden ✝ *Sondra Bullen*

2 (8-ounce) packages cream cheese, softened
2 tablespoons finely diced bell pepper
2 tablespoons finely diced onion
1 cup drained crushed pineapple
1 teaspoon seasoning salt
2 cups finely chopped pecans, divided

Combine all ingredients, except 1 cup pecans. Form into ball and roll in remaining pecans. Chill before serving.

Cheese Ball

First Baptist Byhalia

1 (8-ounce) package cream cheese, softened
1 (5-ounce) jar Old English cheese spread
½ cup mayonnaise
1 teaspoon Worcestershire sauce
⅓ cup grated Parmesan cheese
½ (3-ounce) jar bacon bits
⅓ cup chopped green onions
Garlic salt to taste
½ cup chopped pecans

Combine all ingredients, except chopped pecans. Cover and refrigerate 2 to 4 hours, until firm. Roll into ball. Spread pecans on wax paper and roll cheese ball in nuts until covered. Wrap in plastic wrap and place back in fridge until ready to serve. Serve with crackers.

First Baptist Byhalia

Byhalia

2555 Church Street
Byhalia, MS 38611
662-838-2250
www.facebook.com/firstbaptistbyhalia

Stuart Swicegood, Pastor

First Baptist Church of Byhalia is an exciting family of faith in northwest Mississippi that exists to worship our Lord and bring Him glory by making disciples. Come join us as we journey together as disciples seeking to KNOW God more, to CONNECT with His people, to GROW in our Christlikeness, and to PROMOTE His Gospel truth to the community and beyond.

Cheese Ball

Temple Baptist Church, Hattiesburg † *Deborah Engle*

2 (8-ounce) packages cream cheese,
   softened
1 tablespoon lemon juice
2 cups shredded sharp Cheddar cheese
1 tablespoon Worcestershire sauce
2 tablespoons chopped green onion
Dash cayenne pepper
2 tablespoons chopped pimento
Chopped pecans

Combine all ingredients, except pecans. Form into ball, wrap in plastic wrap and refrigerate at least 2 hours. Remove from plastic and roll in pecans. Serve with your favorite crackers.

Party Cheese Ball

Bethel Missionary Baptist Church, Seminary † *Lena Ellzey*

2 (8-ounce) packages cream cheese,
   softened
¼ cup shredded Cheddar cheese
1 tablespoon finely chopped green bell
   pepper
1 tablespoon grated onion
1 tablespoon Worcestershire sauce
¼ teaspoon garlic powder
Dash cayenne pepper
Dash salt
Chopped pecans and/or chopped parsley
   for coating

Cream all ingredients, except coating, together and shape into 2 balls. Roll in chopped pecans or parsley or 1 ball in each.

Cheese Ring

Calvary Baptist Church, Starkville † *Valaree Tiffin*

1 (16-ounce) block sharp Cheddar cheese, grated
1 cup chopped pecans
¾ cup mayonnaise
1 medium onion, grated
1 clove garlic, minced
½ teaspoon Tabasco
1 cup strawberry preserves

Mix together cheese, pecans, mayonnaise, onion, garlic and Tabasco. Shape into a ring, leaving a hole in the middle. Fill middle with strawberry preserves. Serve with crackers.

Crescent Sausage Squares

First Baptist Church, Eupora † *Jackie Taylor*

1 pound ground pork sausage
1 (8-ounce) package cream cheese, cubed
2 (8-ounce) cans refrigerated crescent dinner rolls

Brown sausage in skillet, crumbling as it cooks; drain. Stir in cream cheese until melted; remove from heat. Open 1 can crescent rolls and place entire piece in a 9x13-inch pan. Spread sausage mixture over dough. Top with 2nd can crescent rolls. Bake in preheated 350° oven for 15 minutes or until golden brown. Slice into squares to serve.

Sausage Balls

Calvary Missionary Baptist Church, Brandon ✝ Delores Ladd

1 pound medium or hot ground pork sausage
8 ounces shredded sharp Cheddar cheese
1 cup Bisquick

Mix all ingredients and form into 1-inch balls. Place on ungreased cookie sheets. Bake at 375° for 12 to 15 minutes or until golden brown. Yields about 4 dozen balls. Can be frozen uncooked.

Calvary Missionary Baptist Church

Brandon

1239 Highway 471
Brandon, MS 39042
601-825-2864

Adair Jernigan, Pastor

"I looked on my right hand, and beheld, but there was no man that would know me; refuge failed me; no man cared for my soul." Psalms 142:4 (KJV)

Calvary Missionary Baptist Church began as a mission February 24, 1974. The organizational meeting was held June 30, 1974. A few weeks later, land was purchased where the church currently stands. The first service in the present building was held in July 1977. Many precious families have given sacrificially in order for this church to continue to serve our community. We have a great desire to honor God by sharing His grace worldwide. God has promised to draw men unto Him as He is exalted. Join us as we strive to worship God biblically and execute a faith that will abide.

Sausage Balls

Goss Baptist Church, Columbia † *Gail McArthur*

1 (8-ounce) block medium or sharp Cheddar cheese
2 to 3 tablespoons milk
1 pound medium or hot ground pork sausage
2 cups Bisquick

Cut cheese into cubes. Place in a microwavable bowl. Add 2 tablespoons milk and microwave until melted, adding an additional tablespoon milk if needed. Remove from microwave and add uncooked sausage to cheese; mix together. Gradually add Bisquick, mixing well. Roll mixture into balls and place on a cookie sheet. Bake at 400° for 10 to 15 minutes, or until golden brown. Can be frozen before baking. Yields about 5 dozen.

Sausage Loaf

Rehobeth Baptist Church, Pelahatchie † *Sarah W. Young*

1 pound ground pork sausage
1 onion, chopped
1 loaf uncut French bread
2 eggs, beaten
¼ cup milk
Velveeta cheese

Brown sausage with chopped onion; drain. Slice French bread lengthwise across the top. Scoop out bread, leaving a shell. Mix bread with eggs, milk and sausage. Put mixture into shell. Bake 20 minutes at 350°. Remove from oven. Cover with cheese and replace top slice of bread. Return to oven until cheese is melted.

Cheddar and Sausage Mini Muffins

Liberty Baptist Church, Waynesboro

1 pound ground pork sausage
1 (10.25-ounce) can Cheddar cheese
  soup, undiluted

1 cup shredded Cheddar cheese
⅔ cup water
3 cups dry biscuit/baking mix

In a large skillet over medium heat, cook sausage until no longer pink; drain. Preheat oven to 350°. In a large bowl, combine soup, shredded cheese and water. Stir in biscuit mix until well blended. Add sausage. Lightly coat mini muffin tin with cooking spray. Fill muffin tins three quarters full. Bake approximately 15 to 20 minutes or until muffins test done. Remove to cooling racks.

Liberty Baptist Church

Waynesboro

485 Old Highway 84 Road
Waynesboro, MS 39367
601-735-2597

Phillip Gandy, Pastor

July 24, 1932, seeing a need for a church in their community, 27 charter members organized Liberty Baptist Church. Over the years the original wooden-framed building has grown to include a cemetery (1949), a new church building (1997), and a 23,341 square-foot addition (2004). We praise God that all facilities are debt free. Many wonderful pastors have served us including are current pastor, Brother Phillip Gandy, who has held the position since May 1990. With a heart for missions, Liberty has been blessed to be personally involved in mission work to Argentina, Chile, China, Ukraine, Mexico and various parts of the United States. We believe in carrying out the Great Commission of Matthew 28:18-20. Liberty has been blessed to see ten men surrender to various areas of ministry from within our fellowship.

"Building a Fellowship of Love" is our motto at Liberty; it is our very reason for being a New Testament Church.

Hot Ham Sandwiches

First Baptist Church, Grenada

2 sticks margarine, melted
1 tablespoon Worcestershire sauce
3 tablespoons poppy seeds
3 tablespoons prepared mustard
1 medium onion, grated
3 packages small dinner rolls, halved (as for a sandwich)
1 pound ham, thinly sliced
½ pound sliced Swiss cheese

Mix margarine with Worcestershire, poppy seeds, mustard and onion. Place bottoms of split rolls on cookie sheet. Brush margarine mixture on inside of both bottom and top rolls. Layer ham and cheese on rolls; add top half of rolls. Cover with foil and bake at 350° for 10 minutes.

Best Ham Sandwiches

Liberty Baptist Church, Waynesboro

2 (12-pack) packages sweet Hawaiian rolls, halved (as for a sandwich)
12 slices Swiss cheese
1½ pounds Virginia ham, sliced
1 stick butter
2 teaspoons Worcestershire sauce
1 teaspoon garlic powder
1 teaspoon onion powder
1 teaspoon poppy seeds

You will need 2 (9x13-inch) pans. Place bottoms of rolls in pans. Cut cheese slices into 4 parts and place 2 parts on rolls. Put a slice of ham over cheese then top with remaining cheese. Melt butter with Worcestershire sauce, garlic powder, onion powder and poppy seeds. Place tops of rolls on sandwich and brush butter mixture on top. Bake at 350° until cheese is melted, about 10 minutes. Serve warm.

Tostados

Shady Grove Missionary Baptist Church, Tishomingo ✝ *Janet Smith*

Refried beans
Tostado chips
Shredded cheese

Sour cream (optional)
Salsa (optional)

Place a teaspoon of refried beans on each chip and place in a baking dish. Top with cheese. Bake in 350° oven until cheese melts. Top with a dollop of sour cream and/or salsa on top, if desired.

Stuffed Mushrooms

Pleasant Home Baptist Church, Laurel ✝ *Karen Matthews*

1 small carton button mushrooms
1 (8-ounce) package cream cheese, softened
¼ cup mayonnaise
3 to 4 green onions, chopped
2 to 3 tablespoons dry ranch dip mix
Pepperidge Farms Herb Seasoned Stuffing Mix for topping
1 stick margarine, melted

Clean outside of mushrooms with cloth; DO NOT WASH. Remove stems and set aside. Combine softened cream cheese, mayonnaise, green onions and ranch dip mix. Stuff mushroom caps with cream cheese mixture. Dip, mixture side down, in herb stuffing mix. Place in casserole dish and drizzle melted butter over top of mushrooms. Bake at 350° for about 30 minutes.

Jalapeño Bites

South Green Baptist Church, Tupelo † *Dot Emison*

1 (8-ounce) package cream cheese, softened
8 ounces Parmesan cheese, grated
1 large egg, beaten

4 tablespoons seeded, chopped jalapeño peppers (about 2)
2 to 3 plain or seasoned breadcrumbs (or panko)

Preheat oven to 350°. Combine cream cheese, Parmesan, egg and jalapeños to form a paste. Shape into balls, using about ½ tablespoon for each (¾-inch balls). Roll balls in breadcrumbs. Place on ungreased baking sheets and bake 10 to 15 minutes, until golden brown. Serve warm. Makes 36 Jalapeño Bites.

South Green Baptist Church
Tupelo

3185 South Green Street • Tupelo, MS 38801
662-842-8447 • Facebook: South-Green-Baptist-Church

Guyton Hinds, Pastor

South Green Baptist Church began on August 8, 1971, as a mission of Monument Drive Baptist Church in Tupelo. The first service was held in the Barbers Milk Company conference room with eighteen people. Two acres of land was purchased on South Green Street as home to the church building. The first unit of the building was started October 1971, consisting of 5,200 square feet with a seating capacity of 225 in the auditorium and nine Sunday school rooms. The first service was held December 12, 1971. November 12, 1972, the church voted to build an education building. October 11, 2015, the church will celebrate 44 years of service to the Lord. We are a small congregation with much love for the Lord. Our pastor, Brother Guyton Hinds preaches the Word as God inspired it to be.

Bacon-Wrapped Cocktails

Union Ridge Baptist Church, Noxapater

1 (16-ounce) package bacon
¾ cup brown sugar
1 (14-ounce) package cocktail sausage

Cut bacon in fourths. Coat in brown sugar. Wrap bacon around sausage and secure with toothpick. Place on a cookie sheet. Bake at 300° for 35 to 40 minutes.

Saucy Cocktail Franks

First Baptist Church, Eupora ✝ *Vera Curry*

1 cup red currant jelly
1 tablespoon yellow mustard
3 drops Tabasco
1 (16-ounce) package franks (I use Oscar Mayer all-beef franks), cut into thirds

Melt jelly in saucepan over medium heat. Blend in mustard and Tabasco. Add franks, stirring occasionally, and cook until completely heated. (They will bulge on ends.) Serve hot. (Hot mustard may be substituted for yellow mustard and Tabasco.)

Give thanks to the Lord for he is good;
his love endures forever. —PSALM 107:1

Glazed Pineapple Kielbasa Bites

New Zion Baptist Church, Crystal Springs

1 (14-ounce) package regular kielbasa, sliced

1 (20-ounce) can pineapple chunks, reserve juice

3 tablespoons teriyaki sauce

1 tablespoon sweet chili sauce

1 tablespoon honey

Preheat oven to 425°. Line a baking sheet with parchment paper. Place a piece of pineapple on top of a slice of kielbasa and stick a toothpick into them. In a small bowl, combine teriyaki sauce, chili sauce and honey; add 1 tablespoon reserved pineapple juice. Mix well. Place kielbasa bites on baking sheet and brush glaze over tops and sides. Bake 15 to 20 minutes, until hot. Cool slightly and serve warm. Makes about 2 dozen.

New Zion Baptist Church

Crystal Springs

12023 New Zion Road
Crystal Springs, MS 39059
601-892-1246

Webb Armstrong, Pastor

"Reaching the lost and growing the saved through Christ-centered relationships."

We are a loving group of Christ followers who are committed to the Kingdom and cause of our Lord and Savior. It is our desire to reach the lost and grow the saved through Christ-centered relationships. This is the end goal of all our ministries. We have labored both near and far in our city, state, and nation as well as around the world. As a group of believers that have been transformed by the Gospel of Jesus Christ, it is our desire to take that same Good News to a world that is desperately searching for hope. Our prayer is that the love and compassion of the Lord will be seen in our actions as well as heard in our words.

Cheese Cookies

Mt. Pisgah Baptist Church, Brandon ✝ Janelle C. Carter

1 pound shredded Cheddar Cheese
1 cup butter, softened
4 cups all-purpose flour
¾ teaspoon salt

1 cup chopped pecans
½ teaspoon red pepper
1 teaspoon garlic powder

Mix all ingredients well (you may adjust the red pepper and garlic powder to taste or leave them out all together). Shape into 2 rolls and slice about ¼ inch thick. Bake at 350° for about 20 minutes or just until brown; do not overbrown as they will taste scorched.

Mt. Pisgah Baptist Church

Brandon

251 Old Highway 43
Brandon, MS 39047
601-825-2887
www.mtpisgahbrandon.com

Mt. Pisgah Baptist Church was founded in 1831 by Reverend William Denson, known fondly as "Parson Bill" by his neighbors. At the time, Mt. Pisgah was the second church founded in Rankin County and is now the oldest Baptist Church in existence in the county. The church has a long history of serving the Lord's people throughout the community, the state, and oftentimes the world. This history is also evident in a continuity in membership of the church with descendants of the original members still on the church rolls. Located in Northern Rankin County, the attic of the present day church contains wood from the original church completed in 1856. Colossians 3:16 tells us, "Let the word of Christ dwell in you richly as you teach and admonish one another with all wisdom, and as you sing psalms, hymns and spiritual songs with gratitude in your hearts to God." With a history stretching back more than 184 years, Mt. Pisgah continues forward with the hands of God upon us to do His work in way that is pleasing and fruitful.

Cheese Straws

Corinth Baptist Church, Magee ✝ *Betty Hall*

¼ pound margarine (1 stick)
1 (5-ounce) jar Kraft Old English sharp
   cheese
1½ cups all-purpose flour

2 tablespoons paprika
¼ teaspoon Tabasco
¼ teaspoon red pepper
2 to 3 tablespoons water

Mix all ingredients until well blended. Using a pastry bag and No. 16 tip, pipe onto ungreased cookie sheet in 3-inch strips. Bake at 350° to 375° until brown and crispy.

Seasoned Crackers

Liberty Baptist Church, Waynesboro

1 (1-ounce) package ranch dressing mix
1½ teaspoons crushed red pepper
1 (16-ounce) box saltine crackers
1½ cups canola oil

Combine dressing mix and red pepper in a gallon plastic container. Add crackers and close lid. Roll and shake to distribute mix over crackers. Open and pour oil over crackers. Close lid and roll and shake to coat crackers with oil. Continue every 5 minutes for about 30 minutes. Enjoy!

Ritz Cracker Snacks

Cash Baptist Church, Lena ✝ *Marisol Brewer*

40 Ritz crackers
1½ cups chopped pecans

2 sticks butter
½ cup sugar

Preheat oven to 350°. Lay Ritz crackers side-by-side on a jellyroll pan. Sprinkle with pecans. Combine butter and sugar in a small saucepan, bring to boil and boil 3 minutes. Pour over crackers. Bake 10 minutes. Remove from oven and cool 5 to 10 minutes. Remove from pan and place on serving tray.

Sweet Trash

Bethel Baptist Church, Heidelburg

1 (12-ounce) box Corn Chex cereal
1 (1.5-ounce) box raisins
1 (12-ounce) can peanuts or mixed nuts
1 cup pecans
1 (12-ounce) bag stick pretzels
1½ pounds CandiQuick vanilla baking bar or almond bark

Pour all ingredients, except CandiQuick, in a large bowl and mix. Following directions on package, melt CandiQuick. Pour over dry ingredients, gently stirring with a large spoon to mix. Spread out on wax paper to dry. Store in airtight container, if not serving immediately.

Microwave Party Mix

Bethel Baptist Church, Heidelburg

6 tablespoons butter or margarine
4 teaspoons Worcestershire sauce
1 teaspoon seasoned salt
3 cups Corn Chex
3 cups Rice Chex
2 cups thin stick pretzels
1 (12-ounce) container mixed nuts (1½ cups)

In a 9x13-inch dish, place butter, Worcestershire and salt. Microwave 1 minute or until butter is melted. Stir well. Add remaining ingredients and mix thoroughly to coat. Microwave 3 minutes; stir. Microwave 3 more minutes until evenly toasted. Makes about 2½ quarts. Cool before placing in zip-lock bag, or serve immediately.

Soups & Salads

When Jesus spoke again to the people, He said, "I am the light of the world. Whoever follows me will never walk in darkness, but will have the light of life." —JOHN 8:12

Brother Jerry's Veggie Beef Soup

Yellow Leaf Baptist Church, Oxford

1 pound ground beef
1 onion, chopped
½ pound beef tips (optional)
2 (12-ounce) cans tomato juice
1 (14-ounce) can diced tomatoes

1 (16-ounce) package frozen mixed
  vegetables
1 (8.25-ounce) can whole corn (optional)
1 (8.5-ounce) can sweet peas (optional)
1 (15-ounce) can butterbeans (optional)

Brown ground beef with onion; drain. Seer beef tips, if desired. Place all meat in a large stockpot. Add tomato juice plus ½ can water; stir. Add tomatoes, mixed vegetables and canned vegetables, if desired. Bring to boil. Reduce heat to low and simmer at least 1 hour before serving. A long, slow simmer is the secret to great taste for this recipe. Enjoy.

Yellow Leaf Baptist Church

Oxford

50 County Road 435
Oxford, MS 38655
662-234-5116
www.yellowleafbc.com

Yellow Leaf Baptist Church predates the Civil War. Established in 1853, it was attended by both black and white members. It has had a strong and influential history. Situated in the beauty of Lafayatte County, it is one of the larger rural churches in the association. It is well known and respected for its friendly, family-like atmosphere. Members come from all over the area. We have ministries for all age groups and try to reach anyone and everyone with the Gospel of Jesus Christ. God has been perfectly faithful to us and we consider it our greatest privilege to "Know Him and Make Him Known." If you're ever in our neck of the woods, please stop by and worship with us. We'll save you a seat.

Taco Soup

Calvary Missionary Baptist Church, Brandon † *Linda Garrett*

1 pound ground chuck
½ onion, chopped
1 (15-ounce) can whole-kernel corn
2 (15-ounce) cans pinto beans
1 (15-ounce) can red kidney beans
1 (15-ounce) can stewed tomatoes

1 (10-ounce) can Rotel tomatoes
1 (1.25-ounce) package taco seasoning
  mix
1 (1-ounce) package dry ranch dressing
  mix
¼ cup apple cider vinegar

In a large pot, brown ground chuck with onion; drain. Add remaining ingredients. Simmer for 20 to 25 minutes.

Easy Taco Soup

Golden Central Baptist Church, Golden † *Cherrye Greene*

1 pound ground beef
1 (1.25-ounce) package taco seasoning
  mix
 (15-ounce) cans chili beans

1 (15-ounce) can whole-kernel corn,
  drained
31 (10-ounce) can Rotel tomatoes
1½ cups tomato juice

Brown ground beef. Add taco seasoning mix, beans, corn, Rotel and tomato juice. Bring to a boil, then turn heat to low and cook for 20 to 30 minutes. Great served with Mexican cornbread.

Chicken Tortilla Soup

Liberty Baptist Church, Waynesboro

1 (15-ounce) can whole-kernel corn, drained
1 (14-ounce) cup chicken broth
1 (15-ounce) can black beans, drained and rinsed
1 (10.25-ounce) can cream of chicken soup
1 (10-ounce) can Rotel tomatoes
2 (12.5-ounce) cans chicken breast, drained
1 (1-pound) block Velveeta cheese

Combine all ingredients in a slow cooker set to low. Simmer until completely heated through.

Loaded Chicken Soup

White Hill Missionary Baptist Church, Tupelo

4 chicken breasts
1 pinch each: salt and pepper
1 tablespoon garlic powder
4 potatoes, peeled and chopped
2 celery stalks, finely chopped
2 (10.25-ounce) cans cream of chicken soup
2 (10.25-ounce) cans cream of mushroom soup
2 cups bacon bits

Boil chicken in salted water to cover until cooked through. Remove chicken from broth (reserving broth) and chop. Add chopped chicken back into broth. Add salt, pepper, garlic powder, potatoes and celery; bring to a boil and cook about 10 minutes. Add all 4 cans of soup and lower heat to simmer. Cover and simmer on low about 10 minutes. Add bacon bits to individual bowls when serving.

Cream of Chicken Soup

Mt. Pisgah Baptist Church, Brandon † *Sheila Simmons*

2 to 3 boneless, skinless chicken breasts
3 tablespoons olive oil
½ onion, processed in food processor (or very finely chopped)
4 tablespoons all-purpose flour
2 cups milk
1 tablespoon sugar
½ teaspoon salt or to taste
½ teaspoon ground black pepper or to taste
½ teaspoon garlic powder or to taste
3 hard-boiled eggs, chopped (optional)
3 tablespoons freshly chopped parsley (optional)

Cook chicken in salted water to cover. Remove chicken (reserve broth) and finely chop. Heat oil in a 3-quart saucepan. Add onion and stir constantly until soft but not brown. Gradually stir in flour; continue to cook until flour is warm and thick but not brown. Add milk, ½ cup at a time, whisking briskly until fully incorporated. Stir in 2 cups reserved chicken broth (save anything over 2 cups for another use; add milk to make 2 cups, if necessary). Add chicken, sugar, salt, pepper and garlic powder. Mix well and simmer 20 minutes over low heat. Stir in eggs and parsley just before serving, if desired. Serves 4 to 6.

Chicken Noodle Soup

Toxish Baptist Church, Pontotoc

1 whole chicken (or 4 chicken breasts)
Salt and pepper to taste
1 (16-ounce) box Velveeta cheese, cubed
2 (10.25-ounce) cans cream of chicken soup
1 (8-ounce) package egg noodles

Boil chicken in seasoned water to cover. Remove chicken from pot, reserving broth. Cool chicken enough to handle then debone and place meat back into broth. Add Velveeta, both cans cream of chicken soup and noodles. Cook on medium-low heat until cheese is melted and noodles are done.

Note: Butter and milk may be added to get the desired thickness.

Roasted Cauliflower White Cheddar Soup

New Zion Baptist Church, Crystal Springs

1 (2- to 2½-pound) head cauliflower,
  cored and chopped into bite-size pieces
2 tablespoons olive oil
Salt and freshly ground black pepper
3 tablespoons butter
1 cup finely chopped yellow onion
3½ tablespoons all-purpose flour
1 clove garlic, minced
3 cups milk
1 (14-ounce) can low-sodium chicken
  broth
½ cup heavy cream
1 teaspoon dried parsley (or 1 tablespoon
  chopped fresh)
¼ teaspoon (slightly heaping) dried
  thyme (or 1 teaspoon chopped fresh)
1 bay leaf
¼ teaspoon sugar
1 cup shredded sharp white Cheddar
  cheese, plus more for serving
¼ cup grated Parmesan cheese

Preheat oven to 425°. Place cauliflower on baking sheet, drizzle with olive oil and toss to evenly coat. Spread into an even layer and season lightly with salt and pepper. Bake until golden, about 25 minutes. Remove from oven and set aside. In a large pot, melt butter over medium heat. Add onion and sauté until tender, about 4 to 5 minutes. Add in flour and cook, stirring constantly, for 1½ minutes, adding in garlic during last 30 seconds of cooking. While whisking, slowly pour in milk followed by chicken broth and cream. Add in parsley, thyme, bay leaf, sugar, roasted cauliflower and season soup with salt and pepper to taste. (I used ½ teaspoon salt but this may vary depending on how much salt you added to your cauliflower and how much salt you prefer.) Bring to a boil, stirring constantly, then reduce heat to low. Purée 3 cups soup in a blender (being careful as you are working with hot liquids) and return to soup in pot. Remove from heat and stir in Cheddar and Parmesan cheese. Serve warm garnished with additional shredded white Cheddar and croutons, if desired. Yields about 4 servings.

Cheesy Potato Soup

Woodland Baptist Church, Columbus

1 (16-ounce) box Velveeta cheese
2 (10-ounce) cans Rotel tomatoes
8 baked potatoes, cooked, cooled and diced
1 (10.25-ounce) can cream of chicken soup
1 (14-ounce) can chicken broth

Melt cheese with tomatoes. Add remaining ingredients and heat to desired temperature. (I make this in the microwave.)

Potato Cheese Soup

Unity Baptist Church, McHenry

1 large onion, chopped
1 stick butter
10 medium potatoes, cubed
3 (10.25-ounce) cans cream of chicken soup
1 (12-ounce) can evaporated milk
2 to 3 cups milk
1 (16-ounce) box Velveeta cheese, cubed
Salt to taste

Sauté onion in butter. Add cubed potatoes and just enough water to cover. Cook until hot. Add soup, evaporated milk and milk. Continue to cook until potatoes are cooked through. Just before serving, add Velveeta cheese and season to taste. Heat just until cheese melts; serve hot. Makes about 1 gallon.

Potato Soup

Bethel Missionary Baptist Church, Seminary ✝ *Betty Sanford*

8 large potatoes
1 tablespoon butter
2 tablespoons self-rising flour
2 cups half-and-half
Salt and pepper to taste
1 teaspoon chopped fresh parsley

Peel and cube potatoes; cover with water. Bring to a boil and cook until tender. Drain and mash about three quarter of the potatoes; set aside. Melt butter in a separate pan and add flour. Slowly add half-and-half until mixture is thick. Add to potatoes and stir. Season with salt and pepper. Add parsley and serve.

Potato Soup

First Baptist Church, Grenada

½ cup finely chopped onion
½ cup finely chopped carrots
½ stick margarine
2 pounds potatoes, coarsely chopped, boiled until tender and drained
1 (14-ounce) can chicken broth
1 (10.25-ounce) can cream of chicken soup
1 (10.25-ounce) can cream of mushroom soup
¼ to ½ teaspoon salt and pepper
1 (16-ounce) box Velveeta cheese, cubed
2 cups milk

Sauté onion and carrots in margarine until tender and onions are clear. Add cooked potatoes, chicken broth and soups; simmer 20 minutes. Season to taste with salt and pepper. Add cheese and milk; cook on low heat 5 to 10 more minutes or until heated through. (Do not boil after adding milk.) Diced, cooked chicken can also be added to this soup.

Potato Chowder

Rehobeth Baptist Church, Pelahatchie ✝ *Sarah W. Young*

Approximately 2 quarts potatoes,
  peeled and diced
½ cup diced onion
3 tablespoons diced bell pepper
  (optional)

½ stick butter
2 heaping tablespoons flour
1 cup sour cream
2 cups diced ham
Salt and pepper to taste

Cover first 3 ingredients with water and boil until potatoes are done but not falling apart. Turn heat off; leave on burner. Do not drain water off. Melt ½ stick butter in microwave. Add flour. Mix well. Add to potatoes along with sour cream and ham. (Potatoes should still have enough liquid to make a thin soup.) Stir all gently until well mixed. Season with salt and pepper. Cook on low until just bubbly.

Rehobeth Baptist Church
Pelahatchie

446 Rehobeth Road
Pelahatchie, MS 39145
601-941-0817

In the spring of 1852, a group of seven Christian men and women set out to give birth to a new Baptist church in rural Rankin County. Securing a parcel of land from Mr. Ned Maum, located nine miles north of Pelahatchie and about one mile east of the present church site, these seven dedicated folks met on Good Friday, April 23rd to worship for the first time. The peculiar name of the church has its origin in the Old Testament, book of Genesis (26:22), where Isaac leads his family to find a place to settle. The name means "plenty of room" in Hebrew; it was the name Isaac chose for their first well. Fifty six ministers have served as pastor to Rehobeth Baptist Church over 163 years. The present church building was erected in 1973.

Corn Chowder

First Baptist Church of Greenville † *Judith Kellebrew*

4 chicken breasts
¾ cup sliced carrots
2 cups cubed potatoes
½ cup chopped onion
1 clove garlic, minced
¼ cup butter
¼ cup all-purpose flour

2 cups milk
Salt, pepper and celery salt to taste
1 (2-ounce) jar pimento
⅛ teaspoon paprika
2 (15-ounce) cans whole-kernel corn, drained
1 (8-ounce) box Velveeta cheese

Boil chicken in water to cover until cooked through. Remove chicken from broth and chop; set aside. Measure broth to 3½ cups (add canned chicken broth if you do not have enough) and return to stockpot. Add carrots, potatoes, onion and garlic; cook until tender. In a separate pot, melt butter and blend in flour. Add milk, pimento, paprika, salt, pepper, and celery salt. Stir until thickened. Add reserved chicken, corn and Velveeta cheese. Cook until cheese melts. Combine mixtures into one pot and mix well before serving.

Shrimp & Corn Chowder

Pleasant Home Baptist Church, Laurel † *Irma Williams*

1 large white onion, chopped
1 stick butter (not margarine)
1 (8-ounce) package cream cheese, cubed
1 (10-ounce) can Rotel tomatoes
2 (11-ounce) cans white shoepeg corn, drained
2 (10.25-ounce) cans cream of potato soup, undiluted
2 (10.25-ounce) cans cream of shrimp soup, undiluted
1 quart half-and-half
1 pound frozen cooked salad shrimp (or more to taste)

Sauté onion in butter; add cream cheese and melt. In a large oval slow cooker (preferably one with a warm setting), place tomatoes, corn and soups. Add cream cheese mixture and half-and-half; mix well. Heat thoroughly on high, 30 minutes to 1 hour. Stir in shrimp and place slow cooker on warm setting. Heat another 20 minutes or until shrimp are heated through. (You may add more half-and-half to achieve the consistency you desire.)

Corn Chowder

Union Ridge Baptist Church, Noxapater

2 (10.25-ounce) cans cream of potato soup
1 (15-ounce) can whole-kernel corn (drained)
1 (15-ounce) can cream-style corn
1 pint half-and-half
1 pound ground pork sausage, browned and drained

Combine all ingredients in a slow cooker and simmer on low heat 2 to 4 hours. Serve with cornbread.

Union Ridge Baptist Church

Noxapater

1765 Union Ridge Road
Noxapater, MS 39346
662-803-9385
www.facebook.com/Union-Ridge-Baptist-Church

Greg Thomas, Pastor

Union Ridge Baptist Church is a community church located in Noxapater. The church was started October 1915, and in 2015, we celebrated out 100th anniversary. Union Ridge is a praying church that is involved in several projects locally throughout the year. One of our main missions is Vacation Bible School. Also, we are very active in Operation Christmas Child. Another mission project is our cookie ministry. We make cookie bags that we deliver to the nursing homes in Louisville and Noxapater. In July, we deliver bags to the Veteran's Home in Kosciusko. Union Ridge is a church where everyone is welcome and everyone is loved.

Crawfish Bisque

Midway Baptist Church, Lucedale

½ cup chopped green onions
½ stick butter
2 (10.25-ounce) cans cream of potato soup
1 (10.25-ounce) can cream of mushroom soup
1 pint half-and-half
1 (15-ounce) can whole-kernel corn, drained
1 (8-ounce) package cream cheese, softened
1 package frozen crawfish tails
½ teaspoon red pepper

Sauté green onions in butter. Combine with all other ingredients in a slow cooker. Heat until warm, about 2 hours.

Seafood Bisque

Pelahatchie Baptist Church, Pelahatchie ✝ Jewel Carter

2 (10.25-ounce) cans potato soup
1 (10.25-ounce) can cream of mushroom soup
1 (8-ounce) package cream cheese, cubed
Chopped green onions to taste
½ stick (4 tablespoons) butter
1 pound cooked shrimp, peeled
1 pound imitation crabmeat
1 (11-ounce) can Mexicorn
½ teaspoon red pepper
Dash Tony Chachere's Creole Seasoning
2 cups half-and-half

Combine all ingredients in a slow cooker. Cook on high for 2 to 3 hours.

Gumbo

North Columbia Baptist Church, Columbia † Charlotte Hibley
(In Loving Memory of Lessie M. Broom)

1 cup oil	2 (8-ounce) cans tomato sauce
1 cup all-purpose flour	2 (14-ounce) cans crushed tomatoes
4 cups chopped onion	Salt and black pepper to taste
1 cup chopped celery	2 tablespoons crab boil
6 cloves garlic, chopped	1 pound crabmeat
1 cup chopped green bell pepper	2 pounds shrimp, peeled
4 quarts water	4 chicken breasts, cooked and chopped
4 cups sliced okra	1 pound smoked sausage, sliced

Combine oil and flour in a cast-iron Dutch oven over medium heat. Cook, stirring constantly, until roux is brown. Add onions, celery, garlic and bell pepper. Cook, stirring constantly, until vegetables are tender. Add water gradually. Add okra, tomato sauce and tomatoes; bring to a boil. Reduce heat; simmer, at least 20 minutes (1 to 1½ hours is better, as the roux develops more flavor). Stir in salt, pepper, crab boil, crab, shrimp, chicken and sausage. Bring to a boil; simmer 10 minutes. Remove from heat and serve over rice.

Seafood Gumbo

Auburn Baptist Church, Tupelo † Cindy Henry

¾ cup each: flour and oil	1 pound white crabmeat
2 medium onions, chopped	Red, white and black pepper to taste
1 stalk celery, chopped	Salt to taste
1 green bell pepper, chopped	½ teaspoon thyme
2 quarts water	1 tablespoon Creole seasoning
1 teaspoon garlic powder	5 green onions, chopped
12 oysters, with juice	3 sprigs parsley
2 pounds peeled shrimp	1 tablespoon Tabasco
1 pound crawfish tails	Filé powder to taste

In a large skillet, make a roux by stirring flour into heated oil until dark brown. Add onions, celery and bell pepper and mix well; remove from heat. Heat water in a large pot to almost boiling; add garlic powder, oyster juice and roux. Bring to a boil then simmer about 45 minutes. Add shrimp, crawfish, crabmeat, oysters and seasonings. Simmer 15 minutes. Add green onions, parsley and Tabasco; simmer 10 minutes. Serve over rice and sprinkle filé over individual servings.

White Chicken Chili

Shady Grove Baptist Church, Lucedale † *Wanda Watson*

1 (32-ounce) carton chicken stock
3 (15-ounce) cans white beans
5 cups chopped cooked chicken
    (rotisserie or boiled)
1 (16-ounce) jar salsa
8 ounces shredded pepper jack
    cheese
2 teaspoons ground cumin
2 cloves garlic, minced
Black or white pepper to taste
½ cup finely crushed corn chips
Sour cream, for garnish

Place all ingredients except corn chips and sour cream in a pot. Cook over medium-high heat until cheese is melted. When chili is ready, add crushed corn chips and simmer 10 minutes to thicken. Garnish with sour cream and serve.

White Chili

First Baptist Byhalia

1 pound dry northern beans, soaked
    overnight in water and drained
6 cups chicken broth
2 tablespoons ground cumin
4 cloves garlic, minced
1 tablespoon dried oregano
2 medium onions, chopped, divided
1 tablespoon olive oil
1 (4-ounce) can chopped green chiles
½ teaspoon cayenne pepper
4 cups diced cooked chicken breast
Monterey jack cheese

Combine beans, chicken broth, cumin, garlic, oregano and half of the onions in large soup pot; bring to a boil. Reduce heat and simmer until beans are very soft, 3 hours or more (add more broth if necessary). In a skillet, sauté remaining onions in oil until tender. Add chiles and cayenne; mix thoroughly. Add to beans. Add chicken and continue to simmer 1 hour. Sprinkle individual servings with desired amount of cheese.

Brother Curt's Big Easy Chili

New Bethel Baptist Church, Philadelphia † *Reverend J. Curtis Pace*

5 pounds lean ground beef
1 (1-gallon) can baked beans
½ gallon tomato juice
1 (32-ounce) bottle ketchup
3 tablespoons chili powder (plus more to taste)

In a 5-gallon, heavy-bottom stockpot, brown meat and then turn heat down to low. Add beans, tomato juice and ketchup; mix. Add 1 gallon water and SLOWLY bring to boil, stirring often. When boiling, add chili powder. Simmer 30 minutes. Add more chili powder to taste. Cool and serve the folks.

This recipe makes about 4 gallons to feed 35 to 40 people, and works well for a Wednesday night fellowship meal.

New Bethel Baptist Church

Philadelphia

11681 Highway 488
Philadelphia, MS 39350
601-656-2301
www.facebook.com/NewBethelSbc

New Bethel Baptist Church, founded in 1954, is located in rural Neshoba County near Philadelphia. Our pastor, the Reverend J. Curtis Pace, has been with us since April 2001. We welcome you to worship with us at 11:00 a.m. and 7:00 p.m. on Sunday; Sunday School is held Sundays at 10:00 a.m.

Fruit Salad

Russell Baptist Church, Meridian † *Dorothy Fleming*

1 (21-ounce) can peach pie filling
1 (15-ounce) can Mandarin oranges, drained
1 (20-ounce) can pineapple chunks, drained
3 bananas, sliced
1 (16-ounce) carton frozen strawberries, thawed

Mix all together, and chill before serving.

Russell Baptist Church

Meridian

1844 Highway 11 And 80
Meridian, MS 39301
601-482-3577
www.russellbaptist.org

Steve Taylor, Pastor

The Word of God instructs us that we are to be "... blameless and harmless, children of God without fault in the midst of a crooked and perverse generation, among whom you shine as lights in the world, holding fast the word of life. ..." (Philippians 2:15-16). At Russell Baptist Church, that is what we are striving to be. Our passion is to be intentional with the truth of the Gospel. We want to share the Gospel with those that don't know Him, and we want to grow deep in our relationship with Him, striving to be the disciples that Christ has called us to be. At Russell Baptist Church we seek to truly live as a light in a dark world. Our purpose is to show the love of Christ, through the Gospel, to a world that does not know Him.

Roquefort Pear Salad

First Baptist Church, Brookhaven † *Kathy Walker*

1 head leafy lettuce, torn bite-size
   (or bag Romaine)
3 pears, peeled, cored and chopped
5 ounces Roquefort cheese, crumbled

1 avocado, peeled, pitted and diced
½ cup thinly diced green onions
¼ cup sugar
½ cup chopped pecans

Layer lettuce, pears, cheese, avocado and green onions in a large bowl. Stir sugar and pecans together in a skillet over medium heat until sugar has caramelized. Sprinkle over salad.

DRESSING:
⅓ cup olive oil
3 tablespoons red wine vinegar
1½ teaspoons sugar
1½ teaspoons prepared mustard

1 clove garlic, chopped fine
½ teaspoon salt
Fresh ground black pepper to taste

Blend olive oil, vinegar, sugar, mustard, garlic, salt and pepper, mixing well. Pour over salad in bowl. Serve immediately.

Simple Fruit Salad

Magnolia Baptist Church, Hattiesburg † *Teri Medenwald*

⅔ cup chopped pecans
1 cup flaked coconut
1 cup marshmallows
1 cup Mandarin oranges

1 cup crushed pineapple
1 cup sour cream
Granulated sugar

Combine all ingredients, except sugar, and mix thoroughly. Dust with sugar to taste.

Strawberry Pretzel Salad

First Baptist Church, Grenada

2 cups crushed pretzels
1½ sticks margarine, melted
1¼ cups sugar, divided
1 (8-ounce) package cream cheese, softened
1 (8-ounce) carton Cool Whip, divided
2 cups pineapple juice
2 (6-ounce) boxes strawberry gelatin
1 (10-ounce) package frozen sliced strawberries. thawed

Combine pretzels, margarine and ¼ cup sugar. Press into a 9x13-inch dish. Bake 10 minutes in a 350° oven; cool completely. Blend cream cheese and remaining 1 cup sugar; fold in three quarters of Cool Whip. Spread on cooled crust. Bring pineapple juice to a boil. Place gelatin in a clean bowl; add juice and stir until completely dissolved. Refrigerate until almost set. Fold in strawberries and spread over cream cheese mixture. Top with remaining Cool Whip, if desired. Refrigerate to set and until ready to serve.

Red Seedless Grape Salad

Mt. Pisgah Baptist Church, Brandon † *Margaret Shedd*

3 pounds red seedless grapes
1 (8-ounce) package cream cheese, softened

1 (8-ounce) container sour cream
½ cup sugar
1 teaspoon vanilla flavoring

Wash grapes and dry completely. Whip together cream cheese, sour cream, sugar and vanilla. Fold in grapes and pour into a 9x13-inch dish.

TOPPING:
½ cup brown sugar

½ cup chopped pecans

Combine Topping ingredients and sprinkle over grape mixture. Refrigerate and serve cold. Better if fixed the day before.

Blueberry Salad

Antioch Baptist Church, Brandon † *Ronnie Bell*

1 (8-ounce) package cream cheese,
  softened
½ cup powdered sugar
½ cup mayonnaise
2 teaspoons lemon juice
1 teaspoon vanilla flavoring

1 (15-ounce) can peaches, cubed
1 (15-ounce) can pineapple tidbits
1 (12-ounce) package fresh blueberries
1 (16-ounce) carton whipped cream
  (or 2 cups)
2 cups mini-marshmallows

Mix cream cheese, powdered sugar and mayonnaise thoroughly. Add remaining items and stir gently until thoroughly mixed. Chill at least 1 hour before serving.

Antioch Baptist Church

Brandon

2350 Highway 43 South
Brandon, MS 39042
601-546-2464
www.antiochbaptistbrandon.org

In 1827, settlers traveled from their homes in South Carolina in search of greater freedom and better opportunities in the wild western frontier of Mississippi. They built homes north of what is now Pelahatchie on the Pelahatchie Creek. By 1836, several of those settlers had moved further south. Desiring to meet more regularly for worship and provide opportunities for their children to gain fuller knowledge of scripture, they formed Antioch Baptist Church on May 5th, 1836. Antioch Baptist Church exists to help people connect to Christ in a life-changing relationship where they can commit to grow into fully devoted followers of Christ who contribute to the Kingdom of God through serving others, teaching the Word of God, and sharing their faith in Christ Jesus in the community.

Apricot Salad

Mt. Pisgah Baptist Church, Brandon † *Georgia Hall*

2 cups boiling water
2 (3-ounce) boxes orange Jell-O
1 (3-ounce) box lemon Jell-O
1 (8-ounce) package cream cheese, cubed
26 ounces apricots and juice
Mayonnaise for garnish
Maraschino cherries for garnish

In a large bowl, stir boiling water into Jell-O until dissolved. Blend Jell-O and cream cheese in blender. Add apricots and juice to blender and blend. Pour in a 9x13-inch casserole dish and chill. Cut in squares and put a teaspoon of mayonnaise and a cherry on each square. Makes a lot.

Orange Salad

Corinth Baptist Church, Magee † *Charlene Loyd*

1 (3-ounce) box orange Jell-O
1 (24-ounce) carton large-curd cottage cheese
1 (15-ounce) can Mandarin oranges, drained
1 (8-ounce) carton Cool Whip
1 (8-ounce) can crushed pineapple, drained

Mix Jell-O and cottage cheese. Add remaining ingredients and mix well. Chill overnight and serve.

Pistachio Fruit Salad

Palestine Baptist Church, Nettleton ✝ Cathy Cody

1 (16-ounce) carton Cool Whip
1 (20-ounce) can crushed pineapple, drained
1 (3.4-ounce) box pistachio instant pudding
½ cup chopped pecans
1 cup miniature marshmallows (optional)

Mix all ingredients. Chill in refrigerator until ready to serve.

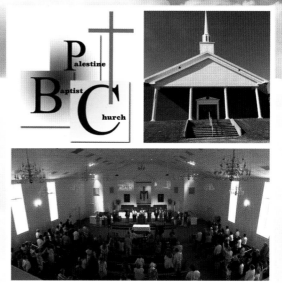

Palestine Baptist Church

Nettleton

730 County Route 598
Nettleton, MS 38862
662-963-2078
facebook.com/pbcnettleton

Nestled back on a county road outside of Nettleton, there stands a red-brick building with a lofty white steeple. On any given day of the week, it stands empty and silent, but on Sunday mornings, the massive wooden double doors swing open to welcome a community of believers eager to worship together. It is here that church and family merge into the children of God, where Jesus is boldly proclaimed Lord and Savior. It is here that members gather to receive the Word of God and disperse to live it out daily. You and your loved ones are always invited to join us in worship at Palestine Baptist Church.

Coca-Cola Salad

Williamsville Baptist Church, Kosciusko ✝ *Era Jean Crowson*

1 (20-ounce) can crushed pineapple, drained (reserve juice)
1 (10-ounce) bottle maraschino cherries, drained (reserve juice) and chopped
2 (3-ounce) packages gelatin, any flavor
1 (12-ounce) can Coca-Cola
1 cup chopped pecans
1 (8-ounce) package cream cheese, softened

Add juice from pineapple and cherries and to a saucepan over medium heat and bring to a boil. Remove from heat and add gelatin, stirring to dissolve. Cool slightly. Add cola, pecans, cherries, pineapple and cream cheese. Mix well. Pour into serving dish. Refrigerate to congeal. Does well in a mold.

Williamsville Baptist Church

Kosciusko

16995 Williamsville Road
Kosciusko, MS 39090
662-289-4294

Junior Davis, Pastor

God has richly blessed Williamsville Baptist for more than one hundred years. Our strength and longevity only comes from Him. The recipes entered in this book represent a long legacy of faithful members throughout those years. You will find no more loving and caring people than in this fellowship. Our goal and passion has been, and will continue to be, to get the Gospel to our community and the world while discipling those God has entrusted to us. These dishes have been used to minister to the sick and grieving while being the hands and feet of Jesus. As you use these recipes, we encourage you to continue to pass the love of Jesus on to others.

Potato Salad

Robinhood Baptist Church, Brandon ✝ *Anita Musgrove*

5 to 6 large potatoes
½ cup diced onions
½ cup diced celery
½ cup chopped dill pickles
3 tablespoons dill pickle juice
1 cup mayonnaise
½ cup mustard
5 boiled eggs, chopped
Salt and pepper to taste

Bake or boil potatoes until done. Cool until you can handle them. Peel and cube potatoes in a bowl. Add onions, celery, pickles and pickle juice; mix gently together. Stir in mayonnaise and mustard. Add eggs, salt and pepper; mix well stirring carefully to not break-up eggs. Serve immediately or refrigerate for a cold salad.

Broccoli Salad

Canaan Baptist Church, Purvis ✝ *Betty Cooper*

1 (10-ounce) bag fresh broccoli florets, chopped
1 Grannie Smith apple, small chopped
⅓ cup diced red onion
¾ cup craisins or raisins
½ cup chopped pecans
⅓ cup bacon bits
Coleslaw dressing to taste

In a large bowl, mix all ingredients. Add enough coleslaw dressing to coat salad well. Chill until served.

Broccoli Salad

Ashland Baptist Church ✝ *Carlie Wilson*

1 bunch fresh broccoli (3 stalks),
   chopped
2 cups shredded mozzarella cheese
½ red onion, chopped

½ cup raisins
½ cup chopped pecans
½ pound bacon, cooked and crumbled

DRESSING:
½ cup mayonnaise
2 tablespoons cider vinegar

½ cup sugar

Mix broccoli, cheese, onion, raisins, pecans and bacon in a serving bowl. Mix Dressing ingredients together and pour over broccoli mixture; toss to mix. Refrigerate until chilled; serve.

Broccoli Salad

Robinhood Baptist Church, Brandon ✝ *Mary Morris*

SALAD:
3 to 4 stalks broccoli with the stems, cut
   in small pieces
1 medium red onion, chopped
½ cup raisins

½ cup sunflower seeds
1 cup chopped pecans
½ to 1 pound bacon, cooked and
   chopped

DRESSING:
1 cup Hellmann's Mayonnaise
¼ cup sugar

¼ cup red wine vinegar

Toss Salad ingredients. Add Dressing ingredients, stir and serve.

Broccoli Salad

Fairfield Baptist Church, Moselle

1 bunch broccoli, finely chopped
1 pound seedless grapes, halved
1 cup finely chopped celery
1 cup finely chopped green onions
1 cup raisins
½ cup chopped nuts (pecans, almonds or walnuts)
½ cup sugar
1 cup mayonnaise
1 tablespoon vinegar
1 tablespoon horseradish sauce
¼ cup cooked and crumbled bacon

Mix all ingredients well and refrigerate overnight.

Fairfield Baptist Church

Moselle

942 Moselle Seminary Road
Moselle, MS 39459
601-752-6366

Brother Brad Brownlee, Pastor

Fairfield Baptist Church is located approximately six miles West of Moselle on Moselle-Seminary Road. It is a fully organized Southern Baptist Church, belonging to the Southern Baptist Convention, the Mississippi Baptist Convention and the Jones County Baptist Association. Sunday Worship begins with Sunday School at 9:00 a.m., then Morning Worship at 10:00 a.m., and Evening Worship at 6:00 p.m. Join us Wednesdays at 5:45 p.m. for Awana, then at 7:00 p.m. for Prayer Meeting and Youth Bible Study.

"For the perfecting of the saints, for the work of the ministry, for the edifying of the body of Christ." Ephesians 4:14

Christmas Crunch Salad

First Baptist Church, Baldwyn

4 cups chopped broccoli and stems
4 cups chopped cauliflower and stems
1 medium red onion, chopped

2 cups chopped cherry tomatoes
Salt and pepper

DRESSING:

1 cup mayonnaise
½ cup sour cream

1 to 2 tablespoons sugar
1 tablespoon vinegar

Combine vegetables and season with salt and pepper to taste. Combine Dressing ingredients and pour over vegetables. Toss to coat well. Chill at least 2 hours before serving.

First Baptist Church of Baldwyn

500 South Fourth Street
Baldwyn, MS 38824
662-365-5201
www.FBCBaldwyn.com

Brother Stanley Huddleston, Pastor

FBC Baldwyn is a Southern Baptist church located in Baldwyn. We are a conservative, Bible-believing church that seeks to honor Jesus Christ in all we do. Our mission is to: "Glorify God by leading people to know Christ through spiritual birth and spiritual growth." Our vision is to: "Become a compassionate, multigenerational, mentoring congregation, actively seeking the unchurched, and expectantly offering each member a place of ministry."

Apple Carrot Raisin Salad

Canaan Baptist Church, Purvis † *Betty Cooper*

2 large crisp apples, chopped
1 cup shredded carrots
½ cup raisins
⅓ cup Miracle Whip

Mix all together, keep chilled until serving.

Chinese Slaw

Cash Baptist Church, Lena † *In Memory of Joyce Rushing*

DRESSING:
Scant cup vegetable oil
⅓ cup white vinegar
½ cup sugar
2 seasoning packages from chicken flavor ramen noodles (reserve noodles for Slaw)

Combine Dressing ingredients and shake until sugar is dissolved; refrigerate. (This can also be done ahead of time.)

SLAW:
Reserved ramen noodles, crushed
¾ cup sunflower seeds
¾ cup slivered almonds
1 (1-pound) package slaw mix (Dole's)
1 bunch green onions (more or less), chopped

Spread noodles, sunflower seeds and almonds on a baking sheet and toast for 20 minutes at 250°, stirring occasionally. (They will burn if the oven is too high. This can be done ahead of time.) Just before serving, combine toasted mixture with slaw mix and onions. Add Dressing and toss.

Cauliflower-Broccoli-Raisin Salad

Shady Grove Missionary Baptist Church, Tishomingo ✝ *Kathy Bobo*

2¼ cups chopped cauliflower florets
2¼ cups chopped broccoli florets
½ cup chopped onion
½ cup raisins
2 tablespoons Hormel bacon bits
½ cup mayonnaise
1 tablespoon vinegar
2 tablespoons sugar

Combine cauliflower, broccoli, onion, raisins and bacon bits in salad bowl. In a small bowl, mix together mayonnaise, vinegar and sugar. Pour over salad. Mix well. Refrigerate at least 2 hours before serving.

Tookie's Sauerkraut Salad

Shady Grove Baptist Church, Lucedale ✝ *Heather Wade*

1½ cups sugar
½ cup white vinegar
1 teaspoon celery seed
1 (20-ounce) can chopped sauerkraut, well drained
1 green bell pepper, chopped
1 cup finely chopped celery
1 cup finely chopped onion
1 (2-ounce) jar chopped pimento

In a heavy saucepan, bring first 3 ingredients to a rolling boil. Mix remaining ingredients in a glass bowl. Pour sauce over vegetables and blend well. Cover tightly and refrigerate overnight.

Cornbread Salad

First Baptist Church, Wiggins

1 (8.5-ounce) package Jiffy corn muffin mix, plus ingredients to prepare
1 medium green bell pepper, chopped
3 to 4 green onions (or 1 medium Vidalia onion), chopped
4 medium tomatoes, chopped
1 cup mayonnaise
½ cup sweet pickle relish
½ cup sweet pickle juice
Bacon bits

Bake cornbread according to package directions. Cool and crumble. Chop bell pepper, onion and tomatoes in separate bowls. Spread crumbled cornbread in a 9x13-inch dish. Layer pepper, onions and tomatoes. Tomatoes should completely cover dish. In a separate bowl, combine mayonnaise, relish and pickle juice. Spread over top of tomatoes. Sprinkle with bacon bits. Chill until ready to serve. Gently toss salad just before serving.

Corn Salad

South Green Baptist Church, Tupelo † *Dot Emison*

2 (15-ounce) cans white shoepeg corn, drained
1 tomato, chopped
2 to 3 green onions, chopped
1 heaping tablespoon mayonnaise
Salt and pepper to taste

Mix all together and chill.

Greek Pasta Salad

Temple Baptist Church, Hattiesburg ✝ *Cindy Hancock*

1 (16-ounce) box vermicelli
½ cup olive oil
3 tablespoons lemon juice
3 tablespoons Greek seasoning

1 (2-ounce) jar chopped pimento
1 (4-ounce) can chopped black olives
4 to 5 green onions, chopped
3 tablespoons mayonnaise

Cook pasta; drain and rinse. Mix with olive oil, lemon juice and Greek seasoning. Marinate overnight, or at least 4 hours. Mix in remaining ingredients. Chill and serve.

Temple Baptist Church

Hattiesburg

5220 Old Highway 11 • Hattiesburg, MS 39402
601-450-3000 • www.tbclife.net

Dr. Darryl Craft, Pastor

Our heart at Temple is to see Life Change, and we see this happening through three key values. Life Worship. We see the body dedicate itself to the teaching of the apostles, to worship, and to prayer. Life Together. We also follow their example of committing themselves to the life together Life Mission. We see that by living out their faith that people in general liked what they saw. Every day their number grew as God added those who were saved. In all that we do, our desire is to equip and inspire healthy family members to live missional, and to leverage their circles of influence for the Gospel.

Greek Pasta Salad

Vardaman Street Baptist Church, Wiggins ✝ Susan Walker/ Louise Crawley

1 (12-ounce) package angel hair pasta
¾ cup olive oil
4½ tablespoons mayonnaise
3 tablespoon Cavender's Greek seasoning
1 (4.25-ounce) can chopped black olives
4 to 5 chopped green onions

Cook pasta according to directions on package; drain well. Mix olive oil, mayonnaise, seasoning, olives and green onions. Add to drained pasta and mix well. Chill 3 to 4 hours before serving. You can add shrimp, ham, pepperoni, etc., if desired.

Garden Fresh Pasta Salad

Mount Helm Baptist Church, Jackson

1 (16-ounce) package bow tie pasta, uncooked
2 cups broccoli florets
1 small red onion, thinly sliced
1 medium red bell pepper, chopped
1 cup halved grape tomatoes
½ cup shredded 100% Parmesan cheese
1 (8-ounce) bottle sun-dried tomato vinaigrette dressing

Cook pasta as directed on package, adding broccoli for the last minute of cooking time. Drain; rinse under cold running water. Drain well. Place pasta mixture in a large bowl. Add onion, bell pepper and grapes; mix lightly. Stir in cheese. Add dressing; toss to coat. Cover and refrigerate at least 1 hour or until ready to serve.

Cajun Shrimp Pasta Salad

First Baptist Church, Orange Grove

2 pounds shrimp, peeled (uncooked)
2 to 3 tablespoons butter
1 teaspoon liquid crab boil
1 (16-ounce) package rotini pasta
1 red bell pepper, chopped

1 bunch green onions, chopped
2 (1-ounce) packets ranch dressing mix
⅓ cup milk
2 tablespoons mayonnaise
1 (16-ounce) carton sour cream

Place shrimp in a skillet with butter and crab boil. Cook over medium heat until shrimp are done. Boil pasta in salted water until tender; drain. In a large serving bowl, combine pasta and shrimp with remaining ingredients; mix well. Serve immediately for a warm salad or refrigerate before serving for more flavor.

First Baptist Church of Orange Grove
Gulfport

15486 Orange Grove Road
Gulfport, MS 39503
228-832-2991
www.fbcorangegrove.com

Christopher Flynn, Pastor

We were founded on November 19, 1959, by Brother W. E. Greenwood, and are in the BMAA (Baptist Missionary Association of America). Having extended the hand to start several churches in the past, we are looking forward to doing it again in the future. Our Vision Statement is: "To magnify Christ, and be a light in our community through evangelism, outreach, and missions. To minister and disciple our members (old and new) to create productive mature Christians for the cause of Christ. To be a support system to our members through leadership, prayer, and love. To carry out the Great Commission by partaking and supporting all aspects of the mission field (local, state, and foreign). To be an example through our lives, words, and actions of a Christian showing God's love to our visitors and community."

Pasta Salad

Calvary Baptist Church, Starkville † *Betty Murphy*

1 (12-ounce) package angel hair pasta
6 green onions, chopped
1 bell pepper, chopped
1 (4-ounce) jar chopped pimento
1 (4.25-ounce) can sliced black olives

½ cup olive oil
3 tablespoons lemon juice
3 tablespoons mayonnaise
¼ cup Cavender's Greek seasoning
1 pound small shrimp, cooked

Cook angel hair pasta per package directions. Combine pasta, onions, bell pepper, pimentos and black olives. In separate bowl, combine olive oil, lemon juice, mayonnaise and Greek seasoning. Pour over pasta and mix. Add shrimp and mix.

Macaroni Salad

Sunrise Baptist Church, Carthage † *Gayle Beckham*

1 (12-ounce) bag elbow macaroni,
  cooked and drained
1¼ cups sweet pickle relish, drained
  (10 ounces)
1 pound longhorn Cheddar cheese, diced

1 onion, chopped
¼ cup finely chopped bell pepper
1 (4-ounce) jar diced pimento
Mayonnaise to taste

Mix all ingredients. Refrigerate overnight.

Shrimp Salad

Community Missionary Baptist Church, Poplarville

1 pound boiled shrimp, peeled and
  deveined
1 (12-ounce) package tri-color noodles,
  prepared
1 cup mayonnaise

4 boiled eggs, peeled and chopped
½ cup pickle relish
1 tablespoon celery salt
2 teaspoons garlic salt
2 teaspoons onion powder

Combine all ingredients and mix well. Refrigerate until ready to serve.

Turkey, Rice, Fruit Salad

Journey Baptist Church, Olive Branch

8 cups fruit (any combination of Mandarin oranges, seedless grapes, apples), drain all liquid

1 (12-ounce) box rice, prepared as directed

6 cup diced cooked turkey or chicken

4 (8-ounce) packages cream cheese, softened

2 (15-ounce) cans cream of coconut

2 cups slivered almonds

Combine fruit, rice and poultry in large bowl. Mix gently, but thoroughly. Place in serving dish. With electric mixer, beat cream cheese and cream of coconut until smooth and the consistency of very thick syrup. Add tablespoons of water until this consistency is obtained. Spread over salad and chill until ready to serve. Top with almonds just before serving. Serves 18 to 20 people. This is a delicious salad and can very easily be halved.

Journey Baptist Church

Olive Branch

7139 Commerce Drive
Olive Branch, MS 38654
662-892-8047
www.journeybaptistchurch.com

Jarrett Jamieson, Pastor

Journey Baptist Church is located in Olive Branch. We are a "contemporary church" with casual dress and a full band. When you walk in our door, you will likely get a hug. Our Pastor, Jarrett Jamieson and his wife planted the church in 2006. A question we ask ourselves often is, "Why another church in Olive Branch?" Our answer is: Because there are still people who do not have a relationship with Jesus, a church home, and/or a family who loves and cares for them. Our mission is to "Reach the most broken people and lead them in a total life-change through Jesus Christ." We believe that there is no life that Jesus cannot change. He loves you regardless of your background, finances, habits, or hang-ups. That is what we are about at Journey. We are simply: Real People, with Real Problems, getting help from a Real God.

Hot Chicken Salad
Star Baptist, Star

1 cup chopped celery
4 tablespoons chopped onions
2 (10.25-ounce) cans cream of chicken soup
¾ cup mayonnaise
½ teaspoon salt
1 cup sliced water chestnuts
4 chicken breasts, cooked and cut in chunks (2 cups)
3 teaspoons lemon juice
2 cups crushed potato chips, divided
1 tablespoon melted butter

Mix all ingredients, except 1 cup potato chips and butter. Pour into buttered casserole dish. Mix remaining 1 cup potato chips with melted butter and sprinkle on top. Bake at 300° for 40 to 45 minutes. (You may fix this the night before, just wait to put chips on top until you bake.)

Chicken Salad
Iuka Baptist Church

SALAD:
5 cups chopped cooked chicken
  (or canned chicken)
1 (14-ounce) can pineapple tidbits,
  drained
2 cups chopped seedless grapes
1 cup chopped celery
1 cup slivered almonds

SAUCE:
2 cup mayonnaise
½ cup margarine, melted
¼ cup chopped parsley
¼ teaspoon curry
¼ teaspoon garlic pepper

Combine Salad ingredients and mix well. In a separate bowl, combine Sauce ingredients. Stir into salad and mix well.

Poppy Seed Chicken Salad

Parkway Baptist Church, Clinton ✝ *Lisa Joyce*

3 pounds chicken breasts, cooked and diced
10 ounces (1¼ cups) poppy seed dressing
5 ounces (about ⅔ cup) sour cream
4 green onions, chopped
½ cup chopped pecans
2 tablespoons chopped dill weed
Salt to taste

Combine all ingredients in a bowl. Serve warm or cold on crackers or crescent rolls.

Parkway Baptist Church

Clinton

802 North Frontage Road • Clinton, MS 39056
601-924-9912 • www.pbcclinton.org

Ken Anderson, Pastor

From the first moment God's hand touched a small group of praying people gathered in a tent meeting in May 1927, through 67 years of ministry on West Capitol Street, to a bright, new Horizon along Interstate 20 west in Clinton, the power and presence of God has been felt in this congregation called Parkway Baptist Church. We are a community chosen by God to follow, reflect, celebrate, and testify to Jesus, our risen Lord and Savior. This calls us to sacrifice, and to put first things first—to prize being over doing, service over being served, in everything we do to be ministry minded. We want everyone to taste and see that the Lord is good.

Mandarin Chicken Salad

Mount Helm Baptist Church, Jackson

1 (8-ounce) can pineapple chunks
3 cups cubed cooked or canned chicken
½ cup seedless raisins or chopped dates
1 (11-ounce) can Mandarin oranges, drained
⅓ cup hoisin sauce

1 (8-ounce) container plain low-fat yogurt
1 teaspoon garlic powder
½ teaspoon dry mustard
2 bananas, sliced
8 cups (about 1 pound) lettuce

Drain pineapple, reserving ¼ cup of juice. Combine pineapple chunks, chicken, raisins and oranges in large serving bowl; set aside. Stir together hoisin sauce, yogurt, reserved pineapple juice, garlic powder and dry mustard in bowl. Spoon over chicken mixture; toss to coat evenly. Cover and chill 1 hour to blend flavors. Add bananas just before serving. Arrange lettuce on serving platter and spoon chicken mixture over salad. Serves 6.

Dorito Salad

Goss Baptist Church, Columbia † *Angi Buckley*

1 (12-ounce) bag Doritos
3 pounds ground beef, cooked and drained
1 (1.25-ounce) package taco seasoning mix
3½ cups sour cream
1 head lettuce, shredded
2½ cups Thousand Island salad dressing
½ cup chopped green onions
½ cup chopped tomatoes
1 cup shredded Cheddar cheese
½ cup sliced jalapeños

Crush Doritos in bottom of serving dish. Mix beef with taco seasoning and sour cream. Put that over Doritos, add a layer of lettuce then cover with Thousand Island. Top with green onions and tomatoes then top with cheese. Place jalapeños over top.

Strawberry Romaine Salad

Farmington Baptist Church, Corinth

1 (12-ounce) package Romaine lettuce, torn into bite-size pieces
1 pint strawberries, sliced
1 medium red onion, sliced
2 tablespoons sesame seeds (may substitute chopped nuts)
¾ cup mayonnaise
⅓ cup sugar or Splenda
¼ cup milk
1 tablespoon vinegar

Toss lettuce, strawberries and onions in a large bowl. Add sesame seeds. Whisk mayonnaise, sugar, milk and vinegar together in a small bowl. Add to salad just before serving or serve on the side.

Italian Bread Salad

Mt. Pisgah Baptist Church, Brandon ✝ Sheila Simmons

1 prebaked 12-inch pizza crust, cubed
1 large tomato, diced
½ cup diced fresh basil
½ cup Italian salad dressing, divided
7 cups ready-to-serve salad greens
1 small green bell pepper, julienned
1 (6-ounce) package sliced pepperoni, chopped
1 cup shredded mozzarella cheese
½ cup grated Parmesan cheese
½ cup sliced ripe olives

In a large salad bowl, combine bread cubes, tomatoes, basil and ¼ cup salad dressing; let stand for 5 minutes. Add salad greens, bell pepper, pepperoni, mozzarella cheese, Parmesan cheese and olives; toss to mix well. Drizzle with remaining salad dressing; toss to coat. Serve with a slotted spoon.

Seven Layer Salad

First Baptist Church, Morton †
Brooke Craig

SALAD:
1 head iceburg lettuce, chopped
1 tomato, peeled and chopped
1 cucumber, peeled and chopped
2 hard-boiled eggs, chopped
½ sweet onion, finely chopped
1 cup shredded Cheddar cheese
½ pound bacon, cooked and chopped

DRESSING:
2 cups mayonnaise
¼ cup sugar
½ cup sour cream
2 teaspoons black pepper

In a glass serving bowl, layer salad ingredients in order. Combine dressing ingredients and mix well. Pour over salad and serve immediately.

For I know the plans I have for you, declares the Lord, plans to prosper you and not to harm you, plans to give you hope and a future. —JEREMIAH 29:11

Taco Salad Catalina

Golden Central Baptist Church, Golden ✝ *Sam Paul*

1 pound ground beef
1 (1.25-ounce) package taco seasoning mix
1 head lettuce, chopped for salad
1 (8-ounce) bag shredded cheese
1 small onion, finely diced
1 (32-ounce) bag plain tortilla chips, crushed
1 (16-ounce) bottle Catalina salad dressing

Brown ground beef; drain. Add taco seasoning to meat per package directions. Set aside to cool slightly. In a large serving bowl, mix together lettuce, cheese, onion, chips and taco meat. Add dressing, mix well and serve immediately.

Taco Salad

Rehobeth Baptist Church, Pelahatchie ✝ *Edna Watts*

1 pound ground beef
1 (1.25-ounce) package taco seasoning
1 (15-ounce) can kidney beans, drained
1 head lettuce, shredded
1 bunch green onions, chopped
2 (4.25-ounce) cans sliced black olives
3 tomatoes, chopped
1 cup grated cheese
1 (32-ounce) bag tortilla chips, crushed
1 cup Hellmann's mayonnaise
1 (8-ounce) jar taco sauce

Brown beef and drain well. Mix in taco seasoning and beans; simmer 10 minutes; cool completely. Toss lettuce, green onions, black olives and tomatoes in a large bowl. Add cheese and crushed chips. Top with meat and bean mixture. Mix mayonnaise and taco sauce for dressing; pour over salad just before serving.

Vegetables & Side Dishes

"I am the vine; you are the branches. If a man remains in me and I in him, he will bear much fruit; apart from me you can do nothing." —JOHN 15:5

Sweet Potato Casserole

Oakland Baptist Church, Vicksburg ✝ *Gladys Baggett*

4 to 6 sweet potatoes
½ cup sugar
1 stick margarine
2 eggs, beaten

1 teaspoon vanilla
⅓ cup milk
Dash of cinnamon

TOPPING:
⅓ cup butter, softened
1 cup brown sugar

½ cup all-purpose flour
1 cup chopped pecans

Boil potatoes whole with skins in water to cover until soft and tender. Drain and peel potatoes. Mash up potatoes and add sugar, margarine, eggs, vanilla, milk and cinnamon. Pour into casserole dish and assemble Topping. Mix all Topping ingredients together until crumbly. Cover casserole with Topping and bake uncovered at 350° for 25 to 30 minutes.

Oakland Baptist Church
Vicksburg

2959 Oak Ridge Road
Vicksburg, MS 39183
601-638-6724

Oakland Baptist Church was organized in 1936. Since its founding, Oakland Baptist Church has served its community well, offering ministry to all age groups, worship, Bible study, and outreach. It is known today for its commitment to missions, giving more than one fourth of its budget to mission endeavors locally, in the state, nation, and around the world. Oakland Baptist also provides activities and ministry for children and youth, as well as senior adults. Our doors are open to all people, with services on Sunday at 10:45 a.m. and 6:00 p.m., and Wednesday night activities for all ages beginning with supper at 5:30 p.m..

Sweet Potato Casserole

Carmel Baptist Church, Monticello ✝ *Alice Givens*

CASSEROLE:
3 cups mashed sweet potatoes
1 stick margarine, melted
3 eggs, beaten
1½ cups sugar
½ cup evaporated milk
1 cup flaked coconut (optional)
1 teaspoon vanilla
½ teaspoon salt

Mix all Casserole ingredients together. Pour into buttered casserole dish.

TOPPING:
1 cup self-rising flour
1 cup sugar
1½ sticks margarine, softened
1 cup chopped nuts
2 tablespoons water

Mix all Topping ingredients and sprinkle over potato mixture. Bake at 350° for 1 hour, or until top is crunchy.

Sweet Potato Casserole

Farmington Baptist Church, Corinth

1 (29-ounce) can sweet potatoes
1 cup sugar
2 eggs, beaten
1 stick margarine, divided (½ softened and ½ melted)
1 teaspoon vanilla
½ teaspoon salt
1 cup brown sugar
⅓ cup all-purpose flour
1 cup chopped nuts (optional)

Mash sweet potatoes. Add sugar, eggs, softened margarine, vanilla and salt; mix well. Pour into a 9x9-inch casserole dish. Combine brown sugar and flour together, adding nuts, if desired. Spread over potato mixture. Pour melted margarine over all. Bake at 350° for 30 minutes.

Candied Yams

Sunrise Baptist Church, Carthage ✝ *Marie Brantley*

4 medium sweet potatoes, peeled and cut like French fries
1 cup sugar
1 tablespoon flour
⅓ cup water
1 tablespoon lemon or orange juice
¾ stick margarine

Place potatoes in a 2-quart baking dish. Mix sugar and flour; sprinkle over potatoes. Mix water and lemon juice; pour over potatoes. Dot with margarine. Cover and bake at 400° for 45 to 60 minutes.

Candied Yams

Toxish Baptist Church, Pontotoc

1 (29-ounce) can yams, drained (reserve ½ cup liquid)
1 (8-ounce) can crushed pineapple
½ cup honey
½ cup brown sugar
¼ cup granulated sugar
¾ cup raisins
½ teaspoon nutmeg
Dash salt
2 tablespoons all-purpose flour
½ cup water

In a saucepan, combine reserved yam liquid, pineapple, honey, sugars, raisins, nutmeg and salt. Bring to a boil. In a small bowl, mix flour and water. Slowly pour into liquid mixture and cook until slightly thickened. Remove from heat and set aside. Arrange yams in a baking dish and pour mixture over all. Place dish on a baking sheet to prevent spills. Bake at 350° for about 35 minutes.

Steamed Cauliflower and Cheese Sauce

1 large head cauliflower, cut into florets
Salt and pepper to taste
2 tablespoons butter
2 tablespoons all-purpose flour
1 cup heavy whipping cream
1 cup shredded Cheddar cheese
2 tablespoons mascarpone cheese

Add cauliflower to a large pot of salted boiling water and cook until tender, about 5 minutes. Drain well, then add back to the pot and continue to cook 3 minutes, or until dry. Season with salt and pepper. Melt butter in a medium sauté pan over medium heat. Sprinkle with flour and stir until pasty, about 1 minute. Slowly add heavy cream whisking constantly until smooth. Continue to cook, stirring constantly, until hot. Stir in mascarpone. Continue to cook and stir until hot and bubbly, just another minute or 2. Drizzle cheese sauce over cauliflower and serve. Serves 4 to 6 people.

Squash Dressing

Vardaman Street Baptist Church, Wiggins † *Debbie Rogers*

2 cups cooked squash
½ stick margarine, melted
1 large onion, chopped
2 cups crumbled cornbread

1 (10.25-ounce) can cream of chicken
  soup
Salt and pepper to taste

Combine all ingredients. Pour into greased 2-quart casserole dish. Bake at 400° for 30 to 40 minutes.

Vardaman Street Baptist Church
Wiggins

334 South Vardaman Street • Wiggins, MS 39577
www.vardamanstreet.org • 601-928-3943

Since the conception of Vardaman Street Baptist Church in September 1946 until the present day, the church has enjoyed many years of fruitfulness and faithfulness. Its current position in the Baptist Missionary Association of America and Southern Baptist Convention is known by almost everyone because of its commitment to missions and service to the association. The church has always stood firm on its commitment to fulfill the Great Commission given to us by the Lord Jesus Christ Himself. Because of the vision and efforts of some 18 people in the beginning, the church now has grown and is active in evangelism, fellowship, and discipleship. Through the church's ministry, hundreds of lives have been touched and many souls have come to know Christ as Lord and Savior. Many families have also found their Christian faith established in the rich history of the church.

Squash Dressing

Farmington Baptist Church, Corinth

1 large onion, chopped
3 cups chopped squash
3 to 5 cups crumbled cornbread
1 stick margarine, melted
1 (10.25-ounce) can cream of celery soup
1 (10.25-ounce) can cream of chicken soup
1 tablespoon rubbed sage, or to taste
Salt and pepper to taste

Cook onion and squash in salted water to cover until tender; drain, reserving water. Mash squash and combine with cornbread, margarine, both soups and sage. Season to taste with salt and pepper. If more liquid is needed, use reserved water from squash and onion. Bake at 350° about 30 minutes or until heated through.

Squash Delight Casserole

Antioch Baptist Church, Brandon ✝ *Betty Bowman*

2 cups cooked squash
½ stick butter, melted
½ cup mayonnaise
Salt and pepper to taste
½ cup grated Cheddar cheese
1 teaspoon sugar
1 onion, chopped
1 egg, beaten
Ritz cracker crumbs

Combine squash, butter, mayonnaise, salt, pepper, cheese, sugar and onion; mix well. Add egg, mixing well. Pour into a 2- to 3-quart baking dish. Top with cracker crumbs and bake at 350° for 35 to 40 minutes.

Squash Dressing

Bethel Missionary Baptist Church, Seminary ✝ *Bernice Morgan*

1 medium onion, chopped
1 stick margarine
2 cups cooked squash
2 cups crumbled cornbread
2 eggs
1 (10.25-ounce) can cream of chicken soup

Sauté onion in butter until soft. Mix with all the other ingredients and bake at 375° about 30 minutes or until brown on top.

Bethel Missionary Baptist Church

Seminary

725 Bethel Church Road
Seminary, MS 39479
601-722-4833

Kevin Sanford, Pastor

Bethel Missionary Baptist Church was organized July 10, 1881. Beginning with a brush arbor, to a log building, to a structure later used as a school, the church house has evolved over the years to the current building, begun in 1950 and expanded in 1991 plus a fellowship hall added in 1977 and steeple in 1995. Bethel has administered baptism according to our Lord's instruction from its very beginning. The first candidates were baptized at the old Sanford Mill and other locations include Bullock Creek at Sanford and the Shows swim hole on Shows Creek. In 1961, a new metal baptistery was installed in the church house and is being used to this date. The first passion of Bethel Baptist Church has always been to fulfill our Lord's command to evangelize the lost, baptize the repentant and equip the Saints. God has graciously rewarded us with souls for our labors.

Squash Casserole

Corinth Baptist Church, Magee ✝ *Doris Tullos*

1 pound yellow squash, chopped
1 medium onion, chopped
1 teaspoon sugar
1 egg, beaten
½ cup mayonnaise
Salt and pepper to taste
1 (8-ounce) can sliced water chestnuts, drained and sliced
1 cup shredded sharp Cheddar cheese
Italian breadcrumbs
½ cup butter

Cook squash and onion until tender; mash and drain. Mix sugar, egg, mayonnaise, salt, pepper, water chestnuts and cheese. Add to squash. Pour into casserole dish and top with breadcrumbs. Dot with butter. Bake at 350° for 30 minutes or until top is lightly brown.

Brussels Sprouts with Bacon

6 slices bacon, chopped
1½ pounds Brussels sprouts
Salt and pepper to taste

In a large nonstick skillet, cook bacon over medium high heat. When fat begins to render, add Brussels sprouts. Sauté until crisp, about 6 minutes. Season with salt and pepper; serve immediately. Makes 4 to 6 servings.

Cabbage Casserole

First Baptist Church, Grenada

1 stick margarine, melted
1½ cups crushed Ritz crackers, divided
4 cups shredded cabbage
½ cup chopped onion
1 (10.25-ounce) can cream of celery soup

½ cup mayonnaise
¼ teaspoon each: salt and pepper
1 cup milk
2 cups grated Cheddar cheese

Mix margarine and crushed crackers. Place half in a greased 2-quart casserole dish. Spread cabbage and onion over top. Mix soup, mayonnaise, salt, pepper and milk; pour over cabbage. Top with cheese and sprinkle remaining crumbs on top. Bake uncovered at 350° for 45 minutes.

First Baptist Church

Grenada

450 Faith Drive
Grenada, MS 38901
662-226-3661

On June 30, 1838, the First Baptist Church of Grenada, Mississippi, was organized. The church has endured through many "dangers, toils and snares," including the Civil War, an epidemic of yellow fever, the Great Depression, a tornado, and fire. First Baptist Church has sent out many men and women to the mission field in our country and abroad. Many ministers have also come from among our congregation. Although we moved our church location in 2012, we are still the same church, with the same mission and ministry of sharing the Gospel of Jesus Christ, more than 175 years later!

The recipes from our church are familiar ones used in many of our Women's Ministry events and church socials. We hope you enjoy them as much as we do!

Sweet and Sour Cabbage

First Baptist Church, Baldwyn

1 cup chopped onions
2 to 3 tablespoons white wine
2 bay leaves
6 teaspoons sugar
1 teaspoon salt
Dash freshly ground pepper
Dash coriander
4 cups thinly sliced red cabbage
1 tablespoon plus 1 teaspoon margarine
2 small green apples, pared, cored and sliced

Combine first 7 ingredients in a large bowl; add cabbage and toss well. Cover and allow to marinate for 1 hour. Melt margarine in a medium skillet. Add cabbage mixture, cover and simmer about 30 minutes. Stir in apples and simmer 1 minute longer.

Eggplant Casserole

Pleasant Home Baptist Church, Laurel † *Linda Clark*

1 medium eggplant
1 cup uncooked rice
1½ pounds ground chuck
1 onion, chopped
½ green bell pepper, chopped
Salt and pepper to taste
Garlic powder to taste
2 (10-ounce) cans Rotel tomatoes
2 cups shredded Cheddar cheese

Peel and cube eggplant; boil until tender. Drain, mash and set aside. Cook rice according to package directions; set aside. Brown meat, onion and bell pepper until meat is no longer pink; drain. Add seasonings and tomatoes. Cook about 30 minutes. Add rice and eggplant; mix well. Pour into casserole dish and top with cheese. Bake at 350° for about 30 minutes.

Yummy Baked Beans

Star Baptist Church, Star

3 (15-ounce) cans pork and beans
1 teaspoon dry mustard
⅛ teaspoon pepper
2 teaspoons salt
¼ cup brown sugar
1 green bell pepper, sliced in rings
1 large onion, sliced in rings

⅛ teaspoon cinnamon
⅛ teaspoon ground cloves
¼ cup ketchup
1 lemon, halved and thinly sliced
3 slices bacon, chopped
1 tablespoon pickle juice

Combine all ingredients; bake in 300° oven for 2 hours or in slow cooker 4 hours.

Star Baptist Church

Star

301 Mangum Drive
Star, MS 39167
601-845-2736
starbaptistchurch.org

In 1906, the New Liberty Baptist Church was organized in Star, and in 1917, the name was changed to Star Baptist Church. A new church building was erected in 1959. The church grew significantly through the coming decades. In 1994, Reverend Victor Bowman was called as pastor and served until 2014. Shortly after his coming, the church building burned and the congregation began meeting in Rankin Academy's facilities. During this time, the church experienced its greatest growth and sweetest fellowship. The church was not rebuilt on the original site, but was blessed to purchase a larger site on which the church could expand. The present building was completed in 1995. The church has a continuing interest in local evangelism, and mission outreach has grown greatly through the years with regular domestic and international mission trips. A Mission Room is maintained at the Christian Life Center to help meet the needs of people in the community.

Green Bean Casserole

Tate Baptist Church, Corinth † *Jannice Shadburn*

4 slices bacon
3 (15-ounce) cans French-style green beans
1 (10.25-ounce) can cream of mushroom soup
1 (8-ounce) package cream cheese, cubed
1 large onion, chopped
½ stick butter
1 (4-ounce) package slivered almonds
1½ cups crushed Ritz crackers

Fry bacon crispy; remove from skillet, reserving fat. Heat beans in fat. Add soup and cream cheese and continue to cook over medium heat to melt cream cheese. Sauté onion in butter. Drain onion, reserving butter. Crumble cooled bacon and add to beans along with onion. Stir in almonds. Place beans in baking dish. Add crackers to reserved butter and mix well. Sprinkle over beans. Bake at 350° until bubbly and brown, about 20 minutes.

Slow Cooker Green Beans

Union Ridge Baptist Church, Noxapater

2 (15-ounce) cans French-style green beans
½ stick butter
½ cup brown sugar
1 (3.5-ounce) package real bacon bits

Put everything except bacon bits in a saucepan. Cook over medium heat until most of liquid is cooked out. Add bacon bits. Transfer to slow cooker and cook 2 to 3 hours. (I usually double this recipe.)

Marinated Green Beans

Liberty Baptist Church, Waynesboro

4 (15-ounce) cans whole green beans, drained and rinsed
½ cup brown sugar
2 tablespoons soy sauce
1 stick butter, melted
4 slices raw bacon

Layer green beans in a large casserole dish. Mix brown sugar, soy sauce and butter. Pour over green beans. Top with bacon slices. Marinate overnight. Bake at 350° for 30 minutes or until bacon is brown.

Sesame Snap Beans

First Baptist Church, Brookhaven † *Leah Stewart*

5 cups fresh green beans
3 tablespoons olive oil
1 tablespoon freshly grated ginger
2 tablespoons minced garlic
½ cup soy sauce
¼ cup sugar
1 teaspoon water
2 teaspoons sesame seeds

In a large wok, sauté beans in olive oil, ginger and garlic about 5 minutes. Mix soy sauce and sugar with water. Add to wok. Stir and cook until beans reach desired tenderness. While stirring, split beans with spatula end allowing sauce to seep into beans for extra flavor. Sprinkle with sesame seeds before serving. These go great with pork.

Hot and Spicy Black-Eyed Peas

Pleasant Home Baptist Church, Laurel ✝ *Beth McBride*

1 (16-ounce) package dried black-eyed peas
4 green onions chopped
1 red bell pepper, chopped
1 jalapeño pepper, diced
1 (3-ounce) package pepperoni slices, diced

2 cups hot water
1 chicken bouillon cube
½ teaspoon salt
¼ teaspoon ground red pepper
1 (14-ounce) can Mexican-style stewed tomatoes
¾ cup uncooked quick rice

Place peas in 5-quart slow cooker. Cover with water 2 inches above peas. Let stand 8 hours; drain. Return peas to slow cooker and add remaining ingredients, except tomatoes and rice. Cover and cook on low 8 hours or until peas are tender. Stir in tomatoes and rice. Cover and cook on low 30 more minutes or until rice is tender.

Pleasant Home Baptist Church

Laurel

386 Matthews Road • Laurel, MS 39443
601-729-2230

Reverend Eric Bean, Pastor

Pleasant Home Baptist Church was organized August 1903, in the rural area of northern Jones County. For over a century, God has richly blessed our church with great, loving pastors, ministers of music, and youth ministers. The congregation is a loving and caring fellowship of believers who remain faithful to His church. Our church has a rich music history, encompassing everything from singing schools to soloists, quartets, ensembles, and a wind ensemble. We are grateful for the contribution all of these make to our worship. There is also a love for missions exhibited by our members. Places the church has served stretch from local ministries in Jones County to areas across the continental United States and beyond. In 2013, we started a food ministry and distributed food boxes to eleven households. That ministry now provides food boxes to over one hundred households each month. We look forward with great anticipation to what God will do in our midst as new staff members are added and as we continue to be faithful and obedient servants.

Broccoli Rice Casserole

Mount Helm Baptist Church, Jackson

3 ounces reduced-fat Cheddar cheese, shredded
½ cup diced onion
1 (4-ounce) can sliced mushrooms, drained
½ cup skim milk
1 tablespoon plus 1 teaspoon diet margarine
½ tablespoon salt
2 (10-ounce) packages frozen chopped broccoli, thawed
1 cup cooked rice

Heat oven to 350°. Spray a 2-quart casserole dish with nonstick spray. In a medium saucepan, combine all ingredients except broccoli and rice. Heat until cheese and margarine are melted. Stir in broccoli and rice and continue to cook 2 minutes. Put in casserole dish and bake 30 minutes. Serves 4.

Roasted Asparagus with Pine Nuts

Mount Helm Baptist Church, Jackson

2 tablespoons pine nuts
1½ pounds asparagus
1 large shallot, thinly sliced
2 teaspoons extra virgin olive oil
¼ teaspoon salt, divided
⅛ teaspoon freshly ground pepper
¼ cup balsamic vinegar

Preheat oven to 350°. Spread pine nuts in a small baking pan and toast in oven until golden and fragrant, 7 to 10 minutes. Transfer to a small bowl to cool. Increase oven temperature to 450°. Snap off the tough ends of asparagus and, if desired, peel stalks. Toss asparagus with shallot, oil, and ⅛ teaspoon salt and pepper. Spread in a single layer on a large baking sheet with sides. Roast, turning twice, until asparagus is tender and browned, 10 to 15 minutes. Bring vinegar and remaining ⅛ teaspoon salt to a simmer, swirling pan occasionally until slightly syrupy and reduced to approximately 1 tablespoon. Cooking time is about 5 minutes. To serve, toss asparagus with reduced vinegar and sprinkle with pine nuts. Serves 4.

Baked Asparagus Fries

New Zion Baptist Church, Crystal Springs

1 cup panko (breadcrumbs)
½ cup grated Parmesan cheese
Kosher salt and freshly ground black
   pepper to taste

1 pound asparagus, trimmed
½ cup all-purpose flour
2 large eggs, beaten

Preheat oven to 425°. Lightly oil a baking sheet or coat with nonstick spray. In a large bowl, combine Panko and Parmesan; season with salt and pepper. Set aside. Working in batches, dredge asparagus in flour, dip into eggs, then dredge in panko mixture, pressing to coat. Place asparagus in a single layer on baking sheet. Place into oven and bake 10 to 12 minutes, or until golden brown and crisp. Serve immediately. Yield 4 servings.

Corn Casserole

Unity Baptist Church, McHenry

½ stick butter
3 tablespoons flour
1 cup whipping cream
2 (11-ounce) cans white corn
1 (6-ounce) can French fried onions

Melt butter in saucepan. Add flour and cook, stirring, over low heat until mixed well. Add cream and stir until thickened. Drain corn and stir into sauce. Place in casserole dish and top with onion rings. Bake at 350° for 15 minutes.

Unity Baptist Church

McHenry

236 Highway 49
McHenry, MS 39561
228-861-4536
www.facebook.com/unitybaptistchurch.mchenry

Neil Tapp, **Pastor**

Unity Baptist Church is a growing body of believers that love serving the Lord. We invite you to come and visit with us and be a part of the many ministries that our church provides. Our Golden Hearts meet every 2nd Tuesday at 10:30 a.m. We work aggressively with youth of all ages, teaching them the Gospel of Jesus Christ, equipping them for the future. The van ministry allows us to reach out to those who are in need of transportation. We have some of the best Sunday School teachers around, with classes for men, ladies, couples, and new converts. There are also Sunday School classes for every youth and children's age group, including a nursery that's staffed and provided for every service. Come and be a part of our services and give us an opportunity to get to know you.

Creamed Corn

Community Missionary Baptist Church, Poplarville

4 pounds sweet corn
2 (8-ounce) packages cream cheese, cubed
1 stick butter
¾ cup heavy whipping cream
4 tablespoons sugar
1 teaspoon pepper
½ teaspoon salt

Mix all together in a slow cooker on low heat; cook 4 hours.

Corn Pudding

First Baptist Byhalia

1 tablespoon bacon drippings
2 eggs
4 tablespoons sugar
4 tablespoons cornstarch
4 tablespoons butter, melted
1 cup milk
1 (15-ounce) can cream-style corn
1 (15-ounce) can whole-kernel corn, drained
½ cup crushed corn chips

Preheat oven to 350° and place a cast-iron skillet with bacon drippings in oven to heat. Beat eggs; add sugar, cornstarch, butter and milk. Mix well. Mix in cans of corn. Place mixture in skillet and bake 30 minutes. Place chips on top and continue to cook 10 minutes, or until middle doesn't jiggle.

Tastes Like Fresh Corn

Journey Baptist Church, Olive Branch

2 (11-ounce) cans white shoepeg corn (Green Giant)
½ pint whipping cream
½ stick REAL butter, melted
3 round tablespoons flour

Combine all ingredients. Bake at 350° for 30 minutes.

Corn Casserole

Woodland Baptist Church, Columbus

1 (8.5-ounce) box Jiffy corn muffin mix
1 (15-ounce) can whole-kernel corn, drained
1 (15-ounce) can cream-style corn
1 stick butter, melted
1 cup sour cream
1 cup grated sharp Cheddar cheese

Mix together and cook in a greased 9x13-inch glass dish at 350° for 35 to 45 minutes, or until golden brown.

Woodland Baptist Church

Columbus

3033 Ridge Road
Columbus, MS 39705
662-327-6689
www.woodlandonline.org

Shelby Hazzard, Pastor

August 1976, Ridgecrest Baptist Church of Columbus and BMA of MS agreed to co-support a mission church in Columbus. The first service was held March 6, 1977, with 15 in Sunday School and 17 in Worship Services. God continued to bless us, and Woodland Mission was organized into Woodland Baptist Church on May 12, 1977, with 59 charter members. The fellowship hall and gym were completed in 1985, and our first note burning was held January 1992. The new sanctuary was completed and dedicated July 1, 2001, with note burning held July 2, 2006. In 2009, the members of Woodland Baptist Church elected to become affiliated with the Southern Baptist Convention. With a focus on missions, the church gives 10% or more for missions. Woodland has made three mission trips to Honduras to help build and establish churches—1992, 1994, and 1996. We have had nine pastors and three interim pastors.

Vegetable Casserole

Liberty Baptist Church, Raleigh † *Kristi Ables*

1 (16-ounce) package frozen mixed vegetables
1 cup chopped celery
1 medium onion, chopped
1 cup shredded cheese
1 cup mayonnaise
1 sleeve Ritz crackers
1 stick margarine, melted

Cook frozen vegetables according to package directions. Drain and place in bottom of casserole dish. Mix celery, onion, cheese and mayonnaise and put on top of vegetables. Combine crackers and margarine; put on top. Bake in 350° oven for about 30 minutes.

Spicy Fried Okra

½ cup cornmeal
1 cup all-purpose flour
¼ teaspoon Cajun seasoning
2 teaspoons seasoned salt
2 pounds fresh okra, sliced ½-inch thick
½ cup buttermilk
Oil, for frying

In a medium bowl, combine cornmeal, flour, Cajun seasoning and seasoned salt. Dip okra in buttermilk and then dredge in cornmeal-flour mixture to coat well. Fry in batches in hot oil removing to a paper towel to drain. Serve immediately drizzled with Spicy Sauce.

SPICY SAUCE:
1 cup mayonnaise
3 tablespoons Thai sweet chili sauce
1 tablespoon garlic chili pepper sauce
⅛ teaspoon Cajun Seasoning

In a small bowl, combine all ingredients, stirring well. Use immediately or cover and chill.

Potato Casserole

Goss Baptist Church, Columbia ✝ *Carolyn Buckley*

2 pounds hash browns
1 onion, grated
3 cups sour cream
2 (10.25-ounce) cans cream of chicken
   soup

3 cups shredded mild Cheddar cheese
½ stick margarine
Salt and pepper to taste
2 cups Frosted Flakes

Grease a large baking dish with butter. Combine hash browns, onion, sour cream, soup, cheese, margarine, salt and pepper. Bake at 350° for 30 minutes. Top with Frosted Flakes and bake another 30 minutes.

Goss Baptist Church
Columbia

20 Mark McArthur Drive
Columbia, MS 39429
601-736-9563
gossbaptist@att.net

Mark McArthur, Pastor

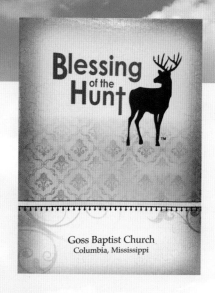

Goss Baptist Church
Columbia, Mississippi

In 2003, God placed a burden on our hearts to minister to the people who enjoy the fruits of God's creation. God led us to offer "The Blessing of the Hunt" as an event through which we could celebrate the opportunity to enjoy the outdoors and share the Gospel Message to provide salvation for all who would believe in Him. God has truly blessed us since that beginning in 2003. The first year, our attendance was numbered at approximately 150. Each year, we have seen the number increase dramatically and in 2014, we saw an attendance of over 3,400 men, women, youth, and children. More than that, through the Blessing of the Hunt, we have seen over 1,400 people either accept Christ as Savior for the first time or renew their commitment to Him. Please join us on the second Thursday of November of each year for The Blessing of the Hunt.

Potato Casserole

Freedom Baptist Church, Burnsville

1 (16-ounce) package shredded potatoes
1 (10.25-ounce) can cream of mushroom soup
1 cup shredded cheese
1 cup chopped onions and peppers mix
1 cup sour cream
Salt and pepper to taste

Mix together all ingredients and place in a casserole dish. Bake at 350° until golden brown, about 35 minutes.

Scalloped Potatoes

2 tablespoons butter
3 tablespoons all-purpose flour
1 teaspoon salt
¼ teaspoon pepper
1½ cups milk
½ cup shredded Cheddar cheese
1¾ pounds potatoes, peeled and thinly sliced
1 medium onion, thinly sliced

Melt butter in a small nonstick skillet. Stir in flour, salt and pepper until smooth; gradually add milk whisking constantly. Bring to a boil. Cook and stir 2 minutes or until thickened. Remove from the heat; stir in cheese and mix until cheese is melted and blends with sauce. Place half the potatoes in a 1½-quart baking dish coated with cooking spray; layer with half the onion and half the cheese sauce. Repeat layers. Cover and bake at 350° for 50 minutes. Uncover; bake 10 to 15 minutes longer or until bubbly and potatoes are tender. Makes 6 servings.

Cheesy Ranch Potatoes

Rehobeth Baptist Church ✝ *Michele Shedd*

6 large potatoes
1 (16-ounce) bottle ranch salad dressing mix
1 package shredded Cheddar cheese
1 (3-ounce) jar bacon bits
1 bunch green onions, chopped

Boil potatoes until tender. Do not overcook. Cut potatoes long ways into halves and place in a baking dish. Pour ranch dressing over each potato and sprinkle with cheese, bacon bits and green onions. Cover with foil and bake at 350° until cheese has melted. Uncover and bake 10 minutes longer. Serves 12.

Ranch Potatoes

Palestine Baptist Church, Nettleton ✝ *Kristy Brown*

5 pounds red or white potatoes
2 cups milk
1 stick butter or margarine, sliced
1 (1-ounce) envelope dry ranch dressing mix
Hormel bacon bits to taste

Cube potatoes (can leave peel on). Place in 9x13-inch pan. Cover with milk. Place butter slices over top. Sprinkle generously with ranch mix. Cover with aluminum foil. Bake at 425° for about an hour. Add bacon bits, if desired. Stir and enjoy.

The Lord is my shepherd, I shall not want. He makes me lie down in green pastures, he leads me beside quiet waters, he restores my soul. He guides me in paths of righteousness for his name's sake.
—Psalm 23:1-3

Mom's Potato Pancakes

Oak Grove Baptist Church, Lucedale ✝ *Dianne Davis*

4 cups peeled and shredded potatoes
  (about 4 large)
1 egg, lightly beaten
3 tablespoons flour

1 tablespoon grated onion
1 teaspoon salt
¼ teaspoon pepper
Oil for frying

Rinse potatoes in cold water; drain well. In a large bowl, combine all ingredients, except oil for frying. In a skillet, heat ¼ inch oil over medium heat. Drop batter by ⅓ cupfuls into hot oil. Flatten to form pancake. When golden brown, turn and brown on other side. Drain on paper towels. Feeds 6.

Oak Grove Missionary Baptist Church

Lucedale

14170 Highway 98
Lucedale, MS 39452
601-947-2803
www.oakgrovemissionarybaptist.org

Oak Grove Missionary Baptist Church, established July 27, 1947, is nestled among numerous oak trees—thus the name Oak Grove. Lucedale is located in George County in southeast Mississippi. Oak Grove has been at the same location since the organization of the church. We are of the Baptist Missionary Association of America (BMAA). The members of Oak Grove have continued to love the Lord and are thankful for the sacrifice that our Lord Jesus Christ made on the cross of Calvary. The Lord continues to bless our country church in many ways. And with the Lord's blessings, Oak Grove believes the commission that Christ gave to the church to go and teach all nations about Christ. Oak Grove supports missionaries to many parts of the world, including those serving in Haiti, Philippines, Panama, India, Ecuador, Ukraine, Mexico, Oregon (US), and Venezuela. Please pray for us as we will pray for you.

Hash Brown Casserole

Big Creek Baptist Church, Soso

1 (32-ounce) package frozen hash brown potatoes, thawed
1 teaspoon salt
½ cup finely chopped onion
2 cups shredded Cheddar cheese
½ cup margarine, melted
½ teaspoon black pepper
1 (10.25-ounce) can cream of chicken soup

Preheat oven to 350°. Combine all ingredients, except hash browns, and mix well. Fold hash browns in last and bake uncovered in a greased 9x13-inch pan for 35 minutes.

Big Creek Baptist Church

Soso

28 Big Creek Church Road
Soso, MS 39480
601-763-8100
www.bigcreeksoso.com

Justin Rhodes, Pastor

Big Creek Baptist Church, located on Highway 84 ten miles west of Laurel, has been in existence for more than 150 years. Big Creek Church has ministered in the Big Creek Community to many families and individuals down through the years, and today the church continues sharing the love of Christ. The church is committed to worship, fellowship, evangelism, discipleship, and sound, biblical preaching. The church is a member of the Baptist Missionary Association of America, the Baptist Missionary Association of Mississippi, and the Big Creek Missionary Baptist Association.

Roasted New Potatoes with Herbs

Auburn Baptist Church, Tupelo ✝ *Lori Robinson*

¼ cup extra virgin oil
4 to 5 large garlic cloves, flattened
20 new potatoes, halved
1 tablespoon chopped fresh rosemary
1½ tablespoons chopped fresh thyme
Salt and pepper to taste

Combine oil and garlic; set aside for at least 1 hour to allow flavors to blend. Preheat oven to 400°. Place potatoes in baking dish and sprinkle with rosemary, thyme, salt and pepper. Pour oil and garlic over potatoes and toss well. Roast, stirring occasionally, about 45 minutes or until tender and crusty. Serves 4 to 6.

Ms. Maggie Black's Hash Brown Casserole

Fairfield Baptist Church, Moselle

1 (32-ounce) package frozen hash browns
2 cups shredded Cheddar cheese
1 cup sour cream
1 (10.25-ounce) can cream of chicken soup
½ teaspoon salt
1½ cups crushed cornflakes
1 stick margarine, melted

Treat a large Pyrex baking dish with nonstick spray. Layer hash browns in the bottom. Mix together cheese, sour cream, soup and salt in saucepan; cook over medium heat until cheese has melted. Pour over hash browns. Sprinkle cornflakes over top and drizzle with margarine. Bake at 350° for 45 minutes.

Slow Cooker Tater Tot Casserole

Russell Baptist Church, Meridian † *Jenifer Robinson*

1 (32-ounce) package frozen tater tots, divided
1 pound lean ground beef or ground turkey, cooked
1 cup sour cream
1 (10.25-ounce) can cream of mushroom soup
Bacon, cooked and crumbled (optional)
2 cups shredded cheese, divided
6 green onions, chopped, divided

Insert a liner in the slow cooker or spray with nonstick cooking spray. Place half the tater tots in slow cooker (only enough to cover the bottom). In a large bowl, mix beef, sour cream, soup, bacon, 1 cup shredded cheese and half the green onions. Pour half of beef mixture over tater tots. Repeat using remaining tater tots and remaining beef mixture; sprinkle top with remaining 1 cup shredded cheese. Cover and cook on high for 3 hours or low for 5 hours. Top with remaining green onions before serving.

Tomato Pie

Robinhood Baptist Church, Brandon † *Mary Morris*

Basil to taste (just a little usually makes it perfect)
4 to 5 fresh tomatoes, chopped and drained
1 pie crust, baked according to directions and cooled
1 cup chopped green onions
Salt and pepper to taste
1 cup shredded mozzarella cheese
1 cup shredded Cheddar cheese
1 cup mayonnaise

Preheat oven to 300°. Mix basil with tomatoes and spread in pie crust. Layer green onions on top and season with salt and pepper. Mix mozzarella cheese, Cheddar cheese and mayonnaise. Pour over top of pie. Bake at 300° until cheese melts, about 35 minutes.

Fried Green Tomatoes with Bacon Vinaigrette and Warm Frisee

Mount Helm Baptist Church, Jackson

4 large green (unripe) tomatoes, sliced crosswise ½ inch thick
1 garlic clove, minced
1 tablespoon extra virgin olive oil
Salt and freshly ground pepper
6 slices thickly sliced bacon (6 ounces), cut crosswise into ½-inch strips
1 tablespoon cider vinegar
1¼ cups all-purpose flour, divided
Cayenne pepper
2 large eggs
1 tablespoon water
1 cup yellow cornmeal
1 teaspoon dried thyme
Canola oil, for frying
1 large head frisée lettuce (½ pound), torn into pieces

In a large bowl, gently toss tomatoes with garlic and olive oil. Season with salt and pepper and let stand for 10 minutes. In a medium skillet, cook bacon over moderately high heat until crisp, about 6 minutes. Drain on paper towels. Pour off all but 2 tablespoons of fat; stir in vinegar. In a pie plate, season ¾ cup flour with salt, pepper and cayenne. In another pie plate, whisk eggs with water. In a third pie plate, mix cornmeal with remaining ¾ cup flour and thyme; season with salt, pepper and cayenne. Line a baking sheet with wax paper. Drain tomatoes. Working with 1 slice at a time, dip tomatoes in flour, tapping off any excess, then dip them in beaten egg, then in cornmeal pressing to help it adhere. Transfer to prepared baking sheet. In a large skillet, heat ¼ inch canola oil until shimmering. Fry tomatoes in batches over moderately high heat, turning once, until golden, 5 to 6 minutes per batch. Transfer to a rack lined with paper towels to drain. Sprinkle with salt. Rewarm bacon fat and vinegar in the skillet over low heat. Add frisee and season with salt and pepper; toss until slightly wilted, about 1 minute. Transfer tomatoes to plates. Top with frisée. Garnish with bacon and serve. Serves 12.

Homemade Mac & Cheese

Parkway Baptist Church, Clinton ✝ *Candy Anderson*

2 cups uncooked elbow macaroni
¼ cup butter or margarine
¼ cup all-purpose flour
½ teaspoon salt
¼ teaspoon pepper
¼ teaspoon ground mustard
¼ teaspoon Worcestershire sauce
2 cups milk
2 cups shredded or cubed Cheddar cheese

Preheat oven to 350°. Cook macaroni as directed on package. While macaroni is cooking, melt butter in a 3 quart saucepan over low heat. Stir in flour, salt, pepper, mustard and Worcestershire sauce. Cook over medium-low heat, stirring constantly, until mixture is smooth and bubbly. Remove from heat. Stir in milk. Heat to boiling, stirring constantly. Boil and stir for 1 minute. Stir in cheese. Cook, stirring occasionally, until cheese is melted. Drain macaroni. Gently stir macaroni into cheese sauce. Pour into an ungreased 2-quart casserole. Bake uncovered for 20 to 25 minutes or until bubbly.

Cheese and Macaroni Casserole

Toxish Baptist Church, Pontotoc

1 (8-ounce) box elbow macaroni, cooked and drained
1 cup mayonnaise
1 (10.25-ounce) can cream of mushroom soup
1 (4-ounce) can mushrooms (ends and pieces)
½ cup chopped onion
1 (4-ounce) jar chopped pimento
1 (16-ounce) package shredded sharp Cheddar cheese
½ cup butter, cut into pats
1 sleeve Ritz Crackers, crumbled

Mix all ingredients, except butter and crackers, and place in a casserole dish. Mix butter pats and crackers and sprinkle on top. Bake at 350° for 30 minutes or until casserole bubbles and is beginning to brown.

3 Cheese Mac 'n Cheese

Oak Grove Baptist Church, Lucedale † *Rhonda Grimes*

1 (16-ounce) package elbow macaroni
½ (16-ounce) package Velveeta cheese, cubed
½ (8-ounce) package cream cheese
1 cup milk
1 stick butter
Salt and pepper to taste
2 cups (8 ounces) shredded Cheddar cheese

Boil macaroni in salted water until done; drain and set aside. Place Velveeta, cream cheese, milk and butter in same pan you used to cook pasta; cook over medium-low heat, stirring constantly, until all are melted and blended. Toss pasta with salt and pepper and put it in a large baking dish. Pour cheese mixture over pasta and stir. Sprinkle shredded Cheddar over top and bake at 350° for 20 to 30 minutes. If pasta is really soupy when you pour the cheese mixture in, extend cooking time by a few minutes and don't add shredded cheese till the last 5 minutes of cook time. Enjoy.

Baked Macaroni Casserole

Liberty Baptist Church, Waynesboro

1 (8-ounce) package macaroni
2 tablespoons margarine
2 tablespoons flour
1 teaspoon salt
2½ cups milk
2 cups shredded Cheddar cheese, divided
1 (10.25-ounce) can Cheddar cheese soup

Cook macaroni as directed on package. Drain. Melt margarine in saucepan. Stir in flour and salt. Add milk. Heat, stirring constantly, until sauce thickens. Add 1 cup cheese and cheese soup; heat until melted and creamy. Combine macaroni and sauce. Pour into greased 2-quart casserole dish. Top with remaining 1 cup cheese. Bake at 375° for 45 minutes.

Cheese Grits with Rotel Tomatoes

First Baptist Church of Greenville † *Tommye Stiles*

3 cups water
2 cups whole milk
1½ cups quick-cooking grits
1½ sticks plus 1 tablespoon butter, divided
⅔ cup chopped green onions
½ teaspoon garlic salt
3 cups grated sharp Cheddar cheese, divided
1½ (10-ounce) cans Rotel tomatoes
2 eggs

Boil water and milk in a medium-size stockpot. Turn temperature down to low and gradually add grits, stirring constantly. Put lid on the pot and let grits cook undisturbed for 3 minutes. Remove cover and stir grits well. Add 1½ sticks butter and stir. Replace lid and simmer 3 more minutes. Sauté green onions in remaining 1 tablespoon butter; add to grits. Add garlic salt and 1½ cups cheese. Stir until cheese melts. Add Rotel tomatoes with juice. Taste to see if dish needs more salt. Beat eggs by hand then mix well into the grits mixture. Pour into a greased 9x13-inch casserole dish and bake at 350° for 30 minutes uncovered. Top with remaining 1½ cups cheese and return to oven long enough to melt the cheese.

Brunch Cheese Grits

Magnolia Baptist Church, Hattiesburg † *Charlotte Townsend*

Cooked grits for 6
1 egg, beaten
¼ stick butter or margarine
1 (8-ounce) package shredded sharp Cheddar cheese
½ teaspoon garlic powder
¼ teaspoon black pepper
1 tablespoon A-1 steak sauce
2 dashes Tabasco

Combine grits with beaten egg, mixing well. Stir in butter, cheese, garlic powder, pepper, A-1 and Tabasco. Pour into a greased glass baking dish. Cover and bake at 350° for 45 minutes. Double recipe for large crowd and double baking time.

Homecoming Chicken Dressing

Carmel Baptist Church, Monticello † *Aline Dunn*

1 large fryer chicken
2 medium onions, chopped
1 cup chopped celery
1 green bell pepper, chopped
2 sticks margarine
3 eggs, beaten
6 boiled eggs, chopped
1 prepared pan cornbread, crumbled

1 cup cooked rice
1 cup evaporated milk
1 (10.25-ounce) can cream of chicken
  soup
1 (2-ounce) package Lipton onion soup
  mix
1 tablespoon poultry seasoning
Salt and pepper to taste

Boil fryer in salted water to cover until done; cool slightly. Debone chicken and cut into small pieces. Save broth. Sauté onions, celery and bell pepper in margarine. In a large baking dish, combine chicken, sautéed vegetables (with butter) and remaining ingredients. Add enough chicken broth to be soupy. Bake at 300° for about an hour or until brown. (Best if mixed the night before and refrigerated before cooking to allow the flavors to blend.)

Carmel Baptist Church
Monticello

1157 Carmel New Hope Road
Monticello, MS 39654
601-587-7145

November 21, 1909, a group of nineteen born-again Christians met under a "brush arbor" to organize a church, which was later named Carmel Baptist Church. After a few meetings under the brush arbor, the worship services were moved into the country school house located just across the road. Within three months, a Building Committee was named, and on August 12, 1912, services were held in the new building. The text for the day was Luke 8:18. "Amazing Grace" was the first hymn sung by the congregation in the new building. The present sanctuary was built in 1954, with the first addition and pastorium being provided in years to follow. The new children's annex was constructed in 1984. A large fellowship hall and kitchen has since been added. Carmel Baptist Church is now debt free.

Holiday Dressing

Pelahatchie Baptist Church, Pelahatchie † *Sylvia Barnes*

The secret to this dressing is baking ingredients in the cornbread. You are going to love it.

Cornbread batter (double batch from your favorite recipe)
6 eggs
4 stalks celery, chopped
1 bunch green onions, chopped (with stems)
1 tablespoon ground sage
Salt to taste
1 stick margarine, melted
1 (10.25-ounce) can cream of chicken soup
Broth from boiled whole chicken

Combine batter, eggs, celery, onions, sage and salt. Pour into hot greased cast-iron skillets (usually takes 2) and bake at 350°, until cornbread is done. Break cornbread in pieces into a large bowl; add margarine, soup and broth as needed to make the dressing very moist; mix well. Pour into a large baking dish. Bake at 350° until set and brown on top.

Spicy Stuffed Peppers

Oakland Baptist Church, Vicksburg † *Grace McCann*

6 green bell peppers
1 pound sweet Italian sausage
  (or regular spicy sausage)
4 cups cooked rice
2 (10-ounce) cans Rotel tomatoes
2 cups shredded Monterey Jack cheese

Preheat oven to 350°. Remove tops and seeds from bell peppers. Blanch peppers in boiling water for 5 minutes and drain. Remove sausage casing and crumble meat into a 5-quart saucepan. Cook over medium heat, stirring, until brown; drain. Stir in rice, tomatoes and cheese. Spoon filling into peppers; place in 8x8-inch baking dish. Bake 20 minutes. Yields 6 servings.

Main Dishes

"*I am the good shepherd. The good shepherd lays down his life for the sheep.*" —JOHN 10:11

Artichoke Chicken Casserole

Magnolia Baptist Church, Hattiesburg ✝ *Charlotte Townsend*

1 (6-ounce) box wild rice
4 cups chopped cooked chicken breast
1 (10.25-ounce) can cream of chicken
   soup
1 (8-ounce) can water chestnuts,
   chopped
1 cup sour cream

1 cup mayonnaise
1 (4-ounce) jar chopped pimento,
   drained
1 (8-ounce) can artichoke hearts (not
   marinated), chopped
1 stick butter
1 sleeve Ritz Crackers, crushed

Cook wild rice as directed on box; add chicken. Mix soup, water chestnuts, sour cream, mayonnaise, pimento and artichoke hearts. Add to rice and chicken. Mix all together well and pour into a greased 3-quart casserole dish. Melt butter and add crushed Ritz crackers. Sprinkle over top of casserole and bake in preheated oven at 350° for 30 minutes.

Magnolia Baptist Church

Hattiesburg

148 King Road
Hattiesburg, MS 39402
601-264-8087
www.magnoliabaptistms.com
Greg Medenwald, Pastor

In October 1950, a small group organized Westside Baptist Church, and in March 1951, the first service was held at the newly purchased property on West 4th Street. November 1975, Greg Medenwald became pastor. November 1994, the church name was changed to Magnolia Baptist Church. Mother's Day 1997 was the final service at the 4th Street location; church services were held at a truck terminal during construction. March 1998 was our first Honduras Medical/Construction Mission Trip. April 19, 1998, was the first service at the new building. October 2000, Magnolia celebrated our 50th anniversary and the 25th anniversary of Pastor Greg. The Lord has truly blessed us with a large membership growth, continued ministry to the people of Honduras and Hattiesburg, three building additions, and in October 2015, we celebrated our 65th anniversary and Pastor Greg's 40th anniversary. We are also soon to construct the Family Ministry Center. Magnolia is truly grateful to God, Jesus Christ, and the Holy Spirit.

Scallopine di Pollo

First Baptist Byhalia

LEMON BUTTER SAUCE:

4 ounces (½ cup) lemon juice
2 ounces (¼ cup) white wine
4 ounces (½ cup) heavy cream

2 sticks butter, melted
Pinch black pepper

Heat lemon juice and wine in a saucepan over medium heat. Bring to boil and reduce by a third. Add cream and continue to stir until mixture thickens, 3 to 4 minutes. Slowly add butter and a pinch of black pepper. Stir until dissolved and reduce heat to low to keep warm.

PASTA:

1 (16-ounce) package angel hair pasta

Cook pasta according to box directions.

CHICKEN:

1 (6- to 8-ounce) chicken breast
   pounded thin (½ inch)
¾ cup flour
2 tablespoons black pepper
1 teaspoon salt
2 tablespoons garlic powder
2 tablespoons olive oil

2 tablespoons butter
6 ounces pancetta
12 ounces fresh mushrooms, sliced
12 ounces artichoke hearts, sliced
1 tablespoon capers
2 tablespoons garlic, minced
Chopped parsley for garnish

Rinse chicken and pat dry. Combine flour, pepper, salt and garlic powder. Heat oil and butter. Dredge chicken in flour mixture and sauté, turning once, until browned on both sides. Remove to a plate. Add remaining ingredients, except parsley. Sauté until mushrooms are soft; place chicken back in pan. Add Lemon Butter Sauce to pan. Place cooked pasta on plate, then chicken; spoon sauce over top according to taste. Garnish with parsley.

Poppy Seed Chicken

First Baptist Church, Grenada

10 pounds boneless, skinless chicken tenders, cooked and chopped
1 (50-ounce) can cream of chicken soup
32 ounces sour cream
¼ cup poppy seeds
Salt and pepper to taste
3 cups crushed butter crackers

Arrange chicken in large hotel-size baking pan. Mix soup, sour cream, poppy seeds, salt and pepper in a large bowl. Spoon over chicken. Top with cracker crumbs. Bake at 350° for 1 hour or until bubbly. Serve over rice.

Poppy Seed Chicken

Mt. Pisgah Baptist Church, Brandon ✝ *Helen Gunn*

5 chicken breasts
½ teaspoon salt
¼ teaspoon pepper
2 (10.25-ounce) cans cream of chicken soup
1 (8-ounce) carton sour cream
1 teaspoon Worcestershire sauce
1 teaspoon celery salt
1 teaspoon minced garlic
1 tablespoon lemon juice
2 cups crushed Ritz crackers
½ cup butter, melted
1 tablespoon poppy seeds

Preheat oven to 350°. Boil chicken in water to cover, salt and pepper until done. Cool slightly then cut into cubes. Place cubed chicken in a 9x13-inch dish. Stir together soup, sour cream, Worcestershire, celery salt, garlic and lemon juice. Pour over chicken. In separate bowl, stir together crushed crackers and melted butter. Spread over chicken and soup mixture. Sprinkle with poppy seeds. Bake 20 to 30 minutes until the top is browned and sauce is bubbly.

Poppy Seed Chicken

Calvary Baptist Church, Starkville † *Jammie Ellis*

2 (10.25-ounce) cans cream of chicken soup
1 cup sour cream
2 cups shredded boiled chicken
1 stick butter, melted
1 sleeve Ritz crackers, crushed
2 tablespoons poppy seeds

Mix together soup, sour cream and chicken. Place in 2-quart casserole dish. Combine melted butter with crushed crackers; spread over chicken mixture. Sprinkle with poppy seeds. Bake at 350° about 30 minutes.

Calvary Baptist Church
Starkville

405 North Jackson Street
Starkville, MS 39759
662-323-1448
www.facebook.com/Calvary-Baptist-
  Church

Dr. Grant Arinder

Today's busy lifestyle makes dinner as a family an occurrence of the past. Calvary Baptist Church's cookbook, *Our Family Table*, sells for $10.00 and is a call to family time at the table—a time of not just food but of sharing the blessings of the day and the goodness of God in our lives. We have included recipes from a cross-section of our church, young and old, and friends, past and present. Our prayer and hope is that these recipes will encourage you to make dinnertime a family time.

Poppy Seed Chicken

First Baptist Church, Orange Grove

3 to 5 chicken breasts
3 to 5 chicken bouillon cubes
1 green bell pepper, sliced
1 yellow onion, quartered,
  divided
2 cups rice
1 (16-ounce) carton sour
  cream
2 (10.25-ounce) cans cream of
  chicken soup
2 teaspoons poppy seeds
2 teaspoons garlic salt
2 sleeves Ritz crackers,
  crushed
1 stick butter, melted

Place chicken, bouillon, bell pepper and half the onion, in a pot. Cover with water and cook over medium-low heat until chicken is tender. (For busy days cook chicken in a slow cooker on low for 8 hours.) While chicken cooks, prepare rice per package directions. Once chicken is tender, remove from broth (reserve broth) and shred. Place shredded chicken, rice, sour cream, soup, poppy seeds, and garlic salt in a large bowl; mix well. Add 1 to 2 cups chicken broth. (I usually do 2 cups, but it does not need to be watery.) Mix well and pour into a 9x13-inch casserole dish. Scatter crushed Ritz crackers over top and drizzle melted butter over crackers. Bake in oven at 350° for 30 minutes or until topping is golden brown.

Country Fried Chicken

1 (2½-pound) chicken
Salt and pepper
3 eggs
⅓ cup water
2 cups self-rising flour
1 teaspoon Cajun seasoning
Oil, for frying (peanut oil is best)

Several hours before serving, cut chicken in pieces. Coat each piece well with salt and pepper. Refrigerate 2 to 3 hours (at least) or until ready to cook. When ready to cook, remove chicken from fridge to sit at room temperature while you prepare to cook. Beat eggs with water in a small bowl. In a separate shallow dish, combine flour and Cajun seasoning. Dip seasoned chicken in egg; coat well in flour. Working in two batches, fry chicken in moderately hot shortening, 350°, in a cast-iron skillet. Place lid on top of skillet and fry until brown and crisp, about 8 to 10 minutes for white meat and 13 to 14 minutes for dark meat.

Oven-Fried Chicken

2 cups panko breadcrumbs
1 cup grated Parmesan cheese
4 tablespoons olive oil, divided
2 tablespoons fresh thyme, minced
Salt and pepper to taste
¼ cup Dijon mustard
2 tablespoons water
2½ pounds boneless skinless chicken breast, pounded to ¼-inch thickness

Preheat oven to 400°. Line a baking sheet with heavy-duty aluminum foil. Place a metal cooling rack over pan and spray rack with nonstick cooking spray. In a shallow dish, combine breadcrumbs, cheese, 2 tablespoons olive oil, thyme, salt and pepper. In a separate shallow dish, combine mustard, water, salt, pepper and remaining olive oil. Coat each chicken breast with mustard mixture then dredge in breadcrumb mixture. Place on prepared rack in pan. Bake 25 to 30 minutes, or until chicken is golden brown. Serve immediately.

Baked Chicken

Sunrise Baptist Church, Carthage † *Nancy Martin*

Season-All seasoned salt
2 chickens, quartered

With seasoned salt, heavily sprinkle each piece of chicken until red. Stack pieces, starting with breasts and wings to the outside, followed by legs and thighs to the outside. Place in a 9x13-inch baking dish with a lip on all sides to allow you to seal container with heavy foil. Put covered dish in oven and set to 300° as you walk out the door for Sunday School. Your meat will be ready after preaching.

Sunrise Baptist Church

Carthage

353 Midway Road
Carthage, MS 39051
601-741-2225
www.sunrisebc.net

Brother David Addy, Pastor

Reverend W.W. Spears spearheaded the move to establish the church eventually to be known as Sunrise. August 22, 1937, a group of elders gathered to organize the church; it was then that the name "Sunrise' was chosen for the new church that made its permanent home in Midway School, built in 1922. The first deacon ever ordained by the church was W.M. Thornton on August 23, 1937. At the present time, there are seven active deacons. The church has had nineteen pastors, including the first pastor, Reverend N.B. Nicholson, and our current pastor, Brother David Addy. Sunrise has always been progressive in its outreach and its buildings. The first new building was in 1964 and the last building was the new sanctuary built in 2013. Through much prayer and dedication, Sunrise Baptist Church was able to construct this building debt free. In 2014, the old education building was remodeled to become our new Children's Department.

Marinated Baked Chicken

Mt. Pisgah Baptist Church, Brandon ✝ *Margaret Shedd*

½ cup Italian salad dressing
½ cup soy sauce
6 bone-in chicken breast halves
⅛ teaspoon onion salt
⅛ teaspoon garlic salt

In a measuring cup, combine salad dressing and soy sauce. Pour ¾ cup into a large re-sealable plastic bag; add chicken. Seal bag and turn to coat; refrigerate for 4 hours or overnight, turning several times. Refrigerate remaining marinade for basting. When ready to cook, drain chicken, discarding marinade. Place chicken, skin side up, on a rack in a roasting pan. Sprinkle with onion salt and garlic salt. Bake uncovered at 350°, brushing occasionally with reserved marinade, for 45 to 60 minutes or until juices run clear and a meat thermometer reads 170°.

Sour Cream Chicken

Iuka Baptist Church

4 boneless chicken breasts
Salt and pepper to taste
1 sleeve Ritz crackers, crushed
Cajun seasoning to taste
1 (16-ounce) carton sour cream
½ stick margarine

Flatten chicken breast to ¼-inch thickness. Season with salt and pepper. In a shallow bowl, combine crushed crackers and Cajun seasoning; mix well. Pour sour cream in another shallow bowl. Completely coat each chicken breast with sour cream, then coat with seasoned crackers. Place on baking sheet. Dab with margarine. Cook at 400° for 30 minutes or until done.

Honey and Spiced Glazed Chicken

Mount Helm Baptist Church, Jackson

¼ cup honey
2 garlic cloves, minced
2 tablespoons fresh lemon juice
2 teaspoons Dijon mustard
1 teaspoon sweet paprika

¼ teaspoon cayenne pepper
4 (10-ounce) bone-in chicken breast
  halves with skin
Salt and freshly ground pepper

Preheat oven to 425°. In a small bowl, mix honey, garlic, lemon juice, mustard, paprika and cayenne. Put chicken breasts on a rimmed baking sheet. Using a sharp knife, make 2 deep slashes in each chicken breast; season with salt and pepper. Brush most of the honey glaze over chicken. Bake 15 minutes. Brush with remaining honey glaze and bake about 10 minutes longer or until cooked through. Remove chicken breasts from oven. Preheat to broil. Brush juices from baking sheet onto chicken and broil about 1 minute, or until skin is crisp. Serve immediately.

Mount Helm Baptist Church

Jackson

300 East Church Street
Jackson, MS 39202
601-353-3981 • www.mthelm.org

CJ Rhodes, Pastor

Mount Helm Baptist Church, the oldest historically black congregation in Mississippi's capital city, humbly began in the basement of First Baptist Jackson during slavery, becoming an independent body of baptized believers named in honor of Thomas and Mary Helm, white Presbyterians who donated the first property. For nearly two centuries, Mount Helm has endured many tests of faith. Even amidst tragedy, God has blessed the church to make history. The General Missionary Baptist State Convention, Church of Christ (Holiness) USA, and Church of God in Christ all trace histories to Mount Helm. For a season in the 1880s, Mount Helm housed Jackson State University. Known for its hospitality and love of European anthems and hymns, Mount Helm embraces its heritage while becoming a vibrant church for the 21st century. Determined to be a leading congregation, Mount Helm exists to the glory of God so that through changed lives can change the world for Jesus Christ.

Crescent Chicken Roll-ups

Golden Central Baptist Church, Golden ✝ *Peggy Sparks*

3 or 4 chicken breasts
1 (8-ounce) package cream cheese, softened
1 medium onion, finely chopped
2 tablespoons pimento
2 (8-ounce) cans crescent rolls
1 (10.25-ounce) can cream of chicken soup
1 (10.25-ounce) can cream of celery soup

Boil chicken in salted water to cover until done; shred and set aside (reserve broth). Spray or grease a 9x13-inch baking dish and set aside. Mix together cream cheese, onion, pimento and chicken. Unroll and separate crescent rolls. Place a heaping spoonful of chicken mixture on wide end. Roll up and place in prepared baking dish. Bake at 375° until browned, about 20 minutes. While that is baking, mix together cream of chicken soup and cream of celery soup with 1½ soup cans reserved broth. Heat on stovetop. When rolls are browned, remove from oven and cover with soup mixture. Return to oven and bake another 30 minutes.

Laura's Chicken

Oakland Baptist Church, Vicksburg ✝ *Jill Marr*

4 whole chicken breasts, cubed
1 (10.25-ounce) can cream of mushroom soup
½ pound fresh mushrooms, sliced
1½ cups chopped celery
1 cup water chestnuts
1 cup nonfat mayonnaise
Seasoned breadcrumbs

Combine all ingredients, except breadcrumbs; mix well. Put into a 2-quart casserole dish. Top with breadcrumbs. Bake at 350° for 45 minutes or until chicken is completely done. Goes great with wild rice.

Chicken Spaghetti Casserole

Bethel Baptist Church, Heidelburg ✝ *Diane Hutcheson*

1 hen or chicken
1 cup chopped onion
2 cups chopped celery
Salt to taste
1 (16-ounce) package spaghetti
1 (10.25-ounce) can cream of mushroom soup
2 cups shredded Cheddar cheese

In a large pot, cover chicken in water and cook with onion, celery and salt. When done, debone chicken and cut into small pieces. Strain broth and cook spaghetti in broth, adding water, if necessary. When spaghettis is done, drain leaving about 1 cup broth; stir in chicken and soup. Put in a casserole dish and cover with cheese. Cook in 400° oven for 30 minutes or until bubbly.

Kate's Potato Chip Chicken

Goss Baptist Church, Columbia ✝ *Brenda Fortenberry*

1 (16-ounce) carton sour cream
2½ pounds chicken tenderloins
Zatarain's Creole seasoning
1 (20-ounce) bag regular Golden Flake salted potato chips, crushed
½ cup (1 stick) butter
1 tablespoon garlic powder (or granulated garlic)
Salsa (optional)

Preheat oven to 450°. Place sour cream in a medium bowl. Sprinkle chicken with Zatarain's Creole seasoning. Dip chicken in sour cream, then coat with potato chips. Place coated chicken on cookie sheet treated with butter-flavored nonstick spray. Bake chicken 5 minutes, then reduce heat to 375° and bake 10 to 12 minutes. While chicken is baking, melt butter; add garlic powder. Return oven to 450° and brush garlic butter over each piece of chicken; bake an additional 5 minutes, or until chicken is golden brown. Serve with salsa, if desired. Makes 12 servings.

FBC Greenville Chicken Casserole

First Baptist Church of Greenville ✝ Hospitality Committee

2 (10.25-ounce) cans cream of chicken soup
1 cup mayonnaise
4 cups chopped cooked chicken (4 to 6 breasts)
2 cups finely chopped celery
1 cup finely chopped onion
1 cup sliced almonds
3 cups cooked rice
2 teaspoons lemon juice
1 teaspoon salt
1 teaspoon pepper
1 cup chicken broth (or enough to make it juicy)
1 (6-ounce) can French fried onion rings

Combine soup with mayonnaise; add remaining ingredients, except broth and onion rings. Add broth to desired consistency. Put in greased 9x13-inch casserole dish. Bake at 350° about 45 minutes to an hour, or until set (shouldn't be jiggly). Top with onion rings; bake 5 minutes or just until onion rings are hot and toasty.

For many years, First Baptist Church of Greenville has been a lunch provider for the Lenten Luncheon, held at the First United Methodist Church. We usually serve this casserole, preparing at least 19 casseroles to feed the 200-plus people who attend the luncheon. It is always a hit; serve with a salad and rolls.

I know what it is to be in need, and I know what it is to have plenty. I have learned the secret of being content in any and every situation, whether well fed or hungry, whether living in plenty or in want. I can do everything through Christ who gives me strength. —PHILIPPIANS 4:13

Chicken Casserole

Franklin Creek Baptist Church, Moss Point

1 whole chicken
1 (12-ounce) bag extra broad noodles
1 medium onion, chopped
½ stick margarine, melted
1 (10-ounce) can Rotel tomatoes
1 (16-ounce) box Velveeta cheese

Boil chicken in salted water to cover until cooked through; remove from broth (reserve broth) and debone. Cook noodles in broth. Sauté onion in melted margarine. Add onion to blender with tomatoes and blend until smooth. Melt cheese. Combine all mixtures then place in a casserole dish. Bake at 350° for 20 minutes or microwave 5 minutes. Extra cheese may be added on top before baking.

Franklin Creek Baptist Church

Moss Point

11505 Independence Road
Moss Point, MS 39562
228-475-3471

Ralph Smith, Pastor

Franklin Creek Baptist Church was formed in 1967 as part of Jackson County Baptist Association. The church originally functioned as a mission. Franklin Creek Baptist Church is a friendly, spiritual church with a desire for souls to be saved and individuals to be equipped to live to their fullest potential in God's will. The church now has a membership upwards of 300 members. They have many active programs for children and youth, including RA's, GA's, and ACTEENS. Worship Services are Sunday at 9:30 a.m. for Sunday School, 11:00 a.m. for Worship Service, and 6:30 p.m. for Evening Worship.

Chicken String Bean Casserole

Zion Hill Baptist Church, Wesson † *Shirley Sandifer*

4 chicken breasts, boiled and deboned
1 (6.9-ounce) box Rice-A-Roni (chicken flavored)
2 (15-ounce) cans cut green beans, drained
1 (15-ounce) jar Cheez Whiz
½ cup mayonnaise
1 (6-ounce) can French fried onions

Dice chicken and set aside. Cook Rice-A-Roni according to package directions. Mix in chicken, beans, Cheez Whiz and mayonnaise. Pour into casserole dish and sprinkle onions on top. Bake at 350° for 1 hour or until onions are golden brown.

Chicken and Vegetable Casserole

Pleasant Home Baptist Church, Laurel † *Sylvia Mauldin*

1 (11-ounce) can white shoepeg corn, drained
1 (15-ounce) can French-style green beans, drained
½ cup sour cream
½ cup chopped onion
1 (4-ounce) jar diced pimento, drained
½ cup shredded sharp Cheddar cheese
1 (10.25-ounce) can cream of celery soup, undiluted
4 cups boiled and chopped chicken breast

Mix all ingredients and place in greased 9x13-inch casserole dish.

TOPPING:
1 cup crumbled Ritz crackers
½ stick butter, melted
½ cup sliced almonds

Mix Topping and sprinkle over casserole. Bake at 350° for 45 minutes or until bubbly.

Chicken Enchiladas

Star Baptist Church, Star

1 (8-ounce) carton sour cream
2 (10.25-ounce) cans cream of chicken soup
2 cups cooked chopped chicken
2 cups shredded Cheddar cheese
1 (4-ounce) can chopped green chiles
Flour tortillas

Mix sour cream and soup; reserve ½ cup for topping enchiladas. Add chicken to remaining mixture and set aside. Mix cheese and chiles. In a tortilla, put a layer of soup mixture and top with cheese mixture. Roll tortilla and place in casserole dish, split side down. Repeat until all filling mixture is used. Top with reserved ½ cup soup mixture. Bake at 400° until heated through.

Chicken Fajita Potatoes

Golden Central Baptist Church, Golden ✝ Cyndi Strickland

4 large baking potatoes
1 medium red or green bell pepper, chopped
1 small onion, chopped
2 tablespoons butter or margarine, melted
1 tablespoon taco seasoning
1½ cups shredded cooked chicken breast
½ cup shredded Cheddar cheese
½ cup shredded Monterey Jack cheese
1 (4.25-ounce) can sliced ripe olives, drained (optional)
2 tablespoons diced green chiles
1 cup salsa, divided (plus additional for serving)
Sour cream (optional)
Guacamole (optional)

Scrub potatoes; pat dry. Wrap in aluminum foil and bake at 400° for 1 hour or until tender (or cook in microwave). Sauté pepper and onion in butter in medium saucepan until tender. Add taco seasoning. Cook 1 minute, stirring constantly; remove from heat. Stir in chicken, cheeses, olives and chiles. Cut a lengthwise slit in top of each potato. Press each potato open. Spoon chicken mixture into potatoes. Spoon ¼ cup salsa over each potato. If desired, serve with sour cream, guacamole and additional salsa. Yields 4 servings.

Chicken Olé

Zion Hill Baptist Church, Wesson ✝ *Candy Walker*

1 box Zatarain's black beans and rice
1 (10-ounce) can Rotel tomatoes
1 (14-ounce) can chicken broth
2 chicken breasts
Shredded Cheddar cheese to taste

Put first 3 ingredients in a 9x13-inch casserole dish. Lay chicken breasts on top. Cover with foil and bake at 350° for 1 hour. After 1 hour, remove foil and top with cheese. Return to oven for about 10 minutes or until cheese is melted.

Welcome to Zion Hill Baptist Church

Zion Hill Baptist Church

Wesson

8081 Martinsville Road
Wesson, MS 39191
601-643-5145

Brother Tom McCormick, Pastor

Motto: "All things through Christ."

Zion Hill is a Bible-believing, praying church family who loves the Lord. We provide several opportunities to come together to worship and praise God. There are ministry opportunities from preschool to senior adults in both music and mission endeavors. God has blessed Zion Hill with so many people who are using their gifts and talents for the glory of God. He is doing a mighty work through their willingness to serve Him. We have a rich history of being a "Light for Christ" in our community and it reaches across the world. God's word tells us "He inhabits the praise of His people" (Psalms 22:3). There is power found there. When we worship and praise Him, He is there.

The Easiest Chicken and Dumplings Ever

North Columbia Baptist Church, Columbia † *Patsy Pittman*

4 (4-ounce) boneless skinless chicken breast halves
1 (13.5-ounce) package fat-free flour tortillas
1 (10.25-ounce) can 99% fat-free cream of chicken soup

Cover chicken with water and boil until tender. Remove from broth and cut into bite-size pieces (reserve broth); set aside. Cut tortillas into approximately 2-inch square pieces. Bring chicken broth to a boil and drop in tortilla pieces one at a time, stirring frequently to keep them from sticking together. Combine cream of chicken soup with ½ cup water. Add to dumplings. Return the chicken pieces to the pot. Serves 6.

Chicken and Dumplings

South Green Baptist Church, Tupelo † *Dot Emison*

1 whole chicken (or 4 to 5 large breasts)
½ cup shortening
2 cups self-rising flour
1½ cups milk, divided
1 (10.25-ounce) can cream chicken soup
1 stick margarine
Salt and pepper to taste

Cover chicken with salted water and boil until done; debone. Set chicken aside, saving broth. Cut shortening into flour and gradually add ¾ cup milk to form a dough. Cover and chill at least 1 hour. Divide dough into 4 balls. Place ball of dough on a floured board; sprinkle top with flour and knead well. Roll dough to ¼-inch thickness and cut into strips. Have broth boiling and add cream of chicken soup. While boiling, pinch strips of dough and drop into broth. Shake pan to stir dough (do not stir with a spoon); continue until all dough is used. Cut up margarine on top. Add remaining ¾ cup milk and shake well. Add salt and pepper. Reduce heat to medium-low. Cover and cook 30 minutes. Shake occasionally to keep from sticking.

Note: If you want a tougher dough, use water instead of milk.

Chicken and Dumplin's

Ashland Baptist Church ✝ *Jo Thompson*

3 to 4 chicken breasts
1 (10.25-ounce) can cream of chicken
   soup
½ stick butter

½ cup milk
1 (12-count) package Aztec Tortillas
   (cut in small pieces)
Salt and pepper to taste

Boil chicken in water to cover until tender; remove chicken to cool, reserving broth. Debone chicken and add back to broth with soup, butter and milk. Bring to a boil. Add tortillas. Cook until done. Salt and pepper to taste.

Ashland Baptist Church

Ashland

173 Church Street
Ashland, MS 38603

Dr. Gerald Hodges, Pastor

Ashland Baptist Church was organized, July 31, 1872, with eleven charter members. Today, we have 510 members. We meet Sunday mornings and Sunday evenings for worship services and on Wednesday night for Prayer Meeting. Our organizations include Sunday School and Discipleship Training for all age groups with special study groups for ladies and men, adult, children's and preschool choirs, Brotherhood, RA's, Baptist Women Actions Mission Friends, and Bible Drills.

To the Glory of God Ashland Baptist Church:
- Ordained four men to the Gospel Ministry
- Two members of the church left to serve as missionaries in Israel in 1988
- A library was established 1963
- A church secretary was employed in 1968
- WMU was first mentioned in the church minutes in 1925
- Brotherhood was organized in 1988
- We have met all of our Mission Goals since churches have set goals

Chicken Pie

Liberty Baptist Church, Waynesboro

1 chicken, boiled and deboned
1 (10.25-ounce) can cream of chicken soup
1 (14-ounce) can plus 2 cups chicken broth
1 stick butter, melted
1½ cups buttermilk
1½ cups self-rising flour

Layer chicken on bottom of casserole dish. Mix soup and 1 can chicken broth; pour over chicken. Combine butter with buttermilk and flour. Spread over top of chicken. Pour remaining 2 cups chicken broth on top of all. Bake at 350° for 1 hour.

Chicken Pot Pie

South Green Baptist Church, Tupelo ✝ Marcelle Bethany

3 to 4 pounds boneless, skinless chicken breasts, cooked and chopped (chop, do not shred)
2 (10.25-ounce) cans cream of chicken soup
1 (10.25-ounce) can cream of celery soup
1 (15-ounce) can tender sweet peas
1 (15-ounce) can sliced carrots
1 teaspoon black pepper
½ teaspoon poultry seasoning (optional)

Combine chicken, soups, peas, carrots and pepper; pour into a greased 9x13-inch casserole dish.

CRUST:
1 cup self-rising flour
1 cup milk
¼ cup mayonnaise

For crust, combine flour, milk and mayonnaise. Mix with a wire whisk to make a thin batter. Pour over chicken/vegetable mixture to cover. Bake at 350° for 1 hour.

I tripled this recipe to feed about 30 people and it was great. After you eat this dish and it seems too thick to heat back up again, just throw in another can of chicken or celery soup, stir, and heat. It may not need it. Depends on how much chicken you use.

Chicken & Spinach Quiche

Calvary Missionary Baptist Church, Brandon † *Diane Jernigan*

1 (10-ounce) package frozen spinach
1 cup chopped cooked chicken
1 cup shredded Swiss cheese
¼ cup chopped onion
2 eggs
¾ cup mayonnaise
¾ cup milk
½ teaspoon dried basil leaves
¼ teaspoon pepper
1 (9-inch) deep-dish pie crust

Cook spinach per package directions and drain well. Combine with remaining ingredients, except pie crust. Pour into pie crust and bake at 350° for 40 minutes.

Slow Cooker Chicken and Dressing

Williamsville Baptist Church, Kosciusko † *Faye Tolleson*

1 whole chicken or 3 chicken breasts
3 celery stalks, chopped
1 onion, chopped
1 stick butter or margarine
½ cup chicken broth
2 (14-ounce) cans chicken broth
1 (10.25-ounce) can cream of chicken soup
1 pan prepared cornbread, crumbled (make with 3 eggs instead of 1)
Salt and pepper
Sage (optional)

Boil chicken in salted water to cover until done; remove from broth (reserve ½ cup broth) and debone. Sauté celery and onion in butter until soft; add reserved ½ cup chicken broth and continue to cook. In a separate pot, bring canned broth and soup to a boil. Pour into a crockpot. Add vegetables, chicken and crumbled cornbread. Season to taste with salt, pepper and sage. Cook on high for 2½ to 3 hours.

Slow Cooker Pulled Chicken

New Zion Baptist Church, Crystal Springs

3 to 4 boneless, skinless chicken breasts
Salt and pepper
1 (18-ounce) bottle Sweet Baby Ray's Barbecue Sauce
¼ cup apple cider vinegar
½ teaspoon red pepper flakes
¼ cup packed brown sugar
1 teaspoon garlic powder

Rinse chicken and pat dry with paper towel. Season chicken on both sides with salt and pepper. In a medium bowl, mix together barbecue sauce, vinegar, red pepper flakes, brown sugar and garlic powder. Mix well. Put a small amount of sauce on bottom of slow cooker. Add chicken. Cover chicken with remaining sauce mixture. Cook on low 4 to 5 hours. Check after 4 hours and see if it pulls apart easily with a fork. If not, allow to cook a while longer. It will get to a point when it just falls apart easily when you use 2 forks (in the same manner a pulled pork does). Once pulled apart, mix well in sauce. Allow to cook on low or warm for few minutes to allow to mix well. Serve on a bun or on slider buns and enjoy

Easy Baked Turkey

South Green Baptist Church, Tupelo ✝ *Josie McCaleb*

1 turkey, thawed (any size turkey will work)
Salt and pepper
1 apple, unpeeled and quartered
1 rib celery, cut in two pieces
1 onion, quartered
1 stick margarine
1 quart warm water

Preheat oven to 475° about 9:00 p.m. or 10:00 p.m. Thanksgiving Eve. Salt and pepper turkey inside and out. Place turkey in roasting pan with cover. (Make sure cover fits tightly.) Place apple, celery and onion in turkey. Melt butter and pour over turkey. Add water to roasting pan. Cover tightly and bake 1 hour. Turn oven off; do not open door. Leave all night. In the morning, turkey will be golden brown, you will have plenty of broth for dressing and gravy, and you'll enjoy a turkey more tender than you have ever tasted.

White Chicken Lasagna

Journey Baptist Church, Olive Branch

1 tablespoon butter
1 onion, chopped
2 tablespoons minced garlic
2 cups shredded (or cubed) cooked chicken
2 (10.25-ounce) cans cream of chicken soup
⅔ cup sour cream
1½ teaspoons oregano
2 tablespoons chopped basil
1½ teaspoons freshly ground black pepper
1½ tablespoons poultry seasoning
1 cup shredded Parmesan, divided
9 oven-ready lasagna noodles (no boil type)
8 ounces fresh mushrooms, sliced
6 ounces fresh baby spinach leaves
2 cups shredded reduced-fat mozzarella, divided

Preheat oven to 350°. Melt butter on medium-low heat, add onion and garlic, cooking until tender and stirring frequently. In a large bowl, mix chicken, cream of chicken soup, sour cream, sautéed onion/garlic mixture, oregano, basil, pepper, poultry seasoning and ¼ cup Parmesan. In a prepared 9x13-inch baking dish, layer ingredients as follows: 3 lasagna noodles on bottom, half the chicken mixture, half mushrooms, then half the spinach. Sprinkle ¼ cup Parmesan and ¼ cup mozzarella over this. Repeat layering. Use last 3 noodles to cover the second layer, then spread entire top of lasagna with remaining 1½ cups mozzarella and ¼ cup Parmesan. Cover with aluminum foil that has been sprayed with oil or cooking spray to prevent sticking and bake 25 minutes. Remove foil and continue to bake 15 to 20 minutes or until cheese begins to brown nicely. Let stand 10 to 15 minutes before serving so lasagna can set as cheese cools.

Tip: you can let this set overnight in fridge and rewarm. This allows for a cleaner cut to lasagna.

Lasagna

Woodland Baptist Church, Columbus

1 pound ground turkey
1 pound ground turkey breakfast sausage
3 (26.5-ounce) cans Hunt's Original Spaghetti Sauce
1 (16-ounce) carton ricotta cheese
½ cup grated Parmesan cheese
2 eggs, beaten
1 teaspoon basil
1 (8-ounce) box oven-ready lasagna noodles
2 (8-ounce) packages shredded mozzarella cheese

Brown meat; drain. Add spaghetti sauce and mix. In a separate bowl, combine ricotta cheese, Parmesan, eggs and basil. Start with a couple ladles of meat mixture in the bottom of a 9x13-inch baking dish. Top with a layer of noodles then a layer of ricotta mixture. Top with more meat mixture then shredded cheese. Repeat layers, ending up with shredded cheese on top. Bake at 350°, uncovered, for 30 to 40 minutes or until bubbly around edges and cheese is brown on top.

Slow Cooker Lasagna

Farmington Baptist Church, Corinth

1½ pounds ground beef
2 jars spaghetti sauce
1 (12-ounce) box lasagna noodles, uncooked
½ cup grated Parmesan cheese
16 ounces shredded Mozzarella cheese
½ (24-ounce) carton cottage cheese

Brown and drain ground beef. Add spaghetti sauce; cook until warm. Spoon layer of meat in a slow cooker. Add a double layer of noodles (breaking to fit). Top with cheeses. Repeat with sauce, noodles and cheeses until all is used to make 3 layers. Make sure noodles are in sauce on top. Cover and cook on low 4 to 5 hours.

Lasagna

Liberty Baptist Church, Waynesboro ✝ *Lena McMichael*

¼ cup oil
1 small onion, chopped
1½ pounds ground beef
½ cup dry red wine
1 (6-ounce) can tomato paste
1 (8-ounce) can tomato sauce
1 (46-ounce) can tomato juice
1 cup water
¼ cup sugar
½ teaspoon salt

4 fresh basil leaves (or ½ teaspoon dried)
2 stems fresh parsley (or ½ teaspoon dried)
½ package McCormick Italian seasoning mix with mushrooms
1 (1-pound) box lasagna noodles
Parmesan cheese to taste
4 to 6 cups shredded Mozzarella cheese
1 (8-ounce) package cream cheese, cut into small pieces

In large pot over medium heat, sauté oil and onion for about 2 minutes. Add ground beef and cook until brown; drain. Add wine and cook about 5 minutes. Add tomato paste, tomato sauce, tomato juice, water, sugar, salt, basil and parsley. Lower heat to low and cook 2 hours, uncovered. Add McCormick seasoning and cook 30 more minutes. Cook lasagna noodles according to package directions. Drain and run under cold water. Put a thin layer of sauce in bottom of a 9x13-inch baking dish, then begin layering. Layer half of the noodles and half of the sauce. Top with a sprinkling of Parmesan cheese then layer half the Mozzarella cheese and all the cream cheese. Repeat layers, except cream cheese. Bake at 350° for 45 minutes or until done. This sauce can also be used for spaghetti.

Lasagna Grilled Cheese

Union Ridge Baptist Church, Noxapater

4 slices thick bread (I use Texas toast)
2 tablespoons butter, softened
2 tablespoons prepared spaghetti sauce
4 large tomato slices (optional)
2 meatballs, sliced (optional)
2 slices mozzarella cheese
2 tablespoons shredded Parmesan cheese
2 tablespoons ricotta cheese

On each slice of bread, spread ½ tablespoon butter, making sure the whole piece is covered evenly. Flip bread so buttered side is facing down. Spread 1 tablespoon spaghetti sauce on each of 2 slices of bread. Top with tomatoes, then meatballs then mozzarella and Parmesan. Spread 1 tablespoon ricotta cheese on each of the other two slices. Place ricotta-cheese-side-down onto a greased and preheated skillet over medium heat; cook each side of the sandwich about 2 to 3 minutes or until bread is golden brown and cheese is melted. Enjoy! Makes 2 sandwiches.

Tangy Meatballs

Shady Grove Missionary Baptist Church, Tishomingo ✝
Barbara Thompson

2 pounds ground beef
1 cup cornflakes
2 tablespoons onion flakes
3 tablespoons soy sauce
¼ teaspoon black pepper
½ teaspoon garlic powder

2 eggs
½ cup ketchup
1 (12-ounce) jar chili sauce
1 (14-ounce) can whole cranberry sauce
2 tablespoons sugar
2 tablespoons lemon juice

In a large bowl combine meat, cornflakes, onion flakes, soy sauce, black pepper, garlic powder, eggs and ketchup, using your hands to mix well. Gently roll into firm (1½-inch) balls. Place in a 9x13-inch baking dish. Prepare sauce by combining chili sauce, cranberry sauce, sugar and lemon juice. Pour over meatballs. Bake at 400° for 35 to 40 minutes.

Swedish Meatballs

Walnut Grove Baptist Church, Fulton

1 (32-ounce) package frozen meatballs
1 (15-ounce) can sauerkraut
2 (14-ounce) cans whole cranberry sauce
1 (12-ounce) jar chili sauce

Place ingredients in a slow cooker and cook on high 4 hours.

Meatloaf

Auburn Baptist Church, Tupelo ✝ Martha Brock

MEATLOAF:
1½ pounds ground beef
1 cup breadcrumbs
½ (8-ounce) can tomato sauce
1 onion, chopped
1 egg, beaten
1½ teaspoons salt
¼ teaspoon pepper

Combine Meatloaf ingredients, mixing well. Form into a loaf in a baking pan.

TOPPING:
½ (8-ounce) can tomato sauce
2 tablespoons brown sugar
1 cup water
2 tablespoons vinegar
2 tablespoons mustard

Mix well and pour over loaf. Bake at 350° for 1½ hours.

Mini Meatloaves

Bethel Baptist Church, Heidelburg † *Diane Hutcheson*

½ cup finely chopped onion
½ cup finely chopped green bell pepper
½ cup dry breadcrumbs
¼ cup barbecue sauce
1 egg, beaten
1½ pounds lean ground beef
Ketchup

In a large bowl, combine the first 5 ingredients. Add beef and mix well. Divide mixture between 6 ungreased muffin cups. Top with ketchup. Bake at 375° for 18 to 20 minutes or until meat is no longer pink.

Old-Fashioned Meatloaf

Mt. Pisgah Baptist Church, Brandon † *Neil Larson*

½ pound ground beef
½ pound ground venison
1 teaspoon salt
⅓ teaspoon ground black pepper
½ cup finely chopped onion
½ cup finely chopped yellow bell pepper
1 egg, lightly beaten
½ (16-ounce) can diced tomatoes (with half the juice)
¼ cup quick-cooking oats

Mix all meatloaf ingredients well and place in a 9x5-inch loaf pan. Shape into a loaf. Bake at 375° for 40 minutes.

TOPPING:
½ cup ketchup
3 tablespoons brown sugar
1 tablespoon prepared mustard

Mix ingredients for Topping and spread on loaf. Bake an additional 10 minutes at 400° or until internal temperature is 160° to 165°. Let stand 15 minutes before serving.

Meatloaf

Community Missionary Baptist Church, Poplarville

MEATLOAF:

1 pound ground beef
1 teaspoon salt
1 teaspoon black pepper
¼ teaspoon paprika
1 cup finely chopped onion

1 small bell pepper, chopped
½ cup milk
½ cup breadcrumbs
1 egg

TOPPING:

2 tablespoons ketchup

2 tablespoons brown sugar

Combine Meatloaf ingredients well and place in a 9x5-inch loaf pan. Shape into a loaf. Mix ingredients for Topping and spread over loaf. Bake at 350° for 45 minutes.

Community Missionary Baptist

Poplarville

886 Barth Road
Poplarville, MS 39470

Bill Cameron, Pastor

At Community Baptist Church, we believe God has placed us here to meet the spiritual needs of our community. Just as most towns and communities have a hospital to help with physical needs, a church is to meet spiritual needs. Someone once said, "The church is a hospital for sinners." Jesus meets spiritual needs through the church, and He came that we might have everlasting life. He said in John 3:16—"For God so loved the world that he gave his only begotten Son, that whosoever believeth in Him should not perish, but have everlasting life." After this short temporary life is over, everyone will live forever in eternity either in heaven or hell. Jesus said, "I am the way, the truth, and the life; no man cometh unto the Father, but by me." If there is any way we can assist you, we hope you will give us a chance.

Spinach Tomato Tortellini

Temple Baptist Church,
Hattiesburg

1 (12-ounce) package tortellini pasta
1½ cups heavy cream
2 tablespoons all-purpose flour
1 tablespoon olive oil
3 garlic cloves, minced
1 (14.5-ounce) can petite diced tomatoes
3 cups roughly chopped spinach
2 teaspoons dried basil
1 teaspoon dried oregano
½ teaspoon dried thyme
¼ teaspoon crushed red pepper flakes
    (optional)
Kosher salt and freshly ground black
    pepper to taste
¼ cup grated Parmesan cheese

In a large pot of boiling salted water, cook pasta according to package instructions; drain well. In a small bowl, whisk together heavy cream and flour; set aside. Heat olive oil in a large skillet over medium-high heat. Add garlic, and cook, stirring frequently, until fragrant, about 1 minute. Stir in tomatoes, spinach, basil, oregano, thyme and red pepper flakes. Season with salt and pepper. Cook, stirring occasionally, until spinach begins to wilt, about 2 minutes. Gradually whisk in heavy cream mixture and Parmesan, and cook, whisking constantly, until slightly thickened, 3 to 4 minutes. Stir in tortellini and gently toss to combine. Serve immediately. Yields 4 servings.

This is the most unbelievably creamy tortellini you will make in just 15 minutes. It doesn't get easier or tastier than this.

Italian Spaghetti

Oakland Baptist Church, Vicksburg ✝ *Linda Edwards*

1 pound ground beef
2 tablespoons oil
1 large onion, chopped
1 green bell pepper, chopped
1 stalk celery, chopped
¼ teaspoon garlic powder
1 teaspoon Italian seasoning
1 teaspoon oregano
3 teaspoons chili powder
1 teaspoon sugar
2 teaspoons salt
1 tablespoon flour
1 (28-ounce) can tomatoes
1 pound spaghetti noodles

Brown beef in oil. When meat is almost done, add onion, bell pepper, and celery. Brown lightly. Add remaining ingredients, except spaghetti; stir well. Cover and simmer 1 hour or longer. Cook spaghetti according to package directions. Serve spaghetti topped with sauce.

Easy Bolognese

Parkway Baptist Church, Clinton ✝ *Stacy Riley*

1 pound ground sirloin
4 garlic cloves, chopped
1 tablespoon oregano
¼ teaspoon red pepper
1 tablespoon salt
1½ teaspoons black pepper
1¼ cups Chianti dry red wine, divided
1 (28-ounce) can crushed tomatoes
2 tablespoons tomato paste
¼ teaspoon nutmeg
¼ cup chopped fresh basil
¼ cup cream
1 (8-ounce) package mini pasta shells, cooked according to package directions
Freshly grated Parmesan

Brown sirloin; drain. Return to skillet; add garlic, oregano, red pepper, salt, black pepper, 1 cup red wine, crushed tomatoes and tomato paste. Stir well and simmer 15 to 20 minutes, stirring occasionally. Add nutmeg, basil, cream and remaining ¼ cup red wine; simmer an additional 8 to 10 minutes. Serve over mini pasta shells with freshly grated Parmesan.

Cheeseburger Casserole

Liberty Baptist Church, Raleigh † *Kristi Ables*

1 pound ground beef
¼ cup chopped onions
1 (8-ounce) can tomato sauce
¼ cup ketchup

Salt and pepper to taste
8 slices cheese
1 (8-count) can crescent rolls

Brown ground beef and onion; drain. Add tomato sauce and ketchup; season with salt and pepper. Simmer 15 minutes. Put half the meat mixture in a casserole dish. Place 4 slices cheese on top of meat mixture. Add remaining meat mixture and remaining 4 slices of cheese on top. Unroll crescent rolls, but do not separate. Place over top of casserole. Bake at 375° for 25 to 30 minutes or until rolls are brown.

Liberty Baptist Church
Raleigh

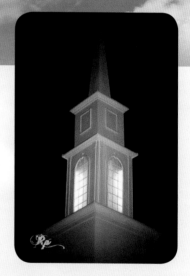

2807 Highway 37
Raleigh, MS 39153
601-467-9224
www.facebook.com/Liberty.BC

Rich Ables, Pastor

Liberty Baptist Church was founded in 1856. The first building was erected in 1859 from logs having a dirt floor. Lighting was provided by coal oil lamps. The church grew, and in 1880 a framed structure was built. In 1907 the third building was built. Baptisms were done in nearby Fisher Creek until the addition of a indoor baptistery was added in 1984. As God continued to work at Liberty, the need arose for more room to accommodate the growth that had begun, and in 2006 a new phase of construction began. The present building can seat 300 people, with a full education department and fellowship hall. Through following the guidance of the Holy Spirit, Liberty has been able to do missions at local and national level even to help start a orphanage in Uganda, Africa. This has proved once again how great God is as He continues to work through Liberty to reach the world.

Cabbage Casserole
Freedom Baptist Church, Burnsville

1 pound ground beef
1 medium onion, chopped
Salt and pepper to taste

1 medium cabbage, chopped
1 cup rice, cooked
1 (14-ounce) can beef broth

Brown beef and onion in a skillet; drain. Season with salt and pepper. In large casserole dish, put cabbage. Spread rice over cabbage. Add meat and onion mixture. Pour broth over all ingredients. Bake at 350° for 1 hour.

HoBo Dinner
Robinhood Baptist Church † *Barbara Long*

2 pounds ground beef
4 potatoes, sliced thin
2 onions, sliced thin

Worcestershire sauce
Cheese slices
Aluminum foil

Form beef into 5 to 8 patties. Tear that many 10x10-inch sheets of aluminum foil. Place a raw beef patty in center of a piece of foil. Place a few potato and onion slices over meat. Cover with Worcestershire sauce. Fold up foil and seal to make a package. Repeat using all meat and vegetables. Place packages in 350° oven until done, about 25 minutes. Open foil package and place 1 to 2 slices of cheese on top. Return to oven—with foil opened—and bake until cheese melts.

Beef Casserole
Rehobeth Baptist Church † *Linda Laster*

1 pound ground beef
1 large onion, chopped
1 (15-ounce) can whole-kernel corn

3 cups raw sliced potatoes
1 (10.25-ounce) can tomato soup
1 cup cubed Velveeta cheese

Brown beef; drain. Add remaining ingredients and mix well. Bake in casserole dish at 350° for 1 hour.

Enchilada Casserole

Robinhood Baptist Church, Brandon ✝ *Mary Morris*

2 pounds ground chuck
2 (10.25-ounce) cans cream of chicken soup
2 (16-ounce) jars picante sauce (mild or hot)
4 large tortillas
1 (12-ounce) package shredded Cheddar cheese
1 (12-ounce) package shredded mozzarella cheese

Brown ground chuck and drain. Add soup and picante sauce and mix well; set aside. Line a 9x13-inch baking dish with 2 large tortillas. Layer with half the beef mixture. Sprinkle with half the cheeses, and put remaining 2 tortillas on top. Spread remaining beef mixture on tortillas. Bake at 350° for about 30 minutes. Top with remaining cheeses and let melt.

Optional: One-half can of Cheddar cheese soup can be added to meat mixture. Makes it cheesy.

Chili Topped Potatoes

Oak Grove Baptist Church, Lucedale ✝ *Josie Grimes*

1 pound ground beef
1 onion, chopped
1 (15-ounce) can chili beans, undrained
1 (15-ounce) can pinto beans, undrained
1 (15-ounce) can whole-kernel corn, drained
1 (10-ounce) can Rotel tomatoes, undrained
1 large tomato, diced
1 (1.25-ounce) envelope taco seasoning mix
1 (1-ounce) envelope ranch dressing mix
2 cups water
4 large baking potatoes
Shredded cheese, sour cream and chopped green onions for topping

Cook ground beef and onion in a Dutch oven; drain and return to pan. Stir in remaining ingredients, except potatoes and toppings. Bring to a boil, stirring occasionally. Reduce heat and simmer about 20 minutes. Bake potatoes in oven or microwave. When done, cut potatoes in half. Place potatoes on plate, spoon chili over potatoes and garnish with toppings.

Texas Hash

Bethel Baptist Church, Heidelburg

1 pound ground chuck
3 large onions, chopped
1 large green bell pepper, chopped
1 (16-ounce) can petite diced tomatoes or 1 (10-ounce) can hot Rotel tomatoes
½ cup uncooked rice
1 to 2 teaspoons chili powder, or to taste
2 teaspoons salt, or to taste
⅛ teaspoon pepper

Preheat oven to 350°. In a large skillet, brown meat, onions and bell pepper; drain. Stir in tomatoes, rice, chili powder, salt and pepper; heat through. Pour into treated 2-quart casserole dish. Cover and bake 1 hour. Makes 4 to 6 servings.

Tater Tot Casserole

Robinhood Baptist Church, Brandon ✝ Barbara Long

1½ pounds hamburger meat
2 (10.25-ounce) cans cream of chicken soup
¾ can water (or milk)
1 (10-ounce) mild Rotel tomatoes
1 (32-ounce) bag frozen tater tots
Salt and pepper to taste
2 cups shredded Cheddar cheese

Cook hamburger meat until lightly browned. Drain off excess grease. Add soup, water and tomatoes. Simmer 5 minutes. Place tater tots in a large casserole dish. Pour meat mixture on top; sprinkle with salt and pepper. Bake at 350° for 40 minutes. Top with shredded cheese and return to oven just until cheese melts.

One Pan Potatoes & Pepper Steak

Midway Baptist Church, Lucedale

4 medium potatoes, sliced ¼ inch thick
1 (1-pound) London broil, thinly sliced
1 tablespoon garlic pepper
2 tablespoons olive oil
1 green bell pepper, cut into thin strips
Salt to taste

Microwave potatoes 6 to 10 minutes. While potatoes are cooking, toss beef with garlic pepper. Heat oil in large skillet over high heat. Add beef and sauté 3 minutes. Remove beef and add bell pepper to skillet. Sauté 3 minutes. Add potatoes and sauté 5 minutes. Return beef to skillet, stirring until heated through. Season with salt. Serves 4.

Upside Down Pizza

First Baptist Church, Eupora ✝ *Lesa Hardin*

1 pound ground beef
1 pound ground sausage
1 medium onion, chopped
1 small bell pepper, chopped
Salt and pepper
2 eggs, divided

1 (15-ounce) jar pizza sauce
1 (4-ounce) can sliced mushrooms
2 cups shredded Cheddar cheese
2 cups shredded mozzarella cheese
1 (8-count) can crescent rolls

Preheat oven to 350°. Spray a 9x13-inch pan with nonstick spray. Brown meats over medium heat with onion and bell pepper; drain. Season with salt and pepper to taste. Beat 1 egg and add to meat mixture. Add pizza sauce and mushrooms. Stir until well blended. Spread in 9x13-inch pan. Sprinkle with Cheddar, then mozzarella. Layer rolls over cheese. Beat remaining egg and brush over rolls. Bake 25 minutes at 350° or until top is brown. Let stand 5 minutes before cutting into squares. Makes 6 to 8 servings.

First Baptist Church

Eupora

520 West Fox Avenue
Eupora, MS 39744
662-258-3491
www.fbceupora.com

Travis Gray, Pastor

Sunday, February 2, 1890, a small group of seven Baptists met with Dr. John T. Christian of the Mississippi Baptist Convention to organize a Baptist church in Eupora. Originally named Eupora Baptist Church, the name was later changed to First Baptist Church. The original church was a white frame building built in 1891. The third and present sanctuary was built in 1949, with an education building being added in 1965. Our latest addition was the Family Life Center, which was built in 1997. Through the years, FBC has continued to grow and develop in ministry and giving. We currently have a full-time staff of five and a part-time staff of three. Today our church is a strong and vital local congregation active in Mississippi Baptist and Southern Baptist life and ministry. It is rich in history, and faith, and glorious accomplishment of work for the Kingdom of Christ.

Italian Steak

First Baptist Church, Eupora ✝ *Jo Faulkenbery*

1 large round steak
Salt and pepper
Flour for coating
½ green bell pepper, chopped
1 medium onion, chopped
2 tablespoons cooking oil
1 (14-ounce) can diced tomatoes

Cut steak into portion sizes. Season with salt and pepper. Dredge in flour and set aside. Sauté bell pepper and onion in oil until soft; remove from oil. Add meat to oil and brown on both sides. Place in 9x13-inch baking dish. Put onion and bell pepper on top. Top with tomatoes, juice and all. Cover and bake at 300° for 1½ hours. Add water, if needed.

Swiss Bliss

Bethel Missionary Baptist Church, Seminary ✝ *Christine McKee*

½ tablespoon butter
2 pounds cube steak, 1 inch thick
1 (2-ounce) envelope dry onion soup mix
1 green bell pepper, chopped
1 (14-ounce) can chopped tomatoes, drained (reserve juice)
1 (8-ounce) can sliced mushrooms
¼ teaspoon salt
Dash pepper
1 tablespoon A-1 steak sauce
1 tablespoon cornstarch
1 tablespoon sugar

Butter a baking dish. Layer steak, onion soup mix, bell pepper, tomatoes and mushrooms. Salt and pepper to taste. Measure out ½ cup reserved tomato juice (add water if needed) and mix with A-1, cornstarch and sugar. Pour over steak. Cover with foil and bake at 375° for 2 hours.

Steak Stir-Fry

White Hill Missionary Baptist Church, Tupelo

1 pound round steak, cut in strips
2 onions, thinly sliced
1 red bell pepper, thinly sliced
1 yellow bell pepper, thinly sliced
1 green bell pepper, thinly sliced
1 teaspoon salt

1 teaspoon pepper
2 teaspoons garlic powder
4 cups Worcestershire sauce
½ (7-ounce) bottle Thai chili sauce
½ cup soy sauce
3 cups water

In a large skillet over medium heat, sauté steak with onions and bell peppers until steak is cooked through. Add salt, pepper and garlic; mix well. Add remaining ingredients and simmer 7 minutes.

White Hill Missionary Baptist Church

Tupelo

1987 South Eason Boulevard • Tupelo, MS 38802
662-842-3738 • www.whitehillmbc.org
www.facebook.com/white-hill-baptist-church

Reverend Jeffery B. Daniel, Pastor

White Hill Missionary Baptist Church is a unique church with rich history and a matchless manner of worship. Founded in 1908 by Reverend Richard Oliver and a handful of faithful members, White Hill has continued to grow spiritually and in numbers throughout the years. Today, under the leadership of Reverend Jeffery Daniel, White Hill has become trailblazers in this community. Jesus said in John 14:12 "Verily, verily, I say unto you, He that believeth on me, the works that I do shall he do also; and greater works than these shall he do; because I go unto my Father." White Hill is striving to fulfill that prophecy. Through the various ministries and community involvement, it is White Hill's vision to reach today's families through tomorrow's generation.

Beef Tips

Cash Baptist Church, Lena ✝ *Betty Gunn*

½ cup all-purpose flour	½ cup oil
Salt and pepper to taste	¼ cup onion flakes or chopped onion
Dash garlic salt	1 cup chopped celery
Dash lemon pepper	½ cup sliced carrots
2 pounds stew meat or sirloin, trimmed	1 to 2 (14-ounce) cans beef broth

Combine flour, salt, pepper, garlic salt and lemon pepper. Roll meat in seasoned flour. Put oil in a large skillet or Dutch oven over medium-high heat. When oil is hot, add meat, onion, celery and carrots. When meat is brown, transfer mixture to a slow cooker. Add beef broth and cook until tender. (This can be cooked in a Dutch oven over low heat.)

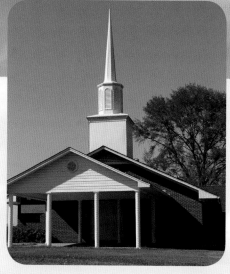

Cash Baptist Church

Lena

1716 Cash Road
Lena, MS 39094

Cash Baptist Church is a close-knit, country church in Scott County that offers sweet, southern hospitality. Since its establishment in 1909, Cash Baptist Church has been known as a center for worship and as a place where food preparation and consumption during fellowship are blessings to be relished by all. Moreover, Cash Baptist Church has always been a loving place that welcomes people as family with open arms. We would love for anyone to not only sample our delicious recipes, but also to join our church family in fellowship with one another and in worship to God from whom these blessings come.

Beef Tips and Rice

Russell Baptist Church, Meridian † *Cynthia Wilson*

2 pounds lean beef tips
2 (10.25-ounce) cans cream of celery soup
1 (10.25-ounce) can cream of
   mushroom soup
1 onion, diced
¾ teaspoon salt
⅛ teaspoon pepper
⅛ teaspoon garlic powder
Cooked rice or egg noodles

In a 5-quart slow cooker, combine beef, soups, onion and seasonings. Cook on low setting for 8 hours, or until beef is tender. Serve over rice or egg noodles.

Italian Beef

Robinhood Baptist Church, Brandon † *Sylvia Shaw*

1 (6- to 7-pound) boneless chuck roast
½ cup water
½ tablespoon garlic powder
1 (12-ounce) jar Guernica peppers, divided
1 (2.5-ounce) package zesty Italian seasoning
1 (1-ounce) package au jus gravy mix
Salt and black pepper to taste

Put roast, water, garlic powder and half the Guernica pepper juice in slow cooker. Sprinkle zesty Italian seasoning on top. Do not stir. Cook about 8 hours. Shred meat using 2 forks. Sprinkle gravy mix on top along with 8 Guernica peppers. Season with salt and black pepper. Do not stir. Cook 1 more hour. Makes about 40 sandwiches.

Pot Roast

Palestine Baptist Church, Nettleton ✝ *Crystal Cody*

1 beef roast
1 onion, peeled and quartered
3 to 5 potatoes, peeled and chopped
1 to 2 sweet potatoes (just trust me), peeled and chopped
½ (16-ounce) bag baby carrots
½ cup Dale's seasoning sauce
1 (10.25-ounce) can cream of mushroom soup

Place all ingredients, except soup, in a large slow cooker. Add about 2 cups water. Cover and cook on low all day (at least 6 hours). Once cooked, add soup for a delicious gravy.

Venison or Beef Roast

First Baptist Church, Wiggins

1 (4- to 6-pound) venison or beef roast (tip, chuck, rump or shoulder)
Santa Maria seasoning (or garlic pepper seasoning and seasoned salt)
4 slices bacon
½ cup Yoshida Original Gourmet marinade and cooking sauce

Coat roast completely with Santa Maria seasoning. Lay bacon slices on top. Pour Yoshida sauce over roast. Top with more seasoning, if desired. Bake in slow oven (250° to 260°) about 5 hours or until tender. Best when cooked very slowly.

Russian Pot Roast

Redemption Church, Diamondhead ✝ *Wanda Bares*

1 (3- to 4-pound) beef roast
4 thin slices pickled pork
1 large onion, sliced
1 large carrot, sliced
½ cup chopped green onions

1 (8-ounce) carton sour cream, room
   temperature
Salt and pepper to taste
1 tablespoon lemon juice
1 tablespoon flour

Brown each side of roast in an oven-ready pot. Place pickled pork, onion, carrot and green onions in pot. Remove from heat and stir in sour cream. Season to taste with salt and pepper. Cover and bake at 350° for 2 to 2½ hours. When roast is finished, remove from pot. Add flour and lemon juice to roast drippings to make a gravy.

REDEMPTION CHURCH
DIAMONDHEAD
———"There's A Place For You"———

Redemption Church

Diamondhead

4401 Park Ten Drive
Diamondhead, MS 39525
228-380-0690
www.facebook.com/RedemptionChurchDmhd

Redemption Church is a faith family of Baptist believers in Diamondhead. Redemption Church is a mission started January 2015 in partnership with the BMA of Mississippi. Brother Wesley Martin is the pastor of the Mission and Campground Baptist Church—our mother church. We are excited about what God is doing in the city of Diamondhead. We are currently the only Baptist church in the city. We are working to reach out to as many people in the city as we can. It is our goal to be a ministry where everyone is welcome and can be active in ministry. We would like to invite you to our Sunday services at 10:30 a.m. We also have small group Bible studies on different nights of the week. We would love for you to visit. You can follow us on Facebook. For more information, you can call 228.380.0690.

Grover's Barbecue Sauce

Mt. Pisgah Baptist Church, Brandon † *Warren Gunn*

2 cups vinegar
½ cups sugar
¾ teaspoon salt
2 ounces chili powder
4 cups water
2 cups oil
3 lemons, diced

½ pound onion, chopped
½ teaspoon red pepper
½ cup Worcestershire sauce
¼ teaspoon black pepper
½ cup mustard
1 to 1½ (12-ounce) jars chili sauce

Combine all ingredients, except chili sauce, in a large boiler. Bring to a boil then reduce heat to simmer for 1 hour. Stir in chili sauce just before serving. Makes nearly a gallon.

Marinated Pork Chops with Herb Salsa

Mount Helm Baptist Church, Jackson

¼ cup extra virgin olive oil
3 tablespoons fresh lemon juice
1 tablespoon chopped rosemary

2 garlic cloves, minced
Freshly ground pepper
6 (5-ounce) boneless pork rib chops

In a large bowl, whisk olive oil with lemon juice, rosemary and garlic; season with pepper. Add pork chops and turn to coat. Let stand in marinade at room temperature for 1 hour.

HERB SALSA:

1 garlic clove, minced
1 tablespoon drained capers
1 tablespoon dry mustard
1 tablespoon white wine vinegar
1 cup flat-leaf parsley leaves

½ cup basil leaves
½ cup mint leaves
2 tablespoons extra virgin olive oil
Salt and pepper to taste

Using a food processor, pulse garlic with capers, mustard and vinegar just to combine. Add parsley, basil and mint and pulse to chop. Add olive oil and pulse just to combine. Transfer salsa to a bowl; season with salt and pepper.

Light a grill. Remove pork from marinade; season with salt. Grill over high heat, turning once, until just cooked, 8 to 9 minutes. Let rest 5 minutes. Serve with Herb Salsa.

Barbecued Pork Chops

Tate Baptist Church, Corinth ✝ *Linda Pratt*

4 large pork chops, thick cut
Salt and pepper to taste
1 lemon, sliced
1 onion, sliced
½ cup ketchup
3 tablespoons Worcestershire sauce
½ teaspoon chili powder
½ teaspoon salt
1 cup water
Dash hot sauce

Place pork chops in a roaster with cover. Salt and pepper to taste. Cover with lemon and onion slices. Cover roaster and bake at 345° for 30 minutes. While chops are cooking in the oven, mix the remaining ingredients and bring to a boil. At the end of the first cooking time, remove chops from oven. Pour ketchup mixture over meat and continue cooking in oven on 300° for 45 minutes.

Family Pork Chops

Unity Baptist Church, McHenry

Salt and pepper to taste
6 pork chops
6 onion slices
¾ cup ketchup
1 cup water
2 tablespoons Worcestershire sauce
2 tablespoons vinegar
2 tablespoons brown sugar
1 teaspoon paprika
1 teaspoon chili powder

Preheat oven to 325°. Salt and pepper chops and place in 9x13-inch baking dish. Top each chop with an onion slice. Combine remaining ingredients in a medium-size bowl and pour over chops. Cover with foil and bake for 1 hour and 10 minutes. Remove foil and bake an additional 20 minutes. Delicious served with juice poured over prepared rice.

Crawfish with Rice

First Baptist Church, Brookhaven ✝ *Alicia Williams*

3 celery stalks, chopped	2 (5-ounce) packages Saffron yellow rice
1 green bell pepper, chopped	1 (10.25-ounce) can cream of mushroom
1 onion, chopped	soup
1 stick margarine or butter	1 cup shredded Cheddar cheese
1 (10-ounce) can Rotel tomatoes	1 (16-ounce) package crawfish tails

Sauté celery, bell pepper and onion in margarine. Combine with tomatoes and steam on low for 10 minutes. Cook rice according to package directions. Mix rice in with tomato mixture. Add soup, cheese and crawfish. Place in greased baking dish and bake at 325° for 40 minutes.

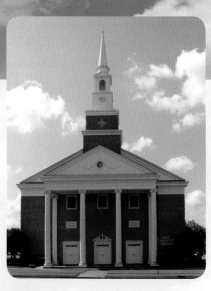

First Baptist Church

Brookhaven

200 East Monticello Street
Brookhaven, MS 39601
601-833-5118
www.fbcbrookhaven.org

Greg Warnock, Pastor

First Baptist Church of Brookhaven began in 1872 with Brother W. P. Farrish as the first pastor and a charter membership of thirteen people. Since then, the congregation has occupied three separate buildings while remaining in the heart of the city. As the church has grown in membership and square footage, the congregation continues to impact Brookhaven, Lincoln County, and beyond with the life-changing Gospel of Jesus Christ. First Baptist encourages everyone to KNOW God through Jesus Christ, GROW in their relationship with God, SERVE God by serving in ministry, and SHARE God's love with others. We are a caring and growing church that is Christ-centered. Our mission is to glorify God through joyous worship, loving fellowship, faithful witness, biblical teaching, and effective training. May all who come behind us find us faithful!

Crawfish Pie

Redemption Church, Diamondhead ✝ *Wanda Bares*

½ stick butter
1 cup chopped onions
½ cup chopped green bell pepper
¼ cup chopped celery
1 teaspoon salt
½ cup chopped tomatoes

1 pound crawfish tails
4 tablespoons flour
½ cup water
2 teaspoons chopped green onions
1 tablespoon chopped parsley
2 (9-inch) pie crusts

Preheat oven to 375°. Melt butter in a large skillet over medium heat. Add onions, bell pepper and celery; sauté 6 to 8 minutes. Add salt and tomatoes and continue to cook, stirring occasionally, for 5 more minutes. Add crawfish tails and cook 10 minutes. Dissolve flour in water and add to pan, continuing to cook, stirring occasionally, until sauce thickens. Add green onions and parsley; remove from heat and cool 30 minutes. Place 1 pie crust into a pie pan and pour sauce in crust. Top with second crust and crimp edges. Make 2 or 3 cuts in the top crust, place pie on a baking sheet, and bake 45 minutes. Cool before serving.

Tricia's Crawfish Mexicala

Pelahatchie Baptist Church, Pelahatchie ✝ *Mary Ann Baker*

1 medium yellow onion, chopped
1 bunch green onions, chopped
1 medium bell pepper, chopped
2 cups chopped celery
1 stick margarine
2 (10.25-ounce) cans cream of mushroom soup
1 (8-ounce) box mild Velveeta cheese, cubed
2 pounds crawfish tails
Salt, black and red pepper to taste
Tony's Chachere's Creole seasoning to taste
Cooked rice or angel hair pasta

Sauté vegetables in margarine until limp. Add soup and cheese; simmer 20 minutes. Add crawfish then season to taste. Simmer 20 more minutes. Serve over rice or angel hair pasta.

Shrimp Casserole

First Baptist Church, Baldwyn

3 cups raw peeled shrimp (about 1½ pounds)
9 tablespoons butter, divided
2 tablespoons liquid shrimp boil
1 cup chopped onion
1 cup chopped green bell pepper
1 cup chopped celery
2 garlic cloves, minced
⅓ cup chopped parsley
1 cup chopped green onion tops
1 (2-ounce) jar pimento
1 (10.25-ounce) can Cheddar cheese soup
1 (10.25-ounce) can cream of shrimp soup
2 cups cooked rice
1 teaspoon salt
1 teaspoon pepper
¼ cup breadcrumbs

Sauté shrimp in 1 tablespoon butter and shrimp boil until pink; set aside. Sauté onion, bell pepper, celery and garlic in remaining 8 tablespoons butter. Add parsley, green onions, pimento, and soups. Drain shrimp and add to soup mixture. Stir in rice, salt and pepper. Pour into a 3-quart casserole and sprinkle with breadcrumbs. Bake at 350° for 30 minutes. Enjoy.

Desserts & Sweets

Jesus said to her, "I am the resurrection and the life. He who believes in me will live, even though he dies." —JOHN 11:25

Kathy's Pecan Pie
Bethel Baptist Church, Heidelburg

¼ cup butter or margarine
1 cup sugar
1 tablespoon flour
1¼ cups white corn syrup
4 eggs
1 cup broken pecans
1 teaspoon vanilla
1 deep-dish pie shell (or 2 regular), unbaked

Cream butter; add sugar and flour, beating until fluffy. Add corn syrup and beat well. Add eggs, 1 at a time beating thoroughly. Add broken pecans and vanilla. Pour into unbaked pie shell(s). Bake at 300° for 50 minutes or until set. (If baking in 2 pie shells, less bake time will be required.)

"No Sugar Added" Pecan Pie
Pleasant Home Baptist Church, Laurel ✝ *Sylvia Mauldin*

3 eggs
¾ cup Splenda
1 cup Honey Tree's Sugar-Free Honey
1 cup chopped pecans
1 teaspoon vanilla
¼ teaspoon salt
1 (9-inch) pie shell, unbaked

Beat eggs and Splenda. Add honey, pecans, vanilla and salt. Pour into unbaked pie shell. Bake at 325° for 50 minutes or until set.

Sweet Potato Pie

Toxish Baptist Church,
Pontotoc

3 cups cooked and mashed
    sweet potatoes
2 cups sugar
4 eggs
1 stick butter or margarine,
    softened
1 (14-ounce) can sweetened
    condensed milk
1 teaspoon vanilla
2 unbaked pie shells

Mix mashed sweet potatoes with sugar, eggs, butter, sweetened condensed milk and vanilla. Pour into unbaked pie shells. Bake at 350° for 45 minutes. Makes 2 pies.

Honey Hush Pie

Robinhood Baptist Church, Brandon ✝ *Sylvia Shaw*

¾ cup sugar
¾ stick butter
3 eggs, beaten
1 tablespoon vinegar

1 (9-inch) pie shell, unbaked
¼ cup chocolate chips
½ cup coconut
½ cup chopped nuts

Mix sugar, butter, eggs and vinegar together and pour into pie shell. Sprinkle chocolate chips over top. Sprinkle coconut on top of that. Sprinkle pecans on top of that. Bake at 350° about 30 minutes, until golden brown.

Chocolate Pie with Meringue

First Baptist Church, Indianola

1¼ cups sugar
3 tablespoons self-rising flour
3 heaping tablespoons cocoa
2½ cups milk, divided

2 egg yolks (reserve egg whites)
1 teaspoon vanilla
½ stick margarine
1 pie crust, baked

Mix sugar, flour and cocoa in a saucepan. Add 2 cups milk and cook over medium-high heat, stirring very frequently, until it begins to thicken. Beat egg yolks (refrigerate whites for meringue) with remaining ½ cup milk; add to saucepan. Continue cooking until very thick. Stir in vanilla and margarine until margarine is melted. Pour into pie crust. Top with Meringue.

MERINGUE:
2 egg whites
½ teaspoon cream of tartar

⅓ cup sugar

Beat egg whites and cream of tartar to soft peaks. Add sugar and beat to stiff peaks. Spread over pie, sealing to edges. Bake at 350° until Meringue is light golden brown, about 10 minutes.

First Baptist Church, Indianola

202 Catchings Avenue
Indianola, MS 38751
662-887-2241
www.facebook.com/fbcindianola

Dr. Guy Burke, Pastor

First Baptist Church is nestled in the historic downtown area of the small town of Indianola. The church building sits around the corner from the famous B.B. King Museum and serves the city of Indianola as a beacon of hope. First Baptist Church exists to cultivate authentic followers of Jesus. We seek to fulfill the Great Commission (Matthew 28:16-20) both locally and globally. We are committed to missions and taking the Gospel to those that need it most as we believe it is the responsibility of every believer. We are a community who firmly believes in God's Word. Come journey with us.

Chocolate Chess Pie

Bethel Baptist Church, Heidelburg

3 cups sugar
1 (12-ounce) can evaporated milk
4 eggs
1 stick butter or margarine, melted

7 teaspoons cocoa
2 teaspoons vanilla
2 pie shells, unbaked (not deep)

Combine all ingredients, expect pie shells. Pour into unbaked pie shells. Bake at 350° about 30 to 40 minutes until slightly firm (will continue to firm while cooling). Cool completely before cutting.

Chocolate Chess Pie

Tate Baptist Church, Corinth † *Susan Beard*

1½ cups sugar
⅓ cup cocoa
2 tablespoons flour
6 tablespoons butter
1 cup evaporated milk

2 eggs, slightly beaten
1 tablespoon vanilla
1 pie shell, unbaked
1 cup chopped pecans

Mix sugar, cocoa and flour; set aside. In a saucepan, melt butter. Add milk, eggs and vanilla; remove from heat. Add flour mixture and beat with an electric mixer for 3 minutes, until very smooth. Pour into pie shell and sprinkle with pecans. Bake at 350° for 40 to 45 minutes.

Chess Pie

First Baptist Church, Eupora † *Ruby Bland*

3 large eggs, room temperature
1 tablespoon cornmeal
½ cup melted butter or margarine
1 tablespoon vinegar

1½ cups sugar
Vanilla to taste
1 (9-inch) pie shell, unbaked

Mix thoroughly all ingredients, except pie shell. Pour into pie shell and bake at 300° for 40 minutes.

Peanut Butter Bacon Pie

Farmington Baptist Church, Corinth

⅓ cup smooth peanut butter
1 cup powdered sugar
1 (8-ounce) package cream cheese, softened
1 (8-ounce) carton whipped topping

½ pound bacon, fried crisp and crumbled (plus more for topping, if desired)
1 chocolate graham cracker crust

Cream peanut butter, sugar and cream cheese. Stir in whipped topping and bacon by hand. (Optional: Use less whipped topping if you want it more like cheesecake.) Pour into crust. Top with additional crumbled bacon, if desired.

This idea came from Sonic's Peanut Butter Bacon milkshake. I love them so much, I thought I'd try a pie. I've taken it to two church functions and it was a hit. Don't knock it till you've tried it.

Farmington Baptist Church

Corinth

84 County Road 106A
Corinth, MS 38834
662-286-8855
www.farmingtonbaptistchurch.com

Jarrod Cox, Pastor

Farmington Baptist Church, established in the early 1800's, has been a beacon of light to the community for well over a century. The church building today, with its white steeple and octagonal sanctuary, looks quite different from the log cabin it was when it began. However, the people inside the church building have remained steadfast in their faith in God and desire to follow Christ and serve others in the community and around the world. Our Children's Choir has performed many musicals to congregations across the mid-South. Our teachers have equipped the children with memory verses so they are able to carry Scripture in their hearts and minds as they walk the halls of their schools. The "Living Last Supper," the Christmas Candlelight Service, and the 4th of July Cookout & Fireworks are favorites of Farmington's annual events. Farmington Baptist Church is a historical landmark and, of course, a church, but many people over the past one hundred years have simply called it "home."

Edith Oliver's Caramel Pie

First Baptist Church, Eupora ✝ *Amy Stephens*

6 eggs, separated
3¼ cups sugar, divided
8 tablespoons cornstarch
2 cups milk

2 sticks margarine
2 teaspoons vanilla
Dash salt
2 pie shells, baked and cooled

Beat egg yolks well (refrigerate egg whites). In a separate bowl, mix 2 cups sugar with cornstarch; add milk and stir. Add beaten egg yolks to this mixture. Cook in large heavy boiler over medium-low heat, stirring constantly. While this is heating, place ½ cup sugar in iron or heavy skillet. Brown sugar until melted and light brown. (If it browns too fast, remove from heat and continue stirring.) Add 2 to 3 tablespoons milk mixture to caramelized sugar then add sugar back into boiler constantly stirring to blend. Add margarine, vanilla and salt, stirring until mixture thickens and is smooth. Stir, stir, stir. Pour into pie shells. Beat cold egg whites until soft peaks form. Slowly add remaining sugar, while beating. Continue to beat until stiff peaks form. Spread meringue over pies, sealing to edge. Bake at 375° in oven until meringue browns, about 10 minutes.

Coconut Pie

4 tablespoons butter, melted
2 eggs, beaten
1 tablespoon all-purpose flour
¾ cup sugar
1 cup shredded sweetened coconut
1 cup milk
1 (9-inch) pie shell, unbaked

Preheat oven to 350°. In a large bowl, combine melted butter, eggs, flour, sugar, coconut and milk. Pour into pie shell. Bake until firm, 45 to 60 minutes.

Egg Custard Pie

Mt. Pisgah Baptist Church, Brandon ✝ *Janelle C. Carter*

1 (5-ounce) can evaporated milk
1 cup milk
2 tablespoons margarine
3 eggs
1 ⅓ cups sugar
1 teaspoon vanilla
1 (9-inch) deep-dish pie crust or 2 (8-inch) pie crusts

Preheat oven to 425°. In a saucepan, heat evaporated milk, milk and margarine to boiling then cool slightly. In the meantime, beat eggs, sugar and vanilla until combine. Slowly pour heated mixture into egg mixture beating continuously to keep eggs from cooking. Pour filling into pie crust and bake 10 minutes. Reduce heat to 400° and bake another 5 minutes. Cool before slicing.

Cornmeal Pie

Sunrise Baptist Church, Carthage ✝ *Martha Lou Beckham*

4 eggs, plus 2 egg whites for top
1 cup plus 2 tablespoons sugar, divided
4 tablespoons cornmeal
¾ cup butter, melted
½ cup milk
1 (9-inch) pie shell

Mix 4 eggs, 1 cup sugar, cornmeal, butter and milk together. Pour into unbaked pie shell. Cook at 350° until firm, about 35 minutes. Beat 2 eggs white with remaining 2 tablespoons sugar until peaks form. Spread on top of pie and bake in oven until golden brown, about 5 minutes.

Lemonade Pie

Walnut Grove Baptist Church, Fulton

1 (6-ounce) can frozen lemonade concentrate, thawed
1 (14-ounce) can sweetened condensed milk
1 (8-ounce) carton Cool Whip
1 (9-inch) graham cracker pie crust

Mix first 3 ingredients. Pour into pie shell. Chill 2 to 4 hours before serving.

Walnut Grove Baptist Church

Fulton

1906 South Adams Street
Fulton, MS 38843

Walnut Grove Baptist Church was built on a desire to see souls saved and to give those who are already saved a place to worship. Our church was built on the philosophy of... Everybody is somebody here. We invite you to join us Sundays at 10:00 a.m. for Sunday School, Morning Worship at 10:40 a.m. and Evening Worship at 5:30 p.m. Wednesday Bible Study begins at 5:30 p.m. The picture here is of our late pastor, Brother James E. Wilson and his wife. We dedicate this page in memory of his dedicated service to the church.

Blueberry Cream Cheese Pie

Mt. Pisgah Baptist Church, Brandon ✝ *Nola Herring*

CRUST:

1¼ cup graham cracker crumbs	½ cup chopped nuts
½ cup brown sugar	½ cup melted butter

Combine crust ingredients and press into a 9x13-inch pan (or 2 pie pans).

FILLING:

1 (8-ounce) package cream cheese, softened	½ cup sugar
	2 eggs, well beaten

Mix filling ingredients thoroughly and pour over crust. Bake at 350° for 20 minutes. Cool before topping. Topping:

4 cups blueberries	1 cup sugar
2 tablespoons cornstarch	1 teaspoon lemon juice

Mix topping ingredients in a medium saucepan. Cook over medium heat until juice thickens. Cool then pour over pie. Refrigerate 1 hour before serving.

Pineapple Cheesecake Pie

Russell Baptist Church, Meridian ✝ *Linda Stuckey*

CRUST:

1¼ cups graham cracker crumbs
2 tablespoons sugar
¼ cup butter, melted

Combine and press into a 9-inch pie plate. Set aside.

CHEESECAKE FILLING:

2 (8-ounce) packages cream cheese, softened
¾ cup sugar
2 eggs, room temperature
1 to 2 teaspoons vanilla extract

Using an electric mixer, beat cream cheese and sugar until combined. Add eggs one at a time, and beat until smooth. Add vanilla; mix well. Pour into Crust. Bake at 350° for approximately 30 minutes or until set. Cool slightly.

SOUR CREAM TOPPING:

1 cup sour cream
2 tablespoons sugar
1 teaspoon vanilla extract

Combine and spread over Cheesecake Filling after it has cooled slightly. Refrigerate.

PINEAPPLE TOPPING:

1 (20-ounce) can crushed pineapple, undrained
½ cup sugar
1 tablespoon cornstarch
1 tablespoon butter, softened
Pinch salt

Combine pineapple, sugar and cornstarch in a small saucepan; cook until thick. Add butter and salt. Refrigerate until cooled and spoon over pie before serving.

Fried Pies

Palestine Baptist Church, Nettleton ✝ *Betty Sue Scribner*

2 cups flour
½ teaspoon salt
1 teaspoon baking soda
4 tablespoons water

1 tablespoon vinegar
1 cup shortening
Desired fruit filling
Oil for frying

Mix first 5 ingredients. Use a fork or pastry blender to work in shortening. Refrigerate 2 hours or longer. Roll out pastry and cut into 4-inch circles. Spread fruit filling over half of each circle. Fold pastry circle over filling and press edges together with a fork. Fry in deep, hot shortening until brown, about 1 minute each.

Fried Pies

South Green Baptist Church, Tupelo ✝ *Dot Emison*

DOUGH:
4½ cups self-rising flour
3 tablespoons sugar
½ cup shortening

2 eggs
1 cup milk

In a large bowl, combine flour and sugar. Cut in shortening. In a separate bowl, combine eggs and milk. Add to flour mixture. Mix until dough forms a ball. Cover and chill several hours.

FRUIT:
Apples, peeled and chopped (or other fruit)
1 cup sugar (or more to taste)

1 teaspoon cinnamon or apple pie spice
1 tablespoon vanilla

While dough is chilling, cook fruit in water to cover until done. Add sugar, cinnamon and vanilla; cool. Taste to make sure fruit is sweet enough. Divide dough into sections. Place each section on a floured board. Roll out and cut into rounds using a small saucer. (I use a Cool Whip lid.) Spoon enough fruit to cover half of dough. Fold together and pinch edges with a fork to seal. Press well. Fry in hot oil, turning until each side is brown. (To bake pies, do as above but brush tops with beaten egg whites; place on cookie sheet and bake at 425° until golden brown.)

Note: Some fruits take more sugar than others, so taste after 1 cup of sugar. For instance, peaches take more than apples. May use Splenda instead of sugar.

Peach Cobbler

Robinhood Baptist Church, Brandon ✝ *Barbara Long*

1 stick margarine
1 (29-ounce) can sliced peaches
1 cup milk
1 cup self-rising flour
1¾ cups sugar, divided
1 teaspoon cinnamon

Melt margarine in a 9x9-inch casserole dish. Pour in peaches with juice; set aside. Mix milk, flour and 1½ cups sugar together. Pour over peaches. Mix remaining ¼ cup sugar and cinnamon together and sprinkle on top. Bake at 350° for 45 to 50 minutes.

Robinhood Baptist Church

Brandon

> 1451 Old Lake Road
> Brandon, MS 39042
> 601-825-0975

David McNeill, Pastor

Robinhood Baptist Church was established in 1964 and is "The little Church with a BIG Heart" sharing God's love. We have a place for you because our church is a place where everyone is Somebody. Come as you are. Jesus is Lord. We hope you will feel right at home as we worship together. Just as Jesus Christ came "not to be ministered unto, but to minister...," we accept our responsibility to reach out in service to others. This applies both within the church family and outside our fellowship. Nothing quite compares to the joy of Christian fellowship. The primary reason we meet together is to focus our attention on God, giving Him our worship and receiving His blessing and inspiration. Our focus at Robinhood Baptist Church is to honor and serve the Lord Jesus Christ first and foremost, then others, and finally ourselves.

Apple Cobbler

Rhymes Baptist Church, Lucedale ✝ *Ruthie Havard*

1 stick butter
2 cups sugar
2 cups water
½ cup shortening
1½ cups flour
½ cup milk
2 cups peeled and chopped apples
1 teaspoon cinnamon

Heat oven to 350°. Melt butter in a 2-quart pan. Dissolve sugar in water in a saucepan over medium heat. Cut shortening in flour until fine particles. Add milk and stir until dough leaves the side of bowl. Turn dough onto floured surface and knead until smooth. Roll dough out into a rectangle. Combine apples and cinnamon; spread over dough. Roll jellyroll style and slice into about 16 slices. Place in pan with melted butter. Pour sugar syrup over and bake 55 minutes.

Rhymes Missionary Baptist Church

Lucedale

1056 Lamar Street
Lucedale, MS 39452

Brother Dale Dean, Pastor

Rhymes Missionary Baptist Church was established in October 1950. Our pastor is Brother Dale Dean and Assistant Pastor is Brother Colon Havard. We are a King James-based church. We have great youth and children programs. Our youth is very involved in all our worship services. We encourage our youth to be involved, for they are the church of tomorrow. If you don't have a home Church, come and worship with us. We would be blessed to have you.

Chocolate Cobbler

6 tablespoons butter
1 cup self-rising flour
1¾ cups sugar, divided
¼ cup plus 1½ tablespoons unsweetened cocoa powder, divided
½ cup milk
1 teaspoon vanilla extract
1½ cups boiling water

Preheat oven to 350°. Melt butter in 8x8-inch baking dish while oven preheats. In a medium bowl, stir together flour, ¾ cup sugar, and 1½ tablespoons cocoa. Whisk in milk and vanilla until smooth. Spoon over melted butter in baking dish. Stir together remaining 1 cup sugar and ¼ cup cocoa powder. Sprinkle over batter. Slowly pour boiling water over top (do not stir). Bake 30 minutes. Serve slightly warm with ice cream.

Tortilla Cobbler

Robinhood Baptist Church, Brandon ✝ Mary Morris

1¾ cups sugar, divided
1½ sticks butter
2 cups water
1 teaspoon vanilla

2 (21-ounce) cans apple pie filling
10 large flour tortillas
¼ teaspoon cinnamon

Bring 1½ cups sugar, butter, water and vanilla to a boil. Cook until sugar is dissolved. Set aside. Divide 1 can apple pie filling between 5 tortillas. Roll pie filling up in tortillas; place seam side down in a 9x13-inch casserole dish. Repeat with remaining tortillas and remaining apple pie filling. When all tortillas have been rolled up, pour sugar mixture over tortillas. Mix cinnamon and remaining ¼ cup sugar together and sprinkle over tortillas before baking. Bake at 350° for 30 minutes.

Butterscotch Bundt Cake

First Baptist Church of Greenville ✝ *Lynn Cox*

1 box yellow cake mix
1 (3.4-ounce) box vanilla instant
  pudding mix
1 (12-ounce) package butterscotch
  chips

1 cup coarsely chopped walnuts
1 cup shredded coconut
4 eggs
1 cup sour cream
⅔ cup oil

Preheat oven to 325°. In a large bowl, stir together dry cake mix, dry pudding mix, butterscotch chips, walnuts and coconut. Blend in eggs, sour cream and oil; mix well. Treat a Bundt pan with nonstick spray; add batter. Bake 1 hour. Cool in pan 5 to 10 minutes before removing to serve.

First Baptist Church of Greenville

407 Main Street
Greenville, MS 38701
662-334-9452
www.fbcgreenville.net

Dr. James L. Nichols, Jr. Pastor

First Baptist Church of Greenville was organized in 1871 with four charter members. The church dealt with a succession of missionary and part-time pastors and had no permanent place of worship, meeting at the Jewish synagogue, the opera house on the corner of Main and Poplar Streets, and at the Presbyterian Church on the east side of Walnut Street. In 1884, a "church house" was completed and was dedicated in 1886 by E.E. King—the church's first full-time pastor. The white frame structure was located on Poplar Street and served the church well until 1906 when the growing congregation moved to the corner of Main and Hinds. Dr. James L. Nichols, Jr. became pastor of First Baptist Church in June 2004. Under his leadership, the church remains a strong and vital force in Greenville. First Baptist Church remains committed to preaching and teaching the Word of God throughout the Delta.

4 Ingredient Butterscotch Cake

Mt. Pisgah Baptist Church, Brandon † *Sheila Simmons*

2 cups milk
1 (3-ounce) box cook-and-serve vanilla pudding mix
1 box yellow cake mix
1 (12-ounce) package butterscotch morsels

In a small boiler over medium-high heat, combine milk and pudding mix; bring to boil. Remove from heat. Add cake mix; mix well. Pour into a prepared 9x13-inch glass baking dish. Sprinkle butterscotch morsels over cake. Bake at 350° for 30 minutes or until done. Cool before serving.

Quite possibly the easiest cake ever...and it tastes GREAT!

Ooey Gooey Butter Cake

Woodland Baptist Church, Columbus

CRUST:

1 box yellow cake mix   1 stick butter, melted
1 egg, beaten

For Crust, combine dry cake mix, egg and butter; press into a greased 9x13-inch baking dish.

TOPPING:

1 (8-ounce) package cream cheese,   2 eggs, beaten
  softened   1 (16-ounce) box powdered sugar
1 stick butter, softened

For Topping, combine cream cheese, butter, eggs and powdered sugar. Pour over crust and bake at 350° for 35 to 45 minutes. Finished cake should be ooey gooey, hence the name, and it is so yummy.

Caramel Cake

Williamsville Baptist Church, Kosciusko ✝ *Gladys McCrory*

1 box yellow cake mix, plus ingredients to prepare

Prepare cake per package directions in a 9x13-inch pan; cool.

ICING:

2½ cups sugar, divided

1 (5-ounce) can evaporated milk

2 sticks margarine

1 teaspoon vanilla

Brown ½ cup sugar in an iron skillet. In a saucepan, combine 2 cups sugar, evaporated milk and margarine; bring to a boil. Boil to soft-ball stage. Add caramelized sugar while continuing to cook and stir until well mixed. Remove from heat and add vanilla. Beat until consistency for spreading. Spread over cooled cake.

Caramel Apple Cake

½ cup butter or margarine

¼ cup whipping cream

1 cup packed brown sugar

½ cup chopped pecans

2 large cooking apples, peeled, cored and thinly sliced

1 box yellow cake mix

1¼ cups water

⅓ cup vegetable oil

3 eggs

¼ teaspoon apple pie spice

Heat oven to 350°. In a heavy saucepan, cook butter, whipping cream and brown sugar over low heat, stirring occasionally, just until butter is melted. Pour into 9x13-inch pan. Sprinkle with pecans; top with sliced apples. In a large bowl, beat cake mix, water, oil, eggs and apple pie spice with electric mixer about 2 minutes. Carefully spoon batter over apple mixture. Bake about 45 minutes or until toothpick inserted near center comes out clean. Cool in pan 10 minutes then flip onto a serving platter leaving pan in place for about 1 minute so caramel can drizzle over cake. Remove pan.

TOPPING:

⅔ cup prepared white frosting

½ cup whipped topping

Caramel topping

In a small bowl, mix frosting and whipped topping. Serve warm cake topped with Topping and drizzled with caramel.

Pecan Pie Cake

Pelahatchie Baptist Church, Pelahatchie † *Mary Ann Baker*

2 cups sugar
1 cup butter or margarine
1½ cups self-rising flour
4 eggs
1 teaspoon vanilla
2 cups chopped pecans

1 (8-ounce) package cream cheese, softened
1 (14-ounce) can sweetened condensed milk
1 (16-ounce) container Cool Whip

Cream sugar and margarine; add flour, eggs, vanilla and pecans. Stir by hand until blended. Pour into greased 9x13-inch baking dish. Bake 30 to 40 minutes in 350° oven; cool. With electric mixer, blend cream cheese, condensed milk and Cool Whip. In separate bowl, crumble cooled cake. In serving dish, layer half the crumbed cake then half Cool Whip mixture. Repeat layers. Chill before serving.

Pelahatchie Baptist Church

300 Church Street
Pelahatchie, MS 39145
601-854-8809

Guy Hughes, Pastor

The Pelahatchie Baptist Church building is beautiful, and the Church is made up of a body of believers who worship and praise their Lord while fellowshipping with each other and reaching out to the community. We provide exciting programs for children, youth, and senior citizens, as well as a men's ministry. Each year in April, our ladies organize a Ladies Evening Out with amazing tablescapes, food, and entertainment. A Holiday Marketplace provides gifts, decorations, canned goods, cakes, and pies for shoppers; usually scheduled for the second Saturday in November, it is a Christmas Wonderland with proceeds paying on our building as will the sales of this cookbook. Through these outreach programs we hope to spread the word that Jesus Christ is Savior and Lord. And He is always enough.

Chocolate Cake

Robinhood Baptist Church, Brandon ✝ *Mary Morris*

1 box yellow cake mix
1 (3.9-ounce) box chocolate instant pudding mix
1 teaspoon cocoa
¾ cup sugar
¾ cup oil
1 teaspoon vanilla
4 eggs
1 (8-ounce) carton sour cream
½ cup flaked coconut
1 cup chopped nuts

Mix all ingredients. Pour into treated tube or Bundt pan. Bake at 325° for 1 hour. If you want icing, this is delicious when frosting with prepared icing while cake is still hot.

Old Time Chocolate Cake

Providence Baptist Church, Amory ✝ *Nan Taylor*

CAKE:

2 cups self-rising flour
1½ cups sugar
3 eggs, beaten
¾ cup oil
1 cup milk
2 teaspoons vanilla

Mix all together. Make 3 or 4 small layers. Bake at 350° until done, about 25 to 30 minutes.

ICING:

2 cups sugar
2 heaping tablespoons cocoa
1 teaspoon baking soda
1 cup milk
1½ sticks margarine
1 teaspoon vanilla
¼ cup Karo light corn syrup

Mix sugar, cocoa and baking soda. Add milk, margarine and vanilla. Cook over low heat until melted then over medium-high heat to a rolling boil. Boil 4 minutes. Cool until spreading consistency. (If too thin, cook a few minutes more.)

Hershey Bar Cake

Liberty Baptist Church, Waynesboro

1 Swiss chocolate cake mix
1 (3.4-ounce) box vanilla instant
   pudding mix

3 eggs, beaten
1½ cups milk
1 cup vegetable oil

Combine dry cake mix with dry pudding mix and eggs. Add milk and oil; mix well. Bake in 3 (8-inch) round cake pans at 350° for 25 to 30 minutes. Cool layers thoroughly before icing.

ICING:

1 cup powdered sugar
1 (8-ounce) package cream cheese,
   softened

1 (12-ounce) carton Cool Whip
½ cup finely chopped pecans
2 (1.55-ounce) Hershey bars, grated

Cream sugar and cream cheese together until smooth. Add Cool Whip, pecans and Hershey bars. Spread icing between each layer and on top only (don't ice sides of cake). Chill until ready to serve.

Chocolate Delight Cake

Parkway Baptist Church, Clinton ✝ *Teresa Floyd*

½ cup warm water
1 (4-ounce) bar German sweet chocolate
11 ounces cream cheese, softened
1¼ cups shortening
2 pounds powdered sugar
3 large eggs

2½ cups all-purpose flour
1 teaspoon baking soda
1 teaspoon salt
1 cup buttermilk
1 tablespoon vanilla

Combine warm water and chocolate. Stir until chocolate is melted and set aside. Combine cream cheese and shortening. Add sugar and mix well. Add melted chocolate and mix well. Set aside half of this mixture for the icing but DO NOT refrigerate. With the other half of the mixture, add eggs (one at a time), beating well. Sift flour with baking soda and salt. Then add flour to chocolate mixture, alternating with buttermilk. Stir in vanilla. Bake in 3 greased and floured round cake pans or two 9x13-inch pans. Bake at 350° for 25 to 30 minutes or until it pulls away from the sides of the pans. Cool in pans for 15 to 20 minutes, then turn out onto cooling racks. When cool, ice with reserved chocolate mixture.

Muscadine Cake

Freedom Baptist Church, Burnsville

1 box yellow cake mix
1 (3.4-ounce) box instant vanilla
  pudding mix
1¼ cups muscadine juice, divided

½ cup oil
4 eggs, beaten
1¾ cups powdered sugar

Heat oven to 350°. In a mixing bowl, combine dry cake mix, dry pudding mix, 1 cup muscadine juice, oil and eggs; beat about 4 minutes. Pour in well-greased and floured tube pan. Bake 40 to 50 minutes or until cake tests done. Cool in pan 5 minutes then flip onto serving plate. Mix powdered sugar with remaining ¼ cup muscadine juice and pour over cake.

Freedom Baptist Church

Burnsville

519 Highway 365 South
Burnsville, MS 38833
662-423-8373

Bobby Elliott, Pastor

Freedom Baptist Mission was started July 2011 in the home of Brother Bobby Elliott (Cairo, Mississippi). He surrendered to the ministry in 1980 at Calvary Baptist Church and was ordained in 1981. He attended Northwest Baptist Institute in Muscle Shoals, Alabama, receiving a Master's Degree in Bible languages. He has pastored churches in Mississippi and Tennessee for 30 years. Brother Elliott and his wife of 37 years, Lesa, have one daughter, Jodi, and two granddaughters, Lauren and Katie. Their primary goal has always been to reach as many homes in the area as possible saying their hearts are touched by the people that "no one else wants." Freedom Baptist witnesses to countless people helping them in different ways. They strive to be a soul-winning, Lord-serving, Bible-believing army to carry on for the Lord.

White Wine Cake

Bethel Missionary Baptist Church, Seminary ✝ Rosie Riels

1 box yellow cake mix
1 (3.4-ounce) box instant vanilla
   pudding and pie filling
¾ cup water
¾ cup oil
4 eggs

¼ cup white wine
2 teaspoons cinnamon
1 teaspoon rum
¼ cup white sugar
¼ cup brown sugar
1 cup chopped nuts

Mix all ingredients together except nuts. Put nuts in the bottom of a treated Bundt pan and pour batter over nuts. Bake at 350° for 1 hour and 10 minutes. Glaze in pan while still hot.

GLAZE:
1 cup sugar
1 stick butter

½ cup white wine

Mix all ingredients in a small saucepan and boil 3 minutes. Remove from heat and pour over cake in pan. Cool 20 minutes and turn out of pan.

Sylvia's Cornbread Cake

Robinhood Baptist Church, Brandon ✝ Sylvia Shaw

1 cup sugar
1 cup brown sugar
4 eggs, beaten
1 cup vegetable oil
1½ cups self-rising flour
1 teaspoon vanilla
2 cups finely chopped pecans
Cool Whip for topping

Preheat oven to 350°. Lightly grease and flour a 9x13-inch baking dish. Stir together sugars, eggs and oil in a medium bowl until smooth. Stir in flour and vanilla. Add pecans and stir until evenly mixed. Pour into prepared dish and bake for 30 to 35 minutes. Serve with a dollop of Cool Whip. This is perfect for potluck suppers or to pack in lunch boxes.

Mother's Strawberry Cake

Golden Central Baptist Church, Golden ✝ *In Memory of Janet Davis*

STRAWBERRY CAKE:

1 box white cake mix
4 eggs
1 (3-ounce) box strawberry Jell-O (reserve 1 tablespoon for frosting)
½ cup water
1 teaspoon vanilla
½ cup vegetable oil
1 (14-ounce) package frozen sliced strawberries, divided (reserve ½ for Frosting)

In the bowl of an electric mixer, combine all ingredients, reserving 1 tablespoon Jell-O and half the strawberries for the Frosting. Beat with mixer 4 minutes. Bake in a greased 9x13-inch pan at 325° until toothpick comes out clean, about 25 minutes. Cool before frosting.

FROSTING:

1 stick margarine, melted
1 box powdered sugar
Frozen strawberries (reserved from cake)
1 tablespoon strawberry Jell-O (reserved from cake)

Mix together all ingredients. Smooth frosting over cooled cake. Enjoy.

Strawberry Cake

Robinhood Baptist Church, Brandon ✝ *Mary Morris*

1 box strawberry cake mix
1 (3.4-ounce) cheesecake instant
  pudding mix
¾ cup sugar
¾ cup oil

1 teaspoon vanilla
4 eggs, beaten
1 (8-ounce) carton sour cream
½ cup flaked coconut
1 cup chopped nuts

Mix all ingredients. Pour batter into greased and floured 9x13-inch baking pan. Bake at 325° for 1 hour.

Mrs. Bailey's Strawberry Cake

Auburn Baptist Church, Tupelo ✝ *Ruth Stanford*

This is Mitch Bailey's grandmother's recipe.

CAKE:

1 box butter cake mix
4 eggs
1 (3-ounce) package strawberry Jell-O
1 cup frozen strawberries, thawed

1 cup cooking oil
1 cup shredded coconut
½ cup milk
1 cup chopped pecans

Combine all cake ingredients; mix well. Pour into a treated 9x13-inch pan. Bake at 350° until middle of cake springs back to the light touch or until an inserted toothpick comes out clean. Cool before icing.

ICING:

1 (16-ounce) box powdered sugar
½ cup shredded coconut
½ cup frozen strawberries, thawed

3 tablespoons cornstarch
½ cup chopped pecans

Mix together and spread over cooled cake.

Auburn Baptist Church

Tupelo

1138 Road 931
Tupelo, MS 38804 • 662-842-5638
www.auburnbaptistchurch.org

Jimmy Henry, Pastor

Auburn Baptist Church and southern cooking go hand in hand. For more than 125 years, Auburn has been nestled on the outskirts of Tupelo sharing the Gospel message to this community. A growing church in a growing community that reaches a multi-generational crowd, Auburn is known far and wide for its hospitality and down-home cooking. One of the key components that makes Auburn a special place is the intentional fellowship of the people. You can find lots of children, students, adults, and senior adults continually growing and serving Jesus together on a regular basis. While worshipping Jesus, discipleship and simply sharing the Good News of Jesus will always remain our mission; the food that comes from the kitchens at Auburn will keep you coming back for more.

Strawberry Cake

Magnolia Baptist Church, Hattiesburg † *Marsha Evans*

1 Duncan Hines strawberry cake mix, plus ingredients to prepare per directions on package
1 (16-ounce) carton frozen strawberries, thawed
½ cup sugar
½ cup powdered sugar
1 (8-ounce) package cream cheese, softened
1 (16-ounce) carton Cool Whip

Bake cake in 2 layers as directed on package; cool. Drain strawberries and mash all liquid out. Combine sugars and cream cheese, mixing well; stir in Cool Whip. Add strawberries and mix. Cut each cake layer in half to make 4 layers. Spread icing between layers, and over top and sides of cake. Keep refrigerated.

Strawberry Cake with Strawberry Cream Cheese Icing

Pleasant Home Baptist Church, Laurel † *Karen Matthews*

1 (6-ounce) carton frozen sweetened strawberries, thawed and drained (reserve liquid)
1 Duncan Hines Strawberry Cake Mix, plus ingredients to prepare per package directions

Mix strawberry cake according to package directions using reserved strawberry juice instead of water; stir in 2 tablespoons drained strawberries (reserve remaining strawberries for icing). Pour batter into 3 (8-inch) round cake pans and bake at 350° until done, about 10 to 15 minutes. Cool before frosting.

STRAWBERRY CREAM CHEESE ICING:
1 cup powdered sugar, sifted
1 cup granulated sugar
1 (8-ounce) package cream cheese, softened
1 (8-ounce) carton Cool Whip

Combine sugars and cream cheese; add reserved strawberries. Combine well and fold in Cool Whip. Frost cake and refrigerate.

Strawberry Short Cake

First Baptist Church, Orange Grove

1 (16-ounce) Sara Lee frozen pound cake, thawed
1 (5.1-ounce) box instant vanilla pudding mix
1 (12-ounce) can evaporated milk, chilled
1 (16-ounce) carton Cool Whip, divided
2 (16-ounce) cartons frozen sweetened sliced strawberries, thawed

Cut pound cake in half lengthwise (into 2 layers). Keeping layers separate, cut each into 1-inch squares. In a large bowl, mix dry vanilla pudding mix with evaporated milk (it will be very thick). Fold about two-thirds of Cool Whip into the pudding mixture with a whisk. In a truffle bowl or clear glass bowl, put 1 layer of pound cake cubes in the bottom. Layer 1 carton strawberries over pound cake (use juice or not; however you like it). Layer half the pudding mixture on top. Repeat layers then top off with remaining Cool Whip. Cover with plastic wrap and refrigerate until ready to use.

Vanilla Wafer Cake

Shady Grove Baptist Church, Lucedale † *Audra Rouse*

2 cups sugar
1 (15-ounce) box vanilla wafers, crushed
2 sticks margarine, softened
1 (7-ounce) box flaked coconut
6 eggs, beaten
1½ cups chopped nuts
½ cup milk

Combine all ingredients. Pour in a tube or Bundt pan; bake at 350° for 1 hour.

Fresh Apple Cake

Robinhood Baptist Church, Brandon ✝ *Peggy Ann Cooke*

½ cup oil
3 eggs, beaten
2 cups sugar
2½ cups self-rising flour
1 teaspoon cinnamon
1 cup chopped nuts
1 teaspoon vanilla

Mix oil, eggs and sugar with electric mixer. Add remaining ingredients and mix until smooth. Pour into a treated tube pan. Bake at 350° for 45 minutes.

Elvis Presley Cake

Rehobeth Baptist Church ✝ *Dorothy Nelson*

1 box yellow cake mix, plus ingredients to prepare
1 (20-ounce) can crushed pineapple
2 cups sugar
1 stick margarine, softened
1 (8-ounce) package cream cheese, softened
1 (16-ounce) box powdered sugar
1 cup chopped pecans

Bake cake per directions in a 9x13-inch pan. When cake is done, use the handle-end of wooden spoon to punch holes in it. Boil pineapple and sugar for 5 minutes and pour over cake. Beat margarine and cream cheese together. Add powdered sugar and nuts and mix well. Spread over cooled cake.

Pineapple Cake

First Baptist Church, Baldwyn

CAKE:
3 cups all-purpose flour
3 teaspoons baking powder
1⅛ teaspoons salt
1 cup butter or margarine, softened
2 cups sugar
4 eggs
1½ cups milk
1½ teaspoons vanilla

Sift flour, baking powder and salt into a bowl. In another bowl, cream butter and sugar well. Add eggs, beating well after each. Add dry ingredients to creamed mixture alternately with milk; mix well. Stir in vanilla and pour into 2 to 4 greased and floured cake pans. (This makes 3 to 4 layers; pour into 2 pans and split after baking; or divide batter between 3 or 4 pans.) Bake at 325° about 30 minutes. (Cook time will be less if using more than 2 pans.)

ICING:
1 (20-ounce) can crushed pineapple
½ cup sugar
1 (8-ounce) package cream cheese, softened
1 stick butter, softened
1 (16-ounce) box powdered sugar
2 tablespoons milk

In a skillet, cook pineapple and sugar over low heat until thickens into a syrup. In a separate saucepan, combine cream cheese and butter over medium heat to melt. Add powdered sugar a little at a time until well blended. Add milk, if needed, to reach a spreading consistency. Pour pineapple syrup over cake first then spread cream cheese mixture over the top.

Pineapple Upside-Down Cake

Mount Helm Baptist Church, Jackson

¾ cup plus 2 tablespoons light
   brown sugar, divided
1½ sticks unsalted butter,
   softened, divided
1 vanilla bean, split and seeds
   scraped
½ large pineapple, peeled,
   quartered, cored and sliced
   ⅓ inch thick
½ cup sour cream, divided
2 large eggs
1 teaspoon pure vanilla extract
1¼ cups all-purpose flour
¾ cup sugar
½ teaspoon baking powder
¼ teaspoon baking soda
½ teaspoon salt

Preheat oven to 350°. Butter an 8-inch round cake pan. Sprinkle bottom with 2 tablespoons brown sugar. In a large skillet, combine remaining ¾ cup brown sugar, ½ stick butter and vanilla bean and seeds. Cook over moderately low heat until butter is melted. Add pineapple and cook over moderately low heat, stirring occasionally, until tender, about 20 minutes. Using a slotted spoon, arrange slices in prepared cake pan, overlapping if necessary. Remove vanilla bean and pour pan juices over pineapple. In a bowl, whisk ¼ cup sour cream, eggs and vanilla extract. In another bowl, beat flour, granulated sugar, baking powder, baking soda and salt. Add remaining 1 stick butter and remaining ¼ cup sour cream; beat at low speed until smooth, then beat at medium speed until fluffy. Add sour cream mixture and beat until fluffy, 2 minutes. Spoon batter over pineapple and spread evenly. Bake 40 minutes, or until cake is deep golden color. Cool 5 minutes on a rack. Run a knife around edge of cake, invert onto a plate and remove pan. Replace any pineapple that may have stuck to the pan. Serve warm or at room temperature.

Blackberry Upside Down Cake

Mt. Pisgah Baptist Church, Brandon † *Helen Gunn*

1½ cups all-purpose flour
1½ teaspoons baking powder
¼ teaspoon salt
3½ tablespoons unsalted butter, softened, divided
¾ cup sugar
2 large eggs, room temperature
2 teaspoons vanilla
½ cup milk
⅓ cup dark brown sugar
3 cups blackberries

Preheat oven to 350°. Whisk together flour, baking powder and salt. In a large bowl, using a mixer, beat 2 tablespoons butter with sugar on high until light and fluffy, about 6 minutes. Beat in eggs and vanilla. With mixer on low, add flour mixture in 2 additions, alternating with milk; beat until combined. In a 10-inch cast-iron skillet, melt remaining butter over medium heat; add brown sugar and cook, stirring, for 30 seconds. Remove from heat and arrange blackberries evenly in skillet. Pour batter over berries and smooth top. Bake until golden brown and a toothpick inserted in center comes out clean, approximately 35 to 40 minutes, rotating halfway through. Cool in skillet on a wire rack for 5 minutes. Run knife around edge and carefully invert cake onto a serving plate. Serve warm or at room temperature.

And everyone who calls on the name of the Lord will be saved. —ACTS 2:21

Lemon Ice Box Cake

Ashland Baptist Church ✝ *Lurline Kimery*

1 box yellow or lemon cake mix (I use lemon) plus ingredients to prepare
2 (14-ounce) cans sweetened condensed milk
⅔ cup lemon juice
1 (8-ounce) carton Cool Whip

Bake cake according to package directions for 2 or 3 layers. Cool completely. While cake is baking, mix condensed milk with lemon juice and refrigerate. If cake was baked as 2 layers, split in half making 4 thin layers. Spread some milk/juice mixture between layers. Combine remaining milk/juice mixture with Cool Whip and spread over top and sides of cake. Keep covered and refrigerated.

Moist 'n Creamy Coconut Cake

Bethel Baptist Church, Heidelburg ✝ *Diane Hutcheson*

1 package yellow cake mix plus
   ingredients to prepare per package
   directions
1½ cups milk

½ cup sugar
2 cups Baker's angel flake coconut,
   divided
1 (8-ounce) container Cool Whip

Prepare cake mix as directed on package, baking in a 9x13-inch pan. Cool 15 minutes then poke holes down through cake with a utility fork. Meanwhile, combine milk, sugar and ½ cup coconut in a saucepan. Bring to a boil, reduce heat and simmer 1 minute. Carefully spoon over warm cake, allowing liquid to soak down through holes. Cool completely. Fold ½ cup coconut into Cool Whip and spread over cake. Sprinkle with remaining 1 cup coconut. Chill overnight. Store leftover cake in refrigerator.

Bethel Baptist Church

Heidelberg

10 Bill Windham Road
Heidelberg, MS 39439
601-428-7167

Wayne Johnson, Pastor

Our first church was built in the year 1881. The church was given the name "Bethel" meaning House of God. Our current brick building is the fourth for our church; the first one was a log building, then two lumber buildings. The first building was begun in the 1800's and the third in 1939. Our present church was started in the year 1965. We have an active membership of 106 with an average attendance of approximately 65. We have recently started a van ministry. We have brought children into our church that would otherwise be unable to attend a church. Our cemetery has members from the Civil War, World War I and World War II. Our services are as follows: Sunday School 10:00 a.m., Sunday Morning Service 11:00 a.m., Sunday Night Service 6:00 p.m., Wednesday Night Service 6:30 p.m.

Orange Slice Cake

North Columbia Baptist Church, Columbia ✝ *Janie Walters*
(In loving memory of Lucille Walters)

1 cup butter
2 cups sugar
4 eggs
1 teaspoon baking soda
½ cup buttermilk
3½ cups all-purpose flour
1 pound orange slice candy, chopped
2 cups chopped nuts
2 cups chopped dates
1 (7-ounce) can flaked coconut

Cream butter and sugar until smooth. Add eggs, one at a time, beating well after each one. Dissolve baking soda in buttermilk and add to creamed mixture. Place flour in a large bowl. Add orange slices, nuts and dates; stir to coat each piece. Add to creamed mixture along with coconut; mix to make a very stiff dough. Put into a greased and floured cake pan. Bake at 250° for 2½ to 3 hours.

ICING:
1 cup orange juice
2 cups powdered sugar

Pour icing onto cake and return to oven, which has been turned off, and let sit all night.

Old-Fashioned Pound Cake

Corinth Baptist Church, Magee † *Mozelle Williamson*

2 sticks margarine or butter, softened
⅓ cup shortening
3 cups sugar
5 eggs

3 cups all-purpose flour
1 cup milk
1 teaspoon vanilla
½ teaspoon baking powder

Cream margarine, shortening and sugar together until light and fluffy. Add eggs, one at a time, beating after each addition. Add flour and milk, alternately. Stir in vanilla and baking powder. Pour into a treated large tube pan. Place in cold oven and set oven at 325°; bake 1 hour and 15 minutes.

Corinth Baptist Church

Magee

207 Church Road
Magee, MS 39111
601-849-2795

"We are therefore Christ's ambassadors, as though God were making his appeal through us. We implore you on Christ's behalf: Be reconciled to God." – 2 Corinthians 5:20 (NIV)

Corinth Baptist Church is based upon Southern Baptist principles and beliefs. We love the Lord and focus fully on His Word for guidance. We have always been a mission-minded church. We are one of the few churches left in our area who still has Acteens, GA's, RA's, and Mission Friends. Our adult mission groups include WMU, Circle 31, and Brotherhood. When our church was destroyed by a tornado almost seven years ago, we stood strong and remained faithful, focused, patient, and together. We received blessings from people all over the country who came to help us rebuild. In return, our church actively participates in the rebuilding of other churches that have also experienced types of destruction. We are a church that is blessed with growth and Godly leadership.

Lemon Cream Cheese Pound Cake

First Baptist Church, Brookhaven ✝ *Erin Waltman*

1 stick margarine, softened
2 sticks butter, softened
1 (8-ounce) package cream cheese,
  softened
3 cups sugar

6 large eggs
3 cups sifted cake flour
1 teaspoon vanilla flavoring
1 teaspoon lemon flavoring

Cream margarine, 2 sticks butter and cream cheese. Slowly add 3 cups sugar, creaming as you go. Add eggs 1 at a time. Mix well and add sifted flour, vanilla and lemon flavoring. Grease and lightly flour Bundt pan. Fill Bundt pan to 1½ inches from the top. (If you have extra batter, place in a small dish and bake separately in a toaster oven.) Place cake in cold oven. Bake 1½ hours at 285°. Do not open oven door while baking. Cool 20 minutes in pan after removing from oven.

GLAZE:
⅜ cup sugar
¼ cup water

2 tablespoons butter
1 teaspoon lemon flavoring

Boil sugar and water for 3 minutes. Add 2 tablespoons butter and 1 teaspoon lemon flavoring. Stir until butter melts. Pour glaze over warm cake.

Cream Cheese Pound Cake

Bethel Baptist Church, Heidelburg ✝ *Diane Hutcheson*

3 sticks butter, softened
3 cups sugar
1 (8-ounce) package cream cheese, softened
6 large eggs
3 cups all-purpose flour
1½ teaspoons vanilla

Grease and flour a tube or Bundt pan and set aside. Cream butter, sugar and cream cheese with electric mixer until well blended. Add eggs one at a time, alternating with flour. Add vanilla and beat well for several minutes. Pour batter into prepared pan and put in cold oven. Turn oven to 300° and bake 1½ hours. Remove from oven and cool in pan for about 5 minutes before turning out onto cake plate.

Cream Cheese Pound Cake

Carmel Baptist Church, Monticello ✝ *Aubilyn Ballard*

1 (8-ounce) package cream cheese, softened
2 sticks margarine, softened
½ cup Crisco shortening
2 teaspoons vanilla
3 cups sugar
6 large eggs
3 cups cake flour

Using an electric mixer, blend cream cheese, margarine, shortening and vanilla until light and fluffy. Add sugar and blend well. While continuing to beat, add eggs, 1 at a time, alternately with flour, until eggs and flour are all used. Continue to beat on medium speed, approximately 2 to 4 minutes, after everything is added. Pour into greased and floured tube pan. Bake at 325° for 1 hour and 45 minutes.

Juanita's Pound Cake

Zion Hill Baptist Church, Wesson ✝ *Juanita Ashley*

8 eggs
2¾ cups plus 6 tablespoons sugar, divided
1 pound butter or margarine, softened
3¼ cups all-purpose flour
½ cup light cream (half-and-half or milk)
1 tablespoon pure vanilla extract
1 tablespoon pure lemon extract

Separate eggs and beat whites stiff, adding 6 tablespoons sugar. Place in refrigerator. Cream egg yolks, butter, and remaining 2¾ cups sugar with mixer. Alternate adding flour and cream, beating well after each addition. Add extracts; mix well. Fold in (if using mixer to fold in, use lowest speed for just a few seconds) stiffly beaten egg whites. Pour into large greased and floured tube pan. Bake at 325° for approximately 1½ hours. Cake will rise 2 inches above pan so be sure to use middle rack. (You can divide batter in half and bake in 2 Bundt pans.)

Sour Cream Pound Cake

Shady Grove Baptist Church, Lucedale ✝ Sandra Holland

1 cup shortening
3 cups sugar
6 eggs, separated
¼ teaspoon baking soda
3 cups all-purpose flour

½ teaspoon salt
1 cup sour cream
1 tablespoon buttermilk
1 teaspoon vanilla

Cream shortening and sugar. Add lightly beaten egg yolks. Mix dry ingredients together in a separate bowl and add alternately with sour cream. Add buttermilk and vanilla; mix well. Beat egg whites until stiff and fold into mixture. Pour batter into 2 greased and floured loaf pans or a 10-inch tube pan. Bake in a preheated oven at 300° for 1 hour and 15 minutes or until done. Extend baking time by 15 minutes for tube pan. Cool cake in pan for 30 minutes.

Shady Grove Baptist Church

Lucedale

14146 Highway 26 West
Lucedale, MS 39452
601-947-3546
www.shadygrovebaptistlife.org

Shady Grove Baptist Church began as a Sunday School class who decided in 1886 they would organize a church. Their first meeting place was a brush arbor. Our present facility has graced the Central Community since 1953. Until that new church was built with an enclosed baptistery, all "baptizings" were held at White's Creek. The congregation stood on the creek bank and sang several songs before the baptismal service was performed. Many, many, faithful Christians, including deacons, Sunday School and Discipleship Training officers and teachers, and other leaders and helpers have worked and served in the church. A story of growth...from a small group of Christians, meeting under a brush arbor, to a wide-awake membership of over five hundred...that is the history of Shady Grove Baptist Church. Thank you, Lord, for all that it means to us.

Old Southern Pound Cake

Robinhood Baptist Church, Brandon ✝ *Anita Musgrove*

3 cups all-purpose flour
2½ cups sugar
Pinch salt
1 cup butter, softened
½ cup shortening
1 cup buttermilk, divided

1 teaspoon vanilla
1 teaspoon lemon extract
1 teaspoon almond extract
1 teaspoon baking powder
¼ teaspoon baking soda
5 eggs

Sift flour, sugar and salt together in a mixing bowl. Add butter, shortening and ¾ cup buttermilk. Beat 3 minutes on medium speed. Add remaining ¼ cup buttermilk, vanilla, extracts, baking powder and baking soda. Beat 3 more minutes. Add eggs, one at a time, beating slightly after each addition. After last egg, beat 3 more minutes. Pour batter into a treated tube pan. Bake at 350° for 1¼ hours.

Caramel Pound Cake

Mt. Pisgah Baptist Church, Brandon ✝ *Nic Williams*

2 sticks margarine, softened
½ cup butter-flavored shortening
1 (16-ounce) box light brown sugar
1 cup sugar
5 eggs

3 cups all-purpose flour
½ teaspoon baking powder
1 cup milk
1 teaspoon vanilla flavoring

Preheat oven to 350°. Cream margarine, shortening and both sugars. Add eggs one a time, beating well after each. Mix flour and baking powder in a separate bowl. Alternate adding a little flour and a little milk beating well after each addition. Add vanilla and continue beating for 2 minutes. Pour into a greased and floured tube pan. Bake 1 hour and 15 minutes.

CARAMEL GLAZE:

1 cup light brown sugar
½ cup evaporated milk
1 teaspoon vanilla

1 cup sugar
1 stick butter
1 cup chopped pecans (optional)

Combine all glaze ingredients (except nuts) in a medium saucepan. Bring to a full rolling boil and boil 2 minutes. Add nuts (if desired) and pour over cake. Cool completely before cutting.

Chocolate Pound Cake

North Columbia Baptist Church, Columbia ✝ *Yvonne G. Walters*

2 sticks butter, softened	½ cup cocoa
½ cup vegetable oil	½ teaspoon salt
3 cups sugar	½ teaspoon baking powder
5 eggs	1¼ cups milk
3 cups all-purpose flour	1½ teaspoons vanilla

With a high speed mixer, cream butter, oil and sugar until light and fluffy. Add eggs one at a time, beating after each one. Sift dry ingredients and add to egg mixture at low speed. Gradually add milk and then vanilla. Pour into a lightly greased tube or Bundt pan. Bake at 350° for 90 minutes. Cool before removing from pan. Delicious served plain or drizzled with a white or chocolate frosting.

North Columbia Baptist Church

Columbia

1527 North Main Street
Columbia, MS 39429
601-736-8635 • www.ncbcms.org

Dr. Joe Wiggins, Pastor

At North Columbia Baptist Church, our mission is be "A place where Jesus is Lord and you are loved.

To WIN people to Jesus Christ, TRAIN believers to become disciples, and SEND disciples out to impact the world."

The purpose of North Columbia Baptist Church:

To encounter God's Presence — Worship

To spread God's Word — Evangelism

To Edify God's People — Discipleship

To Share God's Love — Ministry

"I can do all things through Christ who strengthens me." — Philippians 4:13 (NKJV)

Jewish Pound Cake

Robinhood Baptist Church, Brandon ✝ *Mary Morris*

1 box yellow cake mix
1 (3.4-ounce) box instant vanilla pudding mix
1 teaspoon cinnamon
¾ cup sugar
¾ cup oil
1 teaspoon vanilla
4 eggs, beaten
1 (8-ounce) carton sour cream
½ cup shredded coconut
1 cup chopped nuts

Mix all ingredients. Pour into a treated tube or Bundt pan. Bake at 325° for 1 hour.

Pound Cake

Pearson Baptist Church, Pearl ✝ *Glyndel Bankston*

½ cup shortening
3 cups sugar
1 cup (2 sticks) butter or margarine
5 eggs
1 cup milk, divided
3 cups all-purpose flour
¼ teaspoon baking powder
¼ teaspoon salt
1 teaspoon vanilla flavoring
1 teaspoon maple flavoring

Cream shortening, sugar and margarine. Add 1 egg at a time and blend well after each. Add ¾ cup milk. Sift together flour, baking powder and salt. Add a bit at a time to wet mixture and blend well. Add remaining ¼ cup milk and flavorings; mix well. Pour into a treated Bundt pan, and bake at 350° for about an hour and 15 to 20 minutes or until toothpick comes out clean after inserted.

Abbie's Fruit Cake

Fairfield Baptist Church, Moselle

3 cups sugar
2 sticks margarine, softened
3 cups sifted all-purpose flour
3 teaspoons baking powder
½ teaspoon salt
3 large (or 4 medium) eggs
1 teaspoon coconut flavoring
1 teaspoon orange flavoring
1 cup applesauce
1 cup pears preserves (optional)
⅓ (12-ounce) box raisins
1 cup diced candied cherries
2 cups small diced candied pineapple (use all colors)
3 cups chopped pecans

Cream sugar and margarine until smooth. In a separate bowl, combine flour, baking powder and salt; sift. Add 1 cup to margarine mixture and stir until smooth. Add eggs, one at time, and stir until smooth. In a small bowl, add coconut and orange flavoring to applesauce; mix. Add along with pears and another cup flour to batter; stir well. In a separate bowl, toss fruit pieces in the remaining cup flour. Fold flour and fruit into batter. Working with 3 loaf pans, invert and fit tin foil to bottom to make a mold. Line each pan with brown bag paper then place tin foil molds on top. Spray with nonstick spray. Divide batter between the 3 pans. Use a spoon to move batter so the middle is lower (cake will rise in the middle). Arrange a tin foil "tent" over the pans after they have been placed on the top shelf of the oven. Put a pan of water on the lower rack. Bake at 250° for 1 hour. Then bake at 350° for 1 hour. Remove the 'tent' and test for doneness. When a toothpick inserted in the center comes out clean, remove to a cake rack and cool. Mother typed this December 1, 1996, although she had been making it for years; it is very good.

This recipe came from Mother. She made it every Christmas.

Fruit Pizza

First Baptist Church, Morton

CRUST:

1 stick margarine, softened
1 cup sugar
1 egg, beaten
½ teaspoon vanilla
2 cups flour
¼ teaspoon salt
1½ teaspoons baking powder

Cream margarine and sugar. Add egg and vanilla; mix. Sift flour, salt and baking powder together. Add to creamed mixture; mix well. Divide into 2 portions and press each into a 10-inch pizza pan. Bake at 425° for 8 to 10 minutes; cool.

FILLING:

1 (8-ounce) package cream cheese, softened
½ cup sugar
½ teaspoon vanilla

Combine Filling ingredients until mixed well; spread over cooled crusts.

FRUIT TOPPING:

1 pint strawberries
2 to 3 fresh kiwi
1 cup Bing cherries
1 cup blueberries
1½ cups raspberries
2 cups green grapes

While crust is baking, wash fruit and set aside to dry. Just before serving, thinly slice about half the strawberries and quarter the rest. Peel and thinly slice kiwi. Stem and pit cherries, cutting in half. Working from center of 1 pizza, start with a raspberry in the center, circle that with blueberries (4 to 6). Ring blueberries with quartered strawberries then a ring of green grapes. Next, add a ring of raspberries circled with a ring of cherries alternated with blueberries. The last 2 rings should be thinly sliced kiwi then, on the outside, thinly sliced strawberries. Repeat for second pizza. Serve immediately. (You can use any combination of fruit that appeals to you. Pineapple, bananas, Mandarin oranges, purple grapes and maraschino cherries are all good options.)

Oatmeal Cookies

Canaan Baptist Church, Purvis ✝ Betty Cooper

½ cup corn oil
1 cup brown sugar
1 cup Splenda
2 eggs, beaten
½ teaspoon cinnamon

½ teaspoon vanilla
2 cups oatmeal
2 cups Bisquick
1 teaspoon baking soda
1 cup raisins

Mix oil, brown sugar, Splenda, eggs, cinnamon and vanilla. Beat well. Stir in oatmeal. Add Bisquick, baking soda and raisins. Drop by teaspoons on greased cookie sheet. Bake at 350° until brown, about 12 minutes.

Canaan Baptist Church

Purvis

34 Elliott Circle
Purvis, MS 39475
601-436-0664

Brother Mickey Steele, Pastor

Canaan Baptist Church located at 34 Elliott Circle, Purvis was established in 2003. Brother Mickey Steele is currently serving as pastor. Canaan is a member of the Oak Grove Association, BMA of MS, and BMA of America.

"If my people, who are called by my name, will humble themselves and pray and seek my face and turn from their wicked ways, then I will hear from heaven, and I will forgive their sin and will heal their land." 2 Chronicles 7:14 (NIV)

VBS Tea Cakes

Sunrise Baptist Church, Carthage ✝ *Judy Caston*

1½ cups sugar
2 sticks margarine, softened
3 eggs
1 teaspoon vanilla
5 cups self-rising flour
Chopped pecans (optional)

Cream sugar and margarine; add eggs then vanilla beating well. Add flour and mix well. Stir in pecans, if desired. Roll dough out ¼-inch thick and cut into shapes using a cookie cutter. Bake at 350° for 8 minutes. They're best if they don't get brown.

Aunt Jewel's Tea Cakes

Mt. Pisgah Baptist Church, Brandon ✝ *Warren Gunn*

1½ sticks butter, melted
2 cups sugar
4 teaspoons milk
2 eggs, beaten
½ teaspoons vanilla
3 teaspoons baking powder
Dash salt
5 cups all-purpose flour

For this recipe, you should mix everything by hand (no electric mixture). Mix butter and sugar; add milk, eggs and vanilla. In a separate bowl, combine baking soda, salt and flour. Add flour mixture gradually to butter mixture, stirring well with each addition. (This will make a thick dough.) Roll dough to ¼-inch thickness on a lightly floured surface. Cut into rounds. Place tea cakes ½ inch apart on a greased cookie sheet. Bake at 400° until lightly brown.

Brownies

Calvary Missionary Baptist Church, Brandon ✝ Linda Garrett

1½ cups self-rising flour
2 cups chopped pecans
2 sticks margarine, softened
2 cups sugar
5 eggs, beaten
5 tablespoons cocoa
2 teaspoons vanilla

Preheat oven to 350°. Combine all ingredients by hand until mixed well. Bake in a treated 9x13-inch pan for 35 to 40 minutes. Cool before cutting.

Brownie Bites

Mount Helm Baptist Church, Jackson

½ cup plus 2 tablespoons Bob's Red Mill gluten-free, all-purpose flour
½ cup sugar
¼ cup unsweetened cocoa powder
1¼ teaspoons baking powder
⅛ teaspoon baking soda
½ teaspoon salt
¼ teaspoon xanthan gum
½ cup applesauce
¼ cup canola oil
1 tablespoon pure vanilla extract
½ cup dairy-free mini chocolate chips

Preheat oven to 325°. Spray 2 mini-muffin pans with nonstick vegetable oil spray. In a bowl, whisk flour, sugar, cocoa, baking powder, baking soda, salt and xanthan gum. In another bowl, whisk applesauce, oil and vanilla; stir into dry ingredients. Stir in chocolate chips. Spoon batter into muffin pans, filling three-quarters full. Bake 15 minutes, or until set. Let brownies cool in pans for 15 minutes, then turn out onto a rack to cool completely.

Indulgence

Liberty Baptist Church, Raleigh ✝ *Trey Ables*

1 stick butter, softened
1 cup chopped pecans
1 cup all-purpose flour
1 (8-ounce) package cream cheese, softened
2 (8-ounce) cartons Cool Whip, divided
1 cup powdered sugar
2 (3.4-ounce) boxes chocolate instant pudding mix
1 (3.4-ounce) box vanilla instant pudding mix
4 cups cold milk

Mix butter, pecans and flour and pat into deep oblong dish. Bake 25 minutes at 300°, or until light brown. Mix cream cheese, 1 carton Cool Whip and powdered sugar; spread over cooled crust. Combine pudding mixes and milk. Beat with mixer 2 minutes at medium speed. Spread over cream cheese layer. Top with remaining carton Cool Whip. Chill and serve.

Chess Squares

Canaan Baptist Church, Purvis ✝ *Lynn Steele*

CRUST:

1 box cake mix
1 egg, beaten

1 stick margarine, melted

Combine dry cake mix, egg and melted margarine. Pour into bottom of 9x13-inch pan.

FILLING:

1 (16-ounce) box powdered sugar
3 eggs, beaten

1 (8-ounce) package cream cheese
2 teaspoons vanilla

Combine Filling ingredients and pour over Crust. Bake at 350° for 40 minutes.

Cheese Cake Squares

Midway Baptist Church, Lucedale

1 box yellow cake mix
4 eggs, divided
1 stick margarine, melted
1 (16-ounce) box powdered sugar

1 (8-ounce) package cream cheese,
   softened
3 eggs

Mix dry cake mix, 1 egg and margarine; put in a 9x13-inch baking dish. Combine powdered sugar, cream cheese and remaining 3 eggs. Spread over crust. Bake at 350° for 35 to 40 minutes. Cool and cut in squares.

Midway Baptist Church

Lucedale

2206 Howell Tanner Chapel Road • Lucedale, MS 39452
601-947-6877 • www.facebook.com/midway.baptist.lucedale

Phillip Snodgrass, Pastor

Midway is commissioned by God to go and make disciples of all nations. (Matthew 28:18-19) This is the vision for the church, which was given by Christ Himself. We have made it our goal to be a light in our community, sharing with the love and grace of Jesus while reaching out to those in need. God also calls us to worship and glorify Him. We invite you to come and worship with us.

Honey Bars

Farmington Baptist Church, Corinth

¾ cup oil
¼ cup honey
1 cup sugar
1 egg, well beaten
2 cups all-purpose flour
1 teaspoon baking soda

1 teaspoon salt
1 teaspoon cinnamon
¾ cup powdered sugar
2 tablespoons water
2 tablespoons butter, melted
1 teaspoon vanilla

Mix oil, honey, sugar, egg, flour, baking soda, salt and cinnamon together and press into bottom of greased 9x13-inch pan. Bake at 350° for 18 to 25 minutes. Stir powdered sugar, water, butter and vanilla together and pour over warm bars.

Blueberry Buckle

Vardaman Street Baptist Church, Wiggins ✝ *Myrtis Mallett*

½ cup shortening
¾ cup sugar
1 egg
2 cups sifted all-purpose flour

2½ teaspoons baking powder
¼ teaspoon salt
½ cup milk
2 cups fresh blueberries

Thoroughly cream shortening and sugar; add egg and beat till light and fluffy. Sift together flour, baking powder and salt; add to creamed mixture alternately with milk. Spread in greased 11x7-inch pan. Top with berries.

TOPPING:
½ cup sugar
½ cup sifted all-purpose flour

½ teaspoon ground cinnamon
¼ cup butter or margarine

Mix sugar, flour, and cinnamon; cut in butter till crumbly. Sprinkle over berries. Bake at 350° for 45 minutes. Cut into squares. Serve warm.

Easy Apple Dumplings

New Zion Baptist Church, Crystal Springs

2 apples (Golden Delicious or Granny Smith), peeled and cored
2 (8-count) cans crescent rolls
2 sticks butter
1½ cups brown sugar
1 teaspoon vanilla
1 teaspoon cinnamon
1½ cups 7-Up (or other lemon soda)

Preheat oven at 350°. Butter a 9x13-inch baking dish. Cut each apple into 8 slices. Roll each slice in 1 crescent roll and place in a buttered dish. Melt butter in a small saucepan over medium heat; stir in sugar, vanilla and cinnamon. Cook until thickened, remove from heat and pour over dumplings. Pour soda in middle and along edges of a pan (not over rolls). Bake 35 to 45 minutes, or until golden brown. Serve warm.

White Chocolate Bread Pudding

Star Baptist Church, Star

2 cups sugar
2 cups milk
2 cups whipping cream
3 eggs
1 teaspoon vanilla

4 ounces white chocolate chips or pieces
1 (10-inch) loaf French bread, torn in
 pieces
½ stick butter or margarine, sliced
Cinnamon and sugar to taste

Mix sugar, milk, cream, eggs, vanilla and white chocolate; pour over bread pieces and press down to soak. Pour into a 3-quart baking dish. Dot with butter slices. Sprinkle with cinnamon and sugar. Let sit 30 minutes (up to 2 hours). Bake at 350° for 50 minutes.

SAUCE:

1 stick butter or margarine
6 teaspoons water

1 teaspoon vanilla
4 ounces white chocolate chips or pieces

Mix Sauce ingredients in a saucepan and heat until melted. Pour over top of pudding before serving.

White Chocolate Bread Pudding

Big Creek Baptist Church, Soso

16 slices bread
3 eggs
2 cups sugar
1 quart milk

1 stick butter, melted
1 teaspoon vanilla
Cinnamon

Break bread in pieces place in a 9x13-inch pan that has been sprayed with Pam. Combine remaining ingredients, except cinnamon, and pour over bread. Sprinkle with cinnamon. Bake at 350° for 1 hour.

TOPPING:

1 stick butter
½ (12-ounce) bag white chocolate
 chips

1 cup powdered sugar
½ teaspoon vanilla
6 teaspoons water

In a bowl, melt butter and white chocolate chips in microwave; combine. Add powdered sugar, vanilla, and water. Heat another 2 minutes until smooth and creamy; mix well. Pour over hot bread pudding and serve warm.

Bread Pudding

Russell Baptist Church, Meridian ✝ *Susan Jones*

2 cups half-and-half
¼ cup butter
⅔ cup brown sugar
3 eggs, beaten
2 teaspoons cinnamon
¼ teaspoon ground nutmeg
1 teaspoon vanilla extract
3 cups French bread, torn into small pieces (stale is best)
½ cup raisins
½ cup chopped pecans

In a medium saucepan over medium heat, heat half-and-half until a film forms over top. Remove from heat and add butter, stirring until melted. Cool to lukewarm. In a separate bowl, combine brown sugar, eggs, cinnamon, nutmeg and vanilla. Beat with an electric mixer at medium speed for 1 minute. Slowly add half-and-half mixture, continuing to beat. Place bread in a lightly greased 1½-quart casserole dish. Sprinkle with raisins and pecans. Pour liquid on top. Bake at 350° for 45 to 50 minutes or until set. Serve warm.

BREAD PUDDING SAUCE:
1 cup milk
2 tablespoons butter
⅓ cup brown sugar
1 teaspoon vanilla
1 tablespoon flour
Dash salt

Mix all sauce ingredients together and bring to a boil for 3 to 4 minutes, stirring constantly. Set aside for 5 minutes, then pour on warm bread pudding.

Grandmother Merle's Banana Pudding

Mt. Pisgah Baptist Church, Brandon † *Margaret Shedd's Mother*

1 cup milk
⅓ stick margarine
3 eggs, separated
2 tablespoons flour
¾ cup plus 1 tablespoon sugar, divided
1 teaspoon vanilla
3 to 4 bananas, sliced
1 (16-ounce) bag vanilla wafers

Heat milk and margarine in a saucepan over medium heat until hot, but do not boil. Using an electric mixer, beat egg yolks (refrigerate egg whites); add flour and ¾ cup sugar and beat well. Add vanilla and mix. With mixer running, add egg mixture to warm milk mixture beating until combined. Cook until thick. Layer vanilla wafers, bananas and pudding mixture. Make a meringue by beating cold egg whites and remaining sugar until stiff peaks form. Spread over pudding, sealing to edges. Bake at 350° just until meringue is browned, about 10 minutes.

New-Fashioned Banana Pudding

2 (7.25-ounce) bags Pepperidge Farm Chessmen cookies
6 to 8 very ripe bananas, sliced
2 cups milk
1 (5.1-ounce) box instant French vanilla pudding mix
1 (8-ounce) package cream cheese, softened
1 (14-ounce) can sweetened condensed milk
1 (12-ounce) carton whipped topping

Line the bottom of 9x13-inch dish with 1 bag cookies. Layer bananas on top and set aside. Using an electric mixer, beat milk and pudding until thickened, about 2 minutes. In a separate large bowl, beat cream cheese and condensed milk until smooth. Fold in whipped topping by hand. Fold in pudding mixture and stir gently until well blended. Pour over bananas and cover with remaining cookies. Refrigerate 1 hour or until ready to serve.

Rice Pudding with Cherries

1 cup uncooked long-grain white rice
1 ½ cups milk
1 ½ cups water
½ teaspoon salt
1 (14-ounce) can sweetened condensed milk
⅔ cup dried cherries
2 tablespoons heavy cream
2 tablespoons vanilla extract
Ground nutmeg, for garnish (optional)

Using a double-boiler over lightly simmering water, combine rice, milk, water and salt. Cover and cook until rice is tender. Stir in condensed milk, cherries, and heavy cream. Continue to cook, stirring frequently, about 20 minutes or until pudding thickens slightly. Remove from heat and stir in vanilla. Sprinkle with nutmeg when serving, if desired.

Easy Pineapple Pudding

Mt. Pisgah Baptist Church, Brandon † *Helen Gunn*

1 (5.1-ounce) box instant vanilla pudding plus ingredients to prepare per package
   directions
1 (16-ounce) bag vanilla wafers
1 (20-ounce) can chunk pineapple, well drained
1 (14-ounce) can condensed milk
1 (16-ounce) carton Cool Whip

Prepare pudding as directed; set aside. Place vanilla wafers in a large serving bowl. Pour drained pineapple over wafers. Add condensed milk to pudding mixture; pour over pineapple. Spread Cool Whip on top and chill.

Pineapple Casserole

First Baptist Church, Morton † *Brooke Craig*

6 slices white bread, torn into small pieces
1 (20-ounce) can crushed pineapple, drained
3 eggs, beaten
2 cups sugar
½ cup butter, melted

Mix all ingredients. Pour into a greased 2-quart baking dish. Bake at 350° for 30 minutes.

This recipe makes a great side dish or dessert. It is my go-to for taking a dish because you CAN'T mess it up.

First Baptist Church

Morton

80 Church Street
Morton, MS 39117
601-732-8941
www.facebook.com/First-Baptist-Church-
   Morton-MS

"For where two or three are gathered together in my name, there am I in the midst of them." Matthew 18:20

First Baptist Church of Morton has been gathering the people of our local community together in the name of the Lord for more than 100 years. Our sanctuary fills with a wonderful mix of people—those who have been members for their entire life alongside others who have been a part of it for a short time. Together we make up a strong body of Christ, and our growth comes from showing His love. Through the years we have seen many highs and lows as a church, but with the grace of God, we are still ministering and sharing His love through ministries such as our Celebration Choir, Children's Van Ministry, and a wide variety of Bible study classes. Come and join us anytime you are in the area; we would love to have you.

No Crust Egg Custard

Shady Grove Missionary Baptist Church, Tishomingo † *Shelia Phifer*

4 tablespoons butter

4 small (or 3 large) eggs, beaten

1½ cups sugar

½ cup all-purpose flour

1¾ cups milk

1 teaspoon vanilla flavoring

Combine all ingredients and pour into a greased oven-safe skillet. (A large Pyrex pie plate may be used.) Bake at 350° for 40 minutes.

Shady Grove Missionary Baptist Church
Tishomingo

251 County Road 141, Tishomingo, MS 38873
662-660-3357 or 256-460-9241

Brother Mike Smith, Pastor

Shady Grove Missionary Baptist Church is located in Tishomingo County—the most Northeastern County in our state. Sunday Services include Sunday School at 9:30 a.m. and Worship Service at 10:30 a.m.; evening classes start at 5:00 p.m. and preaching at 6:00 p.m. Wednesday evening Bible Study is at 7:00 p.m. We have a summer and fall revival in June and in October or November, and Vacation Bible School in July. Homecoming Day is the First Sunday in October. Shady Grove Missionary Baptist Church was organized on October 3rd, 1940. The Elder W. C. Patterson was called as her first pastor. She has since called fourteen pastors. Brother Mike Smith is the current pastor of Shady Grove Missionary Baptist Church. We invite you to attend.

Pecan Pie Trifle

Union Ridge Baptist Church, Noxapater

1 (8-ounce) package cream cheese, softened
1½ cups whipping cream
1½ teaspoons vanilla
1 (2-pound) frozen pecan pie, thawed and cubed
Hot fudge ice cream topping, heated
Carmel ice cream topping, heated

Beat cream cheese, whipping cream and vanilla in a large bowl at medium speed for 2 to 3 minutes, until smooth and firm. Set aside. Fill bottom of a trifle bowl with a third of the pecan pie cubes. Top with half the cream cheese mixture and drizzle hot fudge topping and caramel sauce. Repeat layers. Finish with pecan pie cubes.

Pecan Bites

Providence Baptist Church, Amory ✝ *Martha Parker*

1 cup brown sugar
½ cup all-purpose flour
1 cup chopped pecans
⅔ cup butter, melted
2 eggs

Combine all ingredients; mix well. Spray a mini muffin pan; fill two-thirds full. Bake at 350° for 20 minutes.

My command is this: Love each other
as I have loved you. —JOHN 15:12

Texas Millionaires

Calvary Baptist Church, Leakesville ✝ *Annell Walley*

1 cup brown sugar
1 cup sugar
1 cup light corn syrup
2 sticks margarine
1 teaspoon vanilla
1 (12-ounce) can evaporated milk
1 pound pecan halves
¼ stick paraffin wax
1 (12-ounce) bag semisweet chocolate chips

Combine sugars, syrup, margarine, vanilla and 1 cup evaporated milk in saucepan. Stir well. Bring to boil, stirring constantly. Add remaining evaporated milk, gradually, cook to soft-ball stage over low heat. Remove from heat. Add pecans. Pour into large buttered pan. Refrigerate overnight. Cut into squares. Melt chocolate chips and paraffin in double boiler. Dip squares into chocolate and place on wax paper.

Turtle Delight

Calvary Baptist Church, Starkville ✝ *Lynda Gaydon*

17 ice cream sandwiches
1 (12.25-ounce) jar caramel topping
1½ cups chopped pecans, divided
1 (12-ounce) carton Cool Whip
¾ cup hot fudge topping, heated

Place 8½ sandwiches in 9x13-inch baking dish. Spread evenly with caramel topping and sprinkle with 1 cup chopped pecans. Top with ½ carton Cool Whip and remaining ice cream sandwiches. Spread remaining Cool Whip over sandwiches and sprinkle with remaining ½ cup pecans. Cover and freeze at least 2 hours. Remove from freezer and let stand 5 minutes before serving. Cut into squares. Drizzle with hot fudge topping. Serves 10.

New Yorkers

Providence Baptist Church, Amory † *Martha Parker*

1 cup smooth peanut butter
1 cup sugar
1 egg
12 Hershey's Kisses or Reese's Mini Peanut Butter Cups

Spray a mini muffin pan. Combine peanut butter, sugar and egg. Fill cups two-thirds full. Bake at 350° for 10 minutes. While hot, place a Hershey's Kiss or a mini Reese's Peanut Butter Cup on top, pressing down slightly.

Providence Baptist Church

Amory

1311 Highland Drive
Amory, MS 38821
662-256-3623

Praise the Lord; God is so good. Our cup at Providence Baptist Church in Amory is overflowing. In March 1992, the BMA of Mississippi took Providence Baptist Church as one of its mission projects and elected Brother Don Farnham as the missionary there. First Baptist of Manatachie is the mother church. The work of so many volunteers throughout our community and the surrounding areas culminated on November 19, 1992, when Providence Baptist Church held its first of two dedication services. God has richly blessed our church. A sweet spirit is present and love abounds. Please join us.

Fantasy Fudge

Bethel Baptist Church, Heidelburg

1½ sticks butter or margarine
3 cups sugar
1 (5-ounce) can evaporated milk
1 (12-ounce) chocolate chips
1 (7-ounce) jar marshmallow creme
1 cup chopped pecans or walnuts
1 teaspoon vanilla

Spray a foil-lined sheet pan with nonstick spray; set aside. Microwave butter in a 4-quart bowl on high until melted. Add sugar and evaporated milk; mix well. Microwave 5 minutes, stopping after 3 minutes to stir well. Scrape down sides of bowl and microwave 5½ minutes, again stirring after 3 minutes. Let stand 2 minutes; add chocolate chips and marshmallow crème. Stir until melted. Add nuts and vanilla; mix well. Pour immediately into foil-lined pan; spread evenly to cover bottom. Cool at room temperature at least 4 hours; cut into 1-inch squares. Store in airtight container at room temperature.

Velvet Nut Candy

Pleasant Home Baptist Church, Laurel ✝ *Joan Stevens*

1½ pounds vanilla or chocolate candy melts, coarsely chopped
1 (14-ounce) can sweetened condensed milk
¼ teaspoon salt
1 teaspoon vanilla
3 cups coarsely chopped nuts

Line a 10x15-inch pan or dish with wax paper; spray lightly with nonstick spray. Microwave candy melts and sweetened condensed milk in 1-minute intervals, stirring after each, until smooth, 3 to 5 minutes. Stir in salt, vanilla and nuts. Spread onto wax paper, cover and chill 2 hours. Turn onto cutting board, remove paper and cut into squares. Store in covered container at room temperature.

Chocolate Nut Cluster Candy

Pearson Baptist Church, Pearl ✝ *Liz Bailey*

1 (16-ounce) can dry roasted salted peanuts
1 (16-ounce) can dry roasted unsalted peanuts
1 (16-ounce) package white almond bark
1 (12-ounce) package peanut butter chips
1 (12-ounce) package dark chocolate chips
4 ounces German chocolate bar, chopped

Layer all peanuts in a slow cooker. Add remaining ingredients. Place lid on crockpot. Turn on low for 1 hour to 1½ hours without opening lid (so no stirring). It may smell like the nuts are burning, but they are not. DO NOT OPEN LID. When cook time is complete, stir and drop onto wax paper.

Chocolate Chip Dessert Cheese Ball

Vardaman Street Baptist Church, Wiggins ✝ *Malena Martin*

1 (8-ounce) package cream cheese, softened
1 stick butter, softened
¾ cup powder sugar
2 tablespoons brown sugar
¼ teaspoon vanilla
½ (12-ounce) package mini chocolate chips
Crushed pecans for coating

Combine cream cheese, butter, powder sugar, brown sugar, vanilla and chocolate chips; mix well. Put in fridge to harden. Form into a ball and roll in crushed pecans. Refrigerate until ready to eat. Serve with cinnamon sugar graham crackers.

Granny's Crunch

Pearson Baptist Church, Pearl ✝ *Betty Thornhill*

3 cups blueberries (or any fruit, fresh or frozen)
1 (20-ounce) can pineapple chunks
1 cup sugar
1 box yellow cake mix
1 stick margarine
1 cup chopped pecans

Spray a 9x13-inch baking dish with nonstick cooking spray. Place blueberries and pineapple in dish and sprinkle with sugar. Pour dry cake mix over top; do not stir. Melt margarine and drizzle over top. Bake at 350° until lightly brown. Garnish with pecans.

Pearson Baptist Church

Pearl

151 South Pearson Road
Pearl, MS 39208
601-939-3618
www.pbclife.org

Calvin Williams, Pastor

We serve our God and our community faithfully because we know we are only as strong as the community that supports us and the God who gives us strength. We've been called to preach the cross of Christ. We are committed to being the church of Christ. We are commanded to fulfill the commission of Christ. How do we do this? By being the hands and feet of Jesus in our own community, in our neighboring states, and in the foreign field. No matter where you may find yourself, one thing remains the same—people need the Lord. Looking for a place to grow spiritually? Looking for a place to serve? We would love to have you.

Angel Lush with Pineapple

First Baptist Church, Brookhaven ✝ *Linda Edmonson*

1 (20-ounce) can crushed pineapple, undrained
1 (3.4-ounce) package Jell-O instant vanilla pudding and pie filling
1 (8-ounce) carton Cool Whip
1 (10-ounce) round angel food cake, cut into 3 layers
Seasonal berries

Mix pineapple and dry pudding mix in medium bowl. Gently stir in Cool Whip. On a serving platter or cake plate, place 1 layer of cake. Top cake with a third of the pudding mixture. Repeat layers 2 more times ending with pudding. Refrigerate 1 hour or until ready to serve. Garnish with your favorite seasonal berries. Serves 10.

Scalloped Pineapple

Mt. Pisgah Baptist Church, Brandon ✝ *Jane Boyd*

4 cups cubed bread
1 (20-ounce) can tidbit pineapple, drained
1⅔ cups sugar
3 eggs, beaten
½ cup margarine, melted

Put cubed bread in a 2 quart greased casserole dish. Mix pineapple, sugar and eggs together. Stir in melted margarine. Pour over bread. Bake at 350° for 40 to 45 minutes.

Strawberry Supreme

Mt. Pisgah Baptist Church, Brandon ✝ Jane Boyd

1 (14-ounce) can sweetened condensed milk
4 eggs, beaten
1 (16-ounce) package powdered sugar, sifted
1 teaspoon vanilla
2 (12-ounce) boxes vanilla wafers or Graham crackers, crushed
1 cup crushed pecans
2 cups Cool Whip
2 (10-ounce) packages frozen strawberries, thawed

Combine milk, eggs and powdered sugar in a saucepan and cook over low heat until thick. Stir in vanilla. Cool. Spread half of the crushed wafers in a 9x13-inch pan. Pour cooled milk mixture over wafers. Layer all the pecans, then half the Cool Whip, all the strawberries, and remaining Cool Whip. Top with remaining wafers. Cover with foil and freeze. Remove from freezer about 1 hour before serving. Serves 16 to 20.

Strawberry Ice Cream

1 pint fresh strawberries, hulled and chopped
1 tablespoon fresh lemon juice
1 cup sugar, divided
2 large eggs
1 cup milk
1 teaspoon vanilla extract
2 cups heavy whipping cream

Combine strawberries, lemon juice, and ¼ cup sugar in a mixing bowl, set aside in fridge for 1 hour. In large mixing bowl, beat eggs until light and fluffy, about 2 minutes. Gradually add remaining ¾ cup sugar, mixing well. Stir in milk and vanilla; mix well. Add strawberries with juice and mix well. Gently stir in whipping cream just until combined. Pour into ice cream maker and follow manufacturer's instructions.

Homemade Ice Cream

Mt. Pisgah Baptist Church, Brandon ✝ *Warren Gunn*

2 cups sugar
1 (14-ounce) can sweetened condensed
 milk
6 eggs, beaten
2 tablespoons vanilla

Pinch salt
1 pint heavy whipping cream
Milk
Ice
Rock salt

Combine sugar, condensed milk and eggs. Add vanilla and salt; mix thoroughly. Add whipping cream (don't beat or whip cream) and mix thoroughly. Strain into freezer can. Fill freezer can with milk to "fill level" (¾ full). Freeze with ice and rock salt until ice cream sets.

Lemon Delight

Canaan Baptist Church, Purvis ✝ *Gloria Steele*

1ST LAYER:

1 cup all-purpose flour
1 stick margarine, softened

½ cup chopped nuts

Combine all ingredients and spread in a 9x13-inch pan. Bake at 350° for 15 minutes; cool.

2ND LAYER:

1 (8-ounce) package cream cheese,
 softened
1 cup powdered sugar

⅔ (8-ounce) carton Cool Whip
 (reserve remaining for topping)

Beat cream cheese and powdered sugar together; stir in Cool Whip. Spread over cooled crust.

3RD LAYER:

1 (14-ounce) can condensed milk
¼ cup lemon juice

1 egg yolk, beaten

Combine all 3 ingredients and pour over 2nd layer. Top with reserved Cool Whip.

Banana Nut Bread

Calvary Baptist Church, Leakesville ✝ Mildred Stockstill

2 bananas, mashed with fork
⅔ cup brown sugar
⅓ cup white sugar
1½ tablespoons Crisco shortening

1 egg, beaten
1 cup chopped walnuts or pecans
1 tablespoon vanilla
1⅔ cups self-rising flour

Preheat oven to 350°. Combine bananas, sugars, Crisco, egg, nuts and vanilla; mix well. Add flour and mix well. Spread batter in a treated loaf pan (or divide between 12 treated mini-muffin cups) and bake about 50 minutes (18 to 20 minutes for mini muffins).

Calvary Baptist Church

Leakesville

23303 Highway 63 North
Leakesville, MS 39451
601-394-4516

Greg Hillman, Pastor

Calvary Baptist Church in Leakesville, with 85 members at present, was founded 18 years ago and is a thriving congregation. The adults and children of the congregation attend all sermons together; the children are not separated during worship services. The children at Calvary Baptist Church are able to recite numerous Bible verses and have a deep understanding of scriptures. Pastor Greg Hillman believes recent changes in this country are unacceptable in a church setting. He does not believe catering to people and turning a blind eye will save any souls. The Calvary Baptist Church building was once a factory many years ago. The church is under construction at present. Upgrades will include a new school. Calvary is also working to start a bus ministry.

Banana Bread

Robinhood Baptist Church, Brandon ✝ *Peggy Ann Cooke*

2 or 3 bananas, mashed
1 cup sugar
1 cup self-rising flour
2 eggs, beaten

1 stick margarine, melted
2 tablespoons milk
½ cup chopped pecans or raisins

Mix ingredients together and pour into a greased and floured loaf pan. Bake at 325° for 1 hour.

Apple Bread

Providence Baptist Church, Amory ✝ *Nan Taylor*

1½ cups all-purpose flour
½ cup sugar
2 teaspoons baking powder
½ teaspoon cinnamon
¼ teaspoon salt
⅛ teaspoon nutmeg
1 cup chopped apples
½ cup milk
¼ cup oil
1 egg, beaten
½ cup chopped nuts (optional)

In a medium bowl, mix together dry ingredients. Stir in apples; set aside. In a small bowl, combine milk, oil and egg until blended. Add to dry ingredients; stir just until moistened. Pour into greased loaf pan and bake at 350° for 45 to 50 minutes.

Potato Doughnuts

Rhymes Baptist Church, Lucedale ✝ *In memory of Jean McCleery*

1 cup mashed potatoes
1 cup milk
2 eggs, beaten
¼ teaspoon cinnamon
¼ teaspoon ginger
3 teaspoons baking powder
3 to 4 cups flour, divided
Oil for frying
Sugar and cinnamon to taste for dusting

Combine potatoes, milk, eggs, cinnamon and ginger; mix well. Add baking powder to 3 cups flour; add to potato mixture. Mix well. Add additional flour, as needed, to make a soft dough. Roll out and cut into doughnuts. Deep fry until golden brown. Dust immediately with cinnamon/sugar mixture.

Catalog of Churches

*Then Jesus declared, "I am the bread of life. He who comes to me will never go hungry, and he who believes in me will never be thirsty." —*JOHN 6:25

Antioch Baptist Church

2350 Highway 43 South
Brandon, MS 39042
601-546-2464
www.antiochbaptistbrandon.org

Ashland Baptist Church

173 Church Street
Ashland, MS 38603

Dr. Gerald Hodges, Pastor

Auburn Baptist Church

1138 Road 931
Tupelo, MS 38804
662-842-5638
www.auburnbaptistchurch.org

Jimmy Henry, Pastor

Bethel Baptist Church

10 Bill Windham Road
Heidelberg, MS 39439
601-428-7167

Wayne Johnson, Pastor

Bethel Missionary Baptist Church

725 Bethel Church Road
Seminary, MS 39479
601-722-4833

Kevin Sanford, Pastor

Big Creek Baptist Church

28 Big Creek Church Road
Soso, MS 39480
601-763-8100
www.bigcreeksoso.com

Justin Rhodes, Pastor

Calvary Baptist Church

23303 Highway 63 North
Leakesville, MS 39451
601-394-4516

Greg Hillman, Pastor

Calvary Baptist Church

405 North Jackson Street
Starkville, MS 39759
662-323-1448
www.facebook.com/Calvary-Baptist- Church

Dr. Grant Arinder

Calvary Missionary Baptist Church

1239 Highway 471
Brandon, MS 39042
601-825-2864

Adair Jernigan, Pastor

Canaan Baptist Church

34 Elliott Circle
Purvis, MS 39475
601-436-0664

Bro. Mickey Steele, Pastor

Carmel Baptist Church

1157 Carmel New Hope Road
Monticello, MS 39654
601-587-7145

Cash Baptist Church

1716 Cash Road
Lena, MS 39094

Community Missionary Baptist

886 Barth Road
Poplarville, MS 39470

Bill Cameron, Pastor

Corinth Baptist Church

207 Church Road
Magee, MS 39111
601-849-2795

Fairfield Baptist Church

942 Moselle Seminary Road
Moselle, MS 39459
601-752-6366

Bro. Brad Brownlee, Pastor

Farmington Baptist Church

84 County Road 106A
Corinth, MS 38834
662-286-8855
www.farmingtonbaptistchurch.com

Jarrod Cox, Pastor

First Baptist Church, Baldwyn

500 South Fourth Street
Baldwyn, MS 38824
662-365-5201
www.FBCBaldwyn.com

Brother Stanley Huddleston, Pastor

First Baptist Church, Brookhaven

200 East Monticello Street
Brookhaven, MS 39601
601-833-5118
www.fbcbrookhaven.org

Greg Warnock, Pastor

First Baptist Church, Byhalia

2555 Church St.
Byhalia, MS 38611
662-838-2250
www.facebook.com/firstbaptistbyhalia

Stuart Swicegood, Pastor

First Baptist Church, Eupora

520 West Fox Avenue
Eupora, MS 39744
662-258-3491
www.fbceupora.com

Travis Gray, Pastor

First Baptist Church, Greenville

407 Main Street
Greenville, MS 38701
662-334-9452
www.fbcgreenville.net

Dr. James L. Nichols, Jr. Pastor

First Baptist Church, Grenada

450 Faith Drive
Grenada, MS 38901
662-226-3661

First Baptist Church, Indianola

202 Catchings Avenue
Indianola, MS 38751
662-887-2241
www.facebook.com/fbcindianola

Dr. Guy Burke, Pastor

First Baptist Church, Morton

80 Church Street
Morton, MS 39117
601-732-8941
www.facebook.com/First-Baptist-Church-
    Morton-MS

First Baptist Church, Orange Grove

15486 Orange Grove Road
Gulfport, MS 39503
228-832-2991 • www.fbcorangegrove.com

Christopher Flynn, Pastor

First Baptist Church, Wiggins

219 Second Street North
Wiggins, MS 39577
601-928-5226
www.fbcwiggins.org

Franklin Creek Baptist Church

11505 Independence Road
Moss Point, MS 39562
228-475-3471

Ralph Smith, Pastor

Freedom Baptist Church

519 Highway 365 South
Burnsville, MS 38833
662-423-8373

Bobby Elliott, Pastor

Golden Central Baptist Church

13 Red Bay Road
Golden, MS 38847
662-454-7144
www.facebook.com/Central-Baptist-Church

Goss Baptist Church

20 Mark McArthur Drive
Columbia, MS 39429
601-736-9563
gossbaptist@att.net

Mark McArthur, Pastor

Iuka Baptist Church

105 West Eastport Street
Iuka, MS 38852
662-423-5246
www.iukabaptist.com

Johnny Hancock, Pastor

Journey Baptist Church

7139 Commerce Drive
Olive Branch, MS 38654
662-892-8047
www.journeybaptistchurch.com

Jarrett Jamieson, Pastor

Liberty Baptist Church

2807 Highway 37
Raleigh, MS 39153
601-467-9224
www.facebook.com/Liberty.BC

Rich Ables, Pastor

Liberty Baptist Church

485 Old Highway 84 Road
Waynesboro, MS 39367
601-735-2597

Phillip Gandy, Pastor

Magnolia Baptist Church

148 King Road
Hattiesburg, MS 39402
601-264-8087
www.magnoliabaptistms.com

Greg Medenwald, Pastor

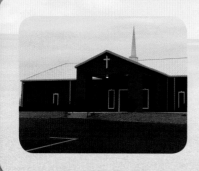

Midway Baptist Church

2206 Howell Tanner Chapel Road
Lucedale, MS 39452
601-947-6877
www.facebook.com/midway.baptist.lucedale

Phillip Snodgrass, Pastor

Mount Helm Baptist Church

300 East Church Street
Jackson, MS 39202
601-353-3981
www.mthelm.org

CJ Rhodes, Pastor

Mt. Pisgah Baptist Church

251 Old Highway 43
Brandon, MS 39047
601-825-2887
www.mtpisgahbrandon.com

New Bethel Baptist Church

11681 Highway 488
Philadelphia, MS 39350
601-656-2301
www.facebook.com/NewBethelSbc

New Zion Baptist Church

12023 New Zion Road
Crystal Springs, MS 39059
601-892-1246

Webb Armstrong, Pastor

North Columbia Baptist Church

1527 North Main Street
Columbia, MS 39429
601-736-8635
www.ncbcms.org

Dr. Joe Wiggins, Pastor

Oak Grove Missionary Baptist Church

14170 Highway 98
Lucedale, MS 39452
601-947-2803
www.oakgrovemissionarybaptist.org

Oakland Baptist Church

2959 Oak Ridge Road
Vicksburg, MS 39183
601-638-6724

Palestine Baptist Church

730 County Route 598
Nettleton, MS 38862
662-963-2078
www.facebook.com/pbcnettleton

Parkway Baptist Church

802 North Frontage Road
Clinton, MS 39056
601-924-9912
www.pbcclinton.org

Ken Anderson, Pastor

Pearson Baptist Church

151 South Pearson Road
Pearl, MS 39208
601-939-3618
www.pbclife.org

Calvin Williams, Pastor

Pelahatchie Baptist Church

300 Church Street
Pelahatchie, MS 39145
601-854-8809

Guy Hughes, Pastor

Pleasant Home Baptist Church

386 Matthews Road
Laurel, MS 39443
601-729-2230

Reverend Eric Bean, Pastor

Providence Baptist Church

1311 Highland Drive
Amory, MS 38821
662-256-3623

Redemption Church

4401 Park Ten Drive
Diamondhead, MS 39525
228-380-0690
www.facebook.com/RedemptionChurchDmhd

Rehobeth Baptist Church

446 Rehobeth Road
Pelahatchie, MS 39145
601-941-0817

Rhymes Missionary Baptist Church

1056 Lamar Street
Lucedale, MS 39452

Bro. Dale Dean, Pastor

Robinhood Baptist Church

1451 Old Lake Road
Brandon, MS 39042
601-825-0975

David McNeill, Pastor

Russell Baptist Church

1844 Highway 11 And 80
Meridian, MS 39301
601-482-3577
www.russellbaptist.org

Steve Taylor, Pastor

Shady Grove Baptist Church

14146 Highway 26 West
Lucedale, MS 39452
601-947-3546
www.shadygrovebaptistlife.org

Shady Grove Missionary Baptist Church

251 County Road 141
Tishomingo, MS 38873
662-660-3357 or 256-460-9241

Brother Mike Smith, Pastor

South Green Baptist Church

3185 South Green Street
Tupelo, MS 38801
662-842-8447
Facebook: South-Green-Baptist-Church

Guyton Hinds, Pastor

Star Baptist Church

301 Mangum Drive
Star, MS 39167
601-845-2736
starbaptistchurch.org

Sunrise Baptist Church

353 Midway Road
Carthage, MS 39051
601-741-2225
www.sunrisebc.net

Brother David Addy, Pastor

Tate Baptist Church

1201 N. Harper Road
Corinth, MS 38834
662-286-2935

Mickey Trammel, Pastor

Temple Baptist Church

5220 Old Highway 11
Hattiesburg, MS 39402
601-450-3000
www.tbclife.net

Dr. Darryl Craft, Pastor

Toxish Baptist Church

1841 Toxish Road
Pontotoc, MS 38863
662-489-5839

Paul Childress, Pastor

Union Ridge Baptist Church

1765 Union Ridge Road
Noxapater, MS 39346
662-803-9385
www.facebook.com/Union-Ridge-Baptist-Church

Greg Thomas, Pastor

Unity Baptist Church

236 Highway 49
McHenry, MS 39561
228-861-4536
www.facebook.com/unitybaptistchurch.mchenry

Neil Tapp, Pastor

Vardaman Street Baptist Church

334 South Vardaman Street
Wiggins, MS 39577
www.vardamanstreet.org
601-928-3943

Walnut Grove Baptist Church

1906 South Adams Street
Fulton, MS 38843

White Hill Missionary Baptist Church

1987 South Eason Boulevard • Tupelo, MS 38802
662-842-3738 • www.whitehillmbc.org
www.facebook.com/white-hill-baptist-church

Reverend Jeffery B. Daniel, Pastor

Williamsville Baptist Church

16995 Williamsville Road
Kosciusko, MS 39090
662-289-4294

Junior Davis, Pastor

Woodland Baptist Church

3033 Ridge Road
Columbus, MS 39705
662-327-6689
www.woodlandonline.org

Shelby Hazzard, Pastor

Yellow Leaf Baptist Church

50 County Road 435
Oxford, MS 38655
662-234-5116
www.yellowleafbc.com

Zion Hill Baptist Church

8081 Martinsville Road
Wesson, MS 39191
601-643-5145

Brother Tom McCormick, Pastor

Index of Churches

A

Amory
Providence Baptist Church 225

Antioch Baptist Church 63
Blueberry Salad 63
Squash Delight Casserole 91

Ashland
Ashland Baptist Church 137

Ashland Baptist Church 137
Broccoli Salad 68
Chicken and Dumplin's 137
Lemon Ice Box Cake 198
Shrimp Dip 25

Auburn Baptist Church 191
Meatloaf 145
Mexican Dip 15
Mrs. Bailey's Strawberry Cake 191
Roasted New Potatoes with Herbs 111
Seafood Gumbo 57

B

Baldwyn
First Baptist Church of Baldwyn 70

Bethel Baptist Church, Heidelberg 199
Chicken Spaghetti Casserole 130
Chocolate Chess Pie 171
Cream Cheese Pound Cake 202
Fantasy Fudge 226
Fruit Dip 24
Kathy's Pecan Pie 168
Mexican Pinwheels 29
Microwave Party Mix 44
Mini Meatloaves 146
Moist 'n Creamy Coconut Cake 199
Sweet Trash 44
Texas Hash 153

Bethel Missionary Baptist Church, Seminary 92
Party Cheese Ball 32
Potato Soup 52
Shrimp Dip 25
Squash Dressing 92
Swiss Bliss 156
White Wine Cake 189

Big Creek Baptist Church 110
Hash Brown Casserole 110
White Chocolate Bread Pudding 217

Brandon
Antioch Baptist Church 63
Calvary Missionary Baptist
Church 34
Mt. Pisgah Baptist Church 42
Robinhood Baptist Church 179

Brookhaven
First Baptist Church 164

Burnsville
Freedom Baptist Church 188

Byhalia
First Baptist Byhalia 31

C

Calvary Baptist Church,
Leakesville 232
Banana Nut Bread 232
Texas Millionaires 224

Calvary Baptist Church,
Starkville 123
Cheese Ring 33
Pasta Salad 77
Poppy Seed Chicken 123
Turtle Delight 224

Calvary Missionary Baptist Church,
Brandon 34
Brownies 212
Chicken & Spinach Quiche 139
Sausage Balls 34
Taco Soup 47

Canaan Baptist Church 210
Apple Carrot Raisin Salad 71
Broccoli Salad 67
Chess Squares 213
Lemon Delight 231
Oatmeal Cookies 210

Carmel Baptist Church 117
Cream Cheese Pound Cake 203
Homecoming Chicken Dressing 117
Smoked Oyster Dip 26
Sweet Potato Casserole 87

Carthage
Sunrise Baptist Church 126

Cash Baptist Church 158
Beef Tips 158
Chinese Slaw 71
Ritz Cracker Snacks 43

Clinton
Parkway Baptist Church 80

Columbia
Goss Baptist Church 106
North Columbia Baptist Church 206

Columbus
Woodland Baptist Church 104

Community Missionary Baptist 147
Creamed Corn 103
Meatloaf 147
Shrimp Salad 77

Corinth
Farmington Baptist Church 172
Tate Baptist Church 21

Corinth Baptist Church 201
Cheese Straws 43
Old-Fashioned Pound Cake 201
Orange Salad 64
Squash Casserole 93

Crystal Springs
New Zion Baptist Church 41

Diamondhead
Redemption Church 161

Eupora
First Baptist Church 155

Fairfield Baptist Church 69
Abbie's Fruit Cake 208
Broccoli Salad 69
Ms. Maggie Black's Hash Brown
Casserole 111

Farmington Baptist Church 172
Buffalo Chicken Dip 18
Honey Bars 215
Peanut Butter Bacon Pie 172
Slow Cooker Lasagna 142
Squash Dressing 91
Strawberry Romaine Salad 82
Sweet Potato Casserole 87

First Baptist Church, Baldwyn 70
Christmas Crunch Salad 70
Pineapple Cake 195
Shrimp Casserole 166
Sweet and Sour Cabbage 95

**First Baptist Church,
Brookhaven 164**
Angel Lush with Pineapple 229
Crawfish with Rice 164
Lemon Cream Cheese Pound
Cake 202
Mexican Fiesta Dip 15
Roquefort Pear Salad 61
Sesame Snap Beans 98

First Baptist Church, Byhalia 31
Cheese Ball 31
Corn Pudding 103
Scallopine di Pollo 121
White Chili 58

First Baptist Church, Eupora 155
Chess Pie 171
Crescent Sausage Squares 33
Edith Oliver's Caramel Pie 173
Italian Steak 156
Saucy Cocktail Franks 40
Upside Down Pizza 155

**First Baptist Church,
Greenville 182**
A Lotta Guacamole 17
Butterscotch Bundt Cake 182
Cheese Grits with Rotel Tomatoes 116
Corn Chowder 54
FBC Greenville Chicken Casserole 131

First Baptist Church, Grenada 94
Cabbage Casserole 94
Hot Ham Sandwiches 37
Poppy Seed Chicken 122
Potato Soup 52
Strawberry Pretzel Salad 62

First Baptist Church, Indianola 170
Chocolate Pie with Meringue 170

First Baptist Church, Morton 221
Fruit Pizza 209
Pineapple Casserole 221
Seven Layer Salad 83

First Baptist Church, Orange Grove 76
Cajun Shrimp Pasta Salad 76
Poppy Seed Chicken 124
Strawberry Short Cake 193

First Baptist Church, Wiggins 27
Cornbread Salad 73
Crab Dip 27
Venison or Beef Roast 160

Franklin Creek Baptist Church 132
Chicken Casserole 132

Freedom Baptist Church 188
Cabbage Casserole 151
Muscadine Cake 188
Potato Casserole 107

Fulton
Walnut Grove Baptist Church 175

G
Golden
Golden Central Baptist Church 14

Golden Central Baptist Church 14
Chicken Fajita Potatoes 134
Crescent Chicken Roll-ups 129
Easy Taco Soup 47
Mother's Hot Dip 14
Mother's Strawberry Cake 190
Pineapple Cheese Ball 30
Taco Salad Catalina 84

Goss Baptist Church 106
Dorito Salad 81
Kate's Potato Chip Chicken 130
Potato Casserole 106
Sausage Balls 35

Greenville
First Baptist Church of Greenville 182

Grenada
First Baptist Church 94

Gulfport
First Baptist Church of Orange Grove 76

H
Hattiesburg
Magnolia Baptist Church 120
Temple Baptist Church 74

Heidelberg
Bethel Baptist Church 199

I
Indianola
First Baptist Church, Indianola 170

Iuka
Iuka Baptist Church 23

Iuka Baptist Church 23
Chicken Salad 79
Sour Cream Chicken 127
Spinach Dip 23

Jackson
Mount Helm Baptist Church 128

Journey Baptist Church 78
Buffalo Chicken Dip 18
Tastes Like Fresh Corn 103
Turkey, Rice, Fruit Salad 78
White Chicken Lasagna 141

Kosciusko
Williamsville Baptist Church 66

Laurel
Pleasant Home Baptist Church 99

Leakesville
Calvary Baptist Church 232

Lena
Cash Baptist Church 158

Liberty Baptist Church, Raleigh 150
Cheeseburger Casserole 150
Indulgence 213
Vegetable Casserole 105

Liberty Baptist Church, Waynesboro 36
Baked Macaroni Casserole 115
Best Ham Sandwiches 37
Cheddar and Sausage Mini Muffins 36
Chicken Pie 138
Chicken Tortilla Soup 48
Hershey Bar Cake 187
Lasagna 143
Marinated Green Beans 98
Seasoned Crackers 43

Lucedale
Midway Baptist Church 214
Oak Grove Missionary Baptist Church 109
Rhymes Missionary Baptist Church 180
Shady Grove Baptist Church 204

Magee
Corinth Baptist Church 201

Magnolia Baptist Church 120
Artichoke Chicken Casserole 120
Boucan Cheese Dip 22
Brunch Cheese Grits 116
Simple Fruit Salad 61
Strawberry Cake 192

McHenry
Unity Baptist Church 102

Meridian
Russell Baptist Church 60

Midway Baptist Church 214
Cheese Cake Squares 214
Crawfish Bisque 56
One Pan Potatoes & Pepper Steak 154

Monticello
Carmel Baptist Church 117

Morton
First Baptist Church 221

Moselle
Fairfield Baptist Church 69

Moss Point
Franklin Creek Baptist Church 132

Mount Helm Baptist Church 128
Broccoli Rice Casserole 100
Brownie Bites 212
Fried Green Tomatoes with Bacon
    Vinaigrette and Warm Frisee 113
Garden Fresh Pasta Salad 75
Honey and Spiced Glazed
    Chicken 128
Mandarin Chicken Salad 81
Marinated Pork Chops with Herb
    Salsa 162
Pineapple Upside-Down Cake 196
Roasted Asparagus with Pine
    Nuts 100
Shrimp Dip 25
Slow Cookery Chili Cheese 20

Mt. Pisgah Baptist Church 42
Apricot Salad 64
Aunt Jewel's Tea Cakes 211
Blackberry Upside Down Cake 197
Blueberry Cream Cheese Pie 176
Caramel Pound Cake 205
Cheese Cookies 42
Cream of Chicken Soup 49
Easy Pineapple Pudding 220
Egg Custard Pie 174
4 Ingredient Butterscotch Cake 183
Grandmother Merle's Banana
    Pudding 219
Grover's Barbecue Sauce 162
Homemade Ice Cream 231
Italian Bread Salad 82
Marinated Baked Chicken 127
Old-Fashioned Meatloaf 146
Poppy Seed Chicken 122
Red Seedless Grape Salad 62
Scalloped Pineapple 229
Strawberry Supreme 230

Nettleton
Palestine Baptist Church 65

New Bethel Baptist Church 59
Brother Curt's Big Easy Chili 59

New Zion Baptist Church 41
Baked Asparagus Fries 101
Easy Apple Dumplings 216
Glazed Pineapple Kielbasa Bites 41
Roasted Cauliflower White Cheddar
    Soup 50
Slow Cooker Pulled Chicken 140

North Columbia Baptist Church 206
Chocolate Pound Cake 206
Easiest Chicken and Dumplings Ever,
   The 136
Gumbo 57
Orange Slice Cake 200

Noxapater
Union Ridge Baptist Church 55

**Oak Grove Missionary Baptist
   Church 109**
Chili Topped Potatoes 153
Mom's Potato Pancakes 109
3 Cheese Mac 'n Cheese 115

Oakland Baptist Church 86
Italian Spaghetti 149
Laura's Chicken 129
Spicy Stuffed Peppers 118
Sweet Potato Casserole 86

Olive Branch
Journey Baptist Church 78

Oxford
Yellow Leaf Baptist Church 46

Palestine Baptist Church 65
Fried Pies 178
LBJ Dip 20
Pistachio Fruit Salad 65
Pot Roast 160
Ranch Potatoes 108

Parkway Baptist Church 80
Chocolate Delight Cake 187
Crab Roll Ups 28
Easy Bolognese 149
Homemade Mac & Cheese 114
Poppy Seed Chicken Salad 80

Pearl
Pearson Baptist Church 228

Pearson Baptist Church 228
Chocolate Nut Cluster Candy 227
Granny's Crunch 228
Pound Cake 207

Pelahatchie
Pelahatchie Baptist Church 185
Rehobeth Baptist Church 53

Pelahatchie Baptist Church 185
Holiday Dressing 118
Onion Dip 22
Pecan Pie Cake 185
Seafood Bisque 56
Tricia's Crawfish Mexicala 165

Philadelphia
New Bethel Baptist Church 59

Pleasant Home Baptist Church 99
Chicken and Vegetable Casserole 133
Eggplant Casserole 95
Hot and Spicy Black-Eyed Peas 99
"No Sugar Added" Pecan Pie 168
Shrimp & Corn Chowder 54
Strawberry Cake with Strawberry
   Cream Cheese Icing 192
Stuffed Mushrooms 38
Velvet Nut Candy 226

Pontotoc
Toxish Baptist Church 19

Poplarville
Community Missionary Baptist 147

Providence Baptist Church 225
Apple Bread 233
New Yorkers 225
Old Time Chocolate Cake 186
Pecan Bites 223

Purvis
Canaan Baptist Church 210

R

Raleigh
Liberty Baptist Church 150

Redemption Church 161
Crawfish Pie 165
Russian Pot Roast 161

Rehobeth Baptist Church 53
Beef Casserole 151
Cheesy Ranch Potatoes 108
Elvis Presley Cake 194
Potato Chowder 53
Sausage Loaf 35
Taco Salad 84

Rhymes Missionary Baptist Church 180
Apple Cobbler 180
Potato Doughnuts 234

Robinhood Baptist Church 179
Banana Bread 233
Broccoli Salad 68
Chocolate Cake 186
Enchilada Casserole 152
Fresh Apple Cake 194
HoBo Dinner 151
Honey Hush Pie 169
Italian Beef 159
Jewish Pound Cake 207
Old Southern Pound Cake 205
Peach Cobbler 179
Potato Salad 67
Redneck Hors d' oeuvres 30
Strawberry Cake 190
Sylvia's Cornbread Cake 189
Tater Tot Casserole 154
Tomato Pie 112
Tortilla Cobbler 181

Russell Baptist Church 60
Beef Tips and Rice 159
Bread Pudding 218
Fruit Salad 60
Pineapple Cheesecake Pie 177
Slow Cooker Tater Tot Casserole 112

S

Seminary
Bethel Missionary Baptist Church 92

Shady Grove Baptist Church, Lucedale 204
Corn Dip 17
Sour Cream Pound Cake 204
Tookie's Sauerkraut Salad 72
Vanilla Wafer Cake 193
White Chicken Chili 58

Shady Grove Missionary Baptist Church, Tishomingo 222
Cauliflower-Broccoli-Raisin Salad 72
No Crust Egg Custard 222
Tangy Meatballs 144
Tostados 38

Soso
Big Creek Baptist Church 110

South Green Baptist Church 39
Chicken and Dumplings 136
Chicken Pot Pie 138
Corn Salad 73
Easy Baked Turkey 140
Fried Pies 178
Jalapeño Bites 39

Star
Star Baptist Church 96

Star Baptist Church 96
Black Bean Dip 16
Chicken Enchiladas 134
Hot Chicken Salad 79
White Chocolate Bread Pudding 217
Yummy Baked Beans 96

Starkville
Calvary Baptist Church 123

Sunrise Baptist Church 126
Baked Chicken 126
Candied Yams 88
Cornmeal Pie 174
Macaroni Salad 77
Polynesian Dip 24
VBS Tea Cakes 211

T

Tate Baptist Church 21
Baked Cheese Dip 21
Barbecued Pork Chops 163
Chocolate Chess Pie 171
Green Bean Casserole 97

Temple Baptist Church 74
Cheese Ball 32
Greek Pasta Salad 74
Spinach Tomato Tortellini 148

Tishomingo
Shady Grove Missionary Baptist Church 222

Toxish Baptist Church 19
Candied Yams 88
Cheese and Macaroni Casserole 114
Chicken Noodle Soup 49
Chicken Rotel Dip 19
Sweet Potato Pie 169

Tupelo
Auburn Baptist Church 191
South Green Baptist Church 39
White Hill Missionary Baptist Church 157

U

Union Ridge Baptist Church 55
Bacon-Wrapped Cocktails 40
Corn Chowder 55
Lasagna Grilled Cheese 144
Pecan Pie Trifle 223
Slow Cooker Green Beans 97

Unity Baptist Church 102
Corn Casserole 102
Family Pork Chops 163
Hot Seafood Dip 26
Potato Cheese Soup 51

V

Vardaman Street Baptist Church 90
Blueberry Buckle 215
Chocolate Chip Dessert Cheese
Ball 227
Greek Pasta Salad 75
Squash Dressing 90

Vicksburg
Oakland Baptist Church 86

W

Walnut Grove Baptist Church 175
Crab Delights 28
Lemonade Pie 175
Swedish Meatballs 145

Waynesboro
Liberty Baptist Church 36

Wesson
Zion Hill Baptist Church 135

**White Hill Missionary Baptist
Church 157**
Chicken Ranch Pinwheels 29
Loaded Chicken Soup 48
Steak Stir-Fry 157

Wiggins
Vardaman Street Baptist Church 90

Williamsville Baptist Church 66
Caramel Cake 184
Coca-Cola Salad 66
Slow Cooker Chicken and
Dressing 139

Woodland Baptist Church 104
Cheesy Potato Soup 51
Chicken Dip 20
Corn Casserole 104
Lasagna 142
Ooey Gooey Butter Cake 183

Y

Yellow Leaf Baptist Church 46
Brother Jerry's Veggie Beef Soup 46

Z

Zion Hill Baptist Church 135
Chicken Olé 135
Chicken String Bean Casserole 133
Juanita's Pound Cake 203
Pink Dip 22

Index of Recipes

A

Abbie's Fruit Cake 208
Almonds
  Chicken and Vegetable Casserole 133
  Chicken Salad 79
  Chinese Slaw 71
  FBC Greenville Chicken Casserole 131
  Green Bean Casserole 97
  Turkey, Rice, Fruit Salad 78
A Lotta Guacamole 17
Angel Lush with Pineapple 229
Appetizers *See also Dips*
  A Lotta Guacamole 17
  Bacon-Wrapped Cocktails 40
  Best Ham Sandwiches 37
  Cheddar and Sausage Mini Muffins 36
  Cheese Ball 31, 32
  Cheese Cookies 42
  Cheese Ring 33
  Cheese Straws 43
  Chicken Ranch Pinwheels 29
  Crab Delights 28
  Crab Roll Ups 28
  Crescent Sausage Squares 33
  Glazed Pineapple Kielbasa Bites 41
  Hot Ham Sandwiches 37
  Jalapeño Bites 39
  Mexican Pinwheels 29
  Microwave Party Mix 44
  Party Cheese Ball 32
  Pineapple Cheese Ball 30
  Redneck Hors d'oeuvres 30
  Ritz Cracker Snacks 43
  Saucy Cocktail Franks 40
  Sausage Balls 34, 35
  Sausage Loaf 35
  Seasoned Crackers 43
  Stuffed Mushrooms 38
  Sweet Trash 44
  Tostados 38

Apples
  Apple Bread 233
  Apple Carrot Raisin Salad 71
  Apple Cobbler 180
  Broccoli Salad 67
  Caramel Apple Cake 184
  Easy Apple Dumplings 216
  Easy Baked Turkey 140
  Fresh Apple Cake 194
  Fried Pies 178
  Sweet and Sour Cabbage 95
  Tortilla Cobbler 181
Apricot Salad 64
Artichokes
  Artichoke Chicken Casserole 120
  Scallopine di Pollo 121
Asparagus
  Baked Asparagus Fries 101
  Roasted Asparagus with Pine Nuts 100
Aunt Jewel's Tea Cakes 211
Avocados
  A Lotta Guacamole 17
  Mexican Fiesta Dip 15
  Roquefort Pear Salad 61

B

Bacon
  Bacon-Wrapped Cocktails 40
  Baked Cheese Dip 21
  Boucan Cheese Dip 22
  Broccoli Salad 67, 68, 69
  Brussels Sprouts with Bacon 93
  Cauliflower-Broccoli-Raisin Salad 72
  Cheese Ball 31
  Cheesy Ranch Potatoes 108
  Chicken Ranch Pinwheels 29
  Chicken Tortilla Soup 48
  Cornbread Salad 73
  Fried Green Tomatoes with Bacon Vinaigrette
      and Warm Frisee 113

Green Bean Casserole 97
Loaded Chicken Soup 48
Marinated Green Beans 98
Peanut Butter Bacon Pie 172
Ranch Potatoes 108
Seven Layer Salad 83
Slow Cooker Green Beans 97
Slow Cooker Tater Tot Casserole 112
Venison or Beef Roast 160
Yummy Baked Beans 96
Baked Asparagus Fries 101
Baked Cheese Dip 21
Baked Chicken 126
Baked Macaroni Casserole 115
Bananas
　Banana Bread 233
　Banana Nut Bread 232
　Fruit Salad 60
　Grandmother Merle's Banana Pudding 219
　Mandarin Chicken Salad 81
　New-Fashioned Banana Pudding 219
Bar Cookies
　Cheese Cake Squares 214
　Chess Squares 213
　Honey Bars 215
　Indulgence 213
Barbecue
　Barbecued Pork Chops 163
　Grover's Barbecue Sauce 162
　Mini Meatloaves 146
　Slow Cooker Pulled Chicken 140
Beans
　Black Bean Dip 16
　Brother Curt's Big Easy Chili 59
　Brother Jerry's Veggie Beef Soup 46
　Chicken and Vegetable Casserole 133
　Chicken Olé 135
　Chicken String Bean Casserole 133
　Chicken Tortilla Soup 48
　Chili Topped Potatoes 153
　Easy Taco Soup 47
　Green Bean Casserole 97

Marinated Green Beans 98
Sesame Snap Beans 98
Slow Cooker Green Beans 97
Taco Salad 84
Taco Soup 47
Tostados 38
White Chicken Chili 58
White Chili 58
Yummy Baked Beans 96
Beef *See also Meatballs, Meatloaf, Roasts, Sausage, Steak*
　Beef Casserole 151
　Beef Tips 158
　Beef Tips and Rice 159
　Brother Curt's Big Easy Chili 59
　Brother Jerry's Veggie Beef Soup 46
　Cabbage Casserole 151
　Cheeseburger Casserole 150
　Chili Topped Potatoes 153
　Dorito Salad 81
　Easy Bolognese 149
　Easy Taco Soup 47
　Eggplant Casserole 95
　Enchilada Casserole 152
　HoBo Dinner 151
　Italian Spaghetti 149
　Lasagna 143
　Mexican Dip 15
　Slow Cooker Lasagna 142
　Slow Cooker Tater Tot Casserole 112
　Slow Cookery Chili Cheese 20
　Taco Salad 84
　Taco Salad Catalina 84
　Taco Soup 47
　Tater Tot Casserole 154
　Texas Hash 153
　Upside Down Pizza 155
Best Ham Sandwiches 37
Bisque
　Crawfish Bisque 56
　Seafood Bisque 56
Black Bean Dip 16
Blackberry Upside Down Cake 197

Blueberries
  Blueberry Buckle 215
  Blueberry Cream Cheese Pie 176
  Blueberry Salad 63
  Fruit Pizza 209
  Granny's Crunch 228
Boucan Cheese Dip 22
Bread *See also Cornbread, Sandwiches*
  Apple Bread 233
  Banana Bread 233
  Banana Nut Bread 232
  Bread Pudding 218
  Cheeseburger Casserole 150
  Chicken Ranch Pinwheel 29
  Cornbread Salad 73
  Crab Delights 28
  Crab Roll Ups 28
  Crescent Chicken Roll-ups 129
  Crescent Sausage Squares 33
  Italian Bread Salad 82
  Mexican Pinwheels 29
  Pineapple Casserole 221
  Sausage Loaf 35
  Scalloped Pineapple 229
  Spinach Dip 23
  Upside Down Pizza 155
  White Chocolate Bread Pudding 217
Broccoli
  Broccoli Rice Casserole 100
  Broccoli Salad 67, 68, 69
  Cauliflower-Broccoli-Raisin Salad 72
  Christmas Crunch Salad 70
  Garden Fresh Pasta Salad 75
Brother Curt's Big Easy Chili 59
Brother Jerry's Veggie Beef Soup 46
Brownies
  Brownie Bites 212
  Brownies 212
Brunch Cheese Grits 116
Brussels Sprouts with Bacon 93
Buckle, Blueberry 215
Buffalo Chicken Dip 18
Butterscotch
  4 Ingredient Butterscotch Cake 183
  Butterscotch Bundt Cake 182

C

Cabbage
  Cabbage Casserole 94, 151
  Chinese Slaw 71
  Swedish Meatballs 145
  Sweet and Sour Cabbage 95
  Tookie's Sauerkraut Salad 72
Cajun Shrimp Pasta Salad 76
Cakes *See also Pound Cakes*
  Abbie's Fruit Cake 208
  Angel Lush with Pineapple 229
  Blackberry Upside Down Cake 197
  Butterscotch Bundt Cake 182
  Caramel Apple Cake 184
  Caramel Cake 184
  Chocolate Cake 186
  Chocolate Delight Cake 187
  Elvis Presley Cake 194
  4 Ingredient Butterscotch Cake 183
  Fresh Apple Cake 194
  Hershey Bar Cake 187
  Lemon Ice Box Cake 198
  Moist 'n Creamy Coconut Cake 199
  Mother's Strawberry Cake 190
  Mrs. Bailey's Strawberry Cake 191
  Muscadine Cake 188
  Old Time Chocolate Cake 186
  Ooey Gooey Butter Cake 183
  Orange Slice Cake 200
  Pecan Pie Cake 185
  Pineapple Cake 195
  Pineapple Upside-Down Cake 196
  Strawberry Cake 190, 192
  Strawberry Cake with Strawberry Cream
    Cheese Icing 192
  Strawberry Short Cake 193
  Sylvia's Cornbread Cake 189
  Vanilla Wafer Cake 193
  White Wine Cake 189
Candied Yams 88
Candy
  Chocolate Nut Cluster Candy 227
  Fantasy Fudge 226
  New Yorkers 225

Pecan Bites 223
Texas Millionaires 224
Velvet Nut Candy 226
Caramel
Caramel Apple Cake 184
Caramel Cake 184
Caramel Pound Cake 205
Edith Oliver's Caramel Pie 173
Turtle Delight 224
Carrots
Apple Carrot Raisin Salad 71
Beef Tips 158
Chicken Pot Pie 138
Corn Chowder 54
Potato Soup 52
Pot Roast 160
Russian Pot Roast 161
Cauliflower
Cauliflower-Broccoli-Raisin Salad 72
Christmas Crunch Salad 70
Roasted Cauliflower White Cheddar Soup 50
Steamed Cauliflower and Cheese Sauce 89
Cheddar and Sausage Mini Muffins 36
Cheese and Macaroni Casserole 114
Cheese Ball 31, 32
Cheese Ball, Chocolate Chip Dessert 227
Cheese Ball, Party 32
Cheese Ball, Pineapple 30
Cheeseburger Casserole 150
Cheese Cake Squares 214
Cheese Cookies 42
Cheese Grits with Rotel Tomatoes 116
Cheese Ring 33
Cheese Straws 43
Cheesy Potato Soup 51
Cheesy Ranch Potatoes 108
Cherries
Abbie's Fruit Cake 208
Apricot Salad 64
Coca-Cola Salad 66
Fruit Pizza 209
Rice Pudding with Cherries 220
Chess Pie 171
Chess Squares 213

Chicken
Artichoke Chicken Casserole 120
Baked Chicken 126
Buffalo Chicken Dip 18
Chicken and Dumplings 136
Chicken and Dumplin's 137
Chicken and Vegetable Casserole 133
Chicken Casserole 132
Chicken Dip 20
Chicken Enchiladas 134
Chicken Fajita Potatoes 134
Chicken Noodle Soup 49
Chicken Olé 135
Chicken Pie 138
Chicken Pot Pie 138
Chicken Ranch Pinwheels 29
Chicken Rotel Dip 19
Chicken Salad 79
Chicken Spaghetti Casserole 130
Chicken & Spinach Quiche 139
Chicken String Bean Casserole 133
Chicken Tortilla Soup 48
Corn Chowder 54, 55
Country Fried Chicken 125
Cream of Chicken Soup 49
Crescent Chicken Roll-ups 129
Easiest Chicken and Dumplings Ever, The 136
FBC Greenville Chicken Casserole 131
Gumbo 57
Homecoming Chicken Dressing 117
Honey and Spiced Glazed Chicken 128
Hot Chicken Salad 79
Kate's Potato Chip Chicken 130
Laura's Chicken 129
Loaded Chicken Soup 48
Mandarin Chicken Salad 81
Marinated Baked Chicken 127
Oven-Fried Chicken 125
Poppy Seed Chicken 122, 123, 124
Poppy Seed Chicken Salad 80
Scallopine di Pollo 121
Slow Cooker Chicken and Dressing 139
Slow Cooker Pulled Chicken 140
Sour Cream Chicken 127
White Chicken Chili 58
White Chicken Lasagna 141
White Chili 58

Chili
  Brother Curt's Big Easy Chili 59
  White Chicken Chili 58
  White Chili 58
Chili Topped Potatoes 153
Chinese Slaw 71
Chocolate
  Brownie Bites 212
  Brownies 212
  Chocolate Cake 186
  Chocolate Chess Pie 171
  Chocolate Chip Dessert Cheese Ball 227
  Chocolate Cobbler 181
  Chocolate Delight Cake 187
  Chocolate Nut Cluster Candy 227
  Chocolate Pie with Meringue 170
  Chocolate Pound Cake 206
  Fantasy Fudge 226
  Hershey Bar Cake 187
  Honey Hush Pie 169
  Indulgence 213
  New Yorkers 225
  Old Time Chocolate Cake 186
  Sweet Trash 44
  Texas Millionaires 224
  Turtle Delight 224
  Velvet Nut Candy 226
  White Chocolate Bread Pudding 217
Chowders
  Corn Chowder 54, 55
  Potato Chowder 53
  Shrimp & Corn Chowder 54
Christmas Crunch Salad 70
Cobbler
  Apple Cobbler 180
  Chocolate Cobbler 181
  Peach Cobbler 179
  Tortilla Cobbler 181
Coca-Cola Salad 66
Coconut
  Butterscotch Bundt Cake 182
  Chocolate Cake 186
  Coconut Pie 173
  Honey Hush Pie 169
  Jewish Pound Cake 207

Moist 'n Creamy Coconut Cake 199
Mrs. Bailey's Strawberry Cake 191
Orange Slice Cake 200
Simple Fruit Salad 61
Strawberry Cake 190
Sweet Potato Casserole 87
Turkey, Rice, Fruit Salad 78
Vanilla Wafer Cake 193
Cookies See also Bar Cookies
  Aunt Jewel's Tea Cakes 211
  Cheese Cake Squares 214
  Chess Squares 213
  Honey Bars 215
  Oatmeal Cookies 210
  VBS Tea Cakes 211
Corn
  Beef Casserole 151
  Black Bean Dip 16
  Brother Jerry's Veggie Beef Soup 46
  Chicken and Vegetable Casserole 133
  Chicken Tortilla Soup 48
  Chili Topped Potatoes 153
  Corn Casserole 102, 104
  Corn Chowder 54, 55
  Corn Dip 17
  Corn Pudding 103
  Corn Salad 73
  Crawfish Bisque 56
  Creamed Corn 103
  Easy Taco Soup 47
  Seafood Bisque 56
  Shrimp & Corn Chowder 54
  Taco Soup 47
  Tastes Like Fresh Corn 103
Cornbread
  Cornbread Salad 73
  Corn Casserole 104
  Holiday Dressing 118
  Homecoming Chicken Dressing 117
  Slow Cooker Chicken and Dressing 139
  Squash Dressing 90, 91, 92
  Sylvia's Cornbread Cake 189
Cornmeal Pie 174
Country Fried Chicken 125

Crabmeat
 Crab Delights 28
 Crab Dip 27
 Crab Roll Ups 28
 Gumbo 57
 Hot Seafood Dip 26
 Seafood Bisque 56
 Seafood Gumbo 57
Cracker Snacks, Ritz 43
Crackers, Seasoned 43
Cranberries
 Swedish Meatballs 145
 Tangy Meatballs 144
Crawfish
 Crawfish Bisque 56
 Crawfish Pie 165
 Crawfish with Rice 164
 Seafood Gumbo 57
 Tricia's Crawfish Mexicala 165
Cream Cheese Pound Cake 202, 203
Creamed Corn 103
Cream of Chicken Soup 49
Crescent Chicken Roll-ups 129
Crescent Sausage Squares 33
Custard
 Egg Custard Pie 174
 No Crust Egg Custard 222

D

Dates
 Mandarin Chicken Salad 81
 Orange Slice Cake 200
Desserts *See also Brownies, Cakes, Candies,*
       Cobblers, Cookies, Ice Cream, Pies
 Angel Lush with Pineapple 229
 Apple Bread 233
 Banana Bread 233
 Banana Nut Bread 232
 Chocolate Chip Dessert Cheese Ball 227
 Granny's Crunch 228
 Lemon Delight 231
 Pecan Bites 223
 Pecan Pie Trifle 223

Pineapple Casserole 221
Potato Doughnuts 234
Scalloped Pineapple 229
Strawberry Supreme 230
Turtle Delight 224
Dips
 A Lotta Guacamole 17
 Baked Cheese Dip 21
 Black Bean Dip 16
 Boucan Cheese Dip 22
 Buffalo Chicken Dip 18
 Chicken Dip 20
 Chicken Rotel Dip 19
 Corn Dip 17
 Crab Dip 27
 Fruit Dip 24
 Hot Seafood Dip 26
 LBJ Dip 20
 Mexican Dip 15
 Mexican Fiesta Dip 15
 Mother's Hot Dip 14
 Onion Dip 22
 Pink Dip 22
 Polynesian Dip 24
 Shrimp Dip 25
 Slow Cookery Chili Cheese 20
 Smoked Oyster Dip 26
 Spinach Dip 23
Dorito Salad 81
Doughnuts, Potato 234
Dressing
 Holiday Dressing 118
 Homecoming Chicken Dressing 117
 Slow Cooker Chicken and Dressing 139
 Squash Dressing 90, 91, 92
Dumplings
 Chicken and Dumplings 136
 Chicken and Dumplin's 137
 Easiest Chicken and Dumplings Ever, The 136
 Easy Apple Dumplings 216

E

Easiest Chicken and Dumplings Ever, The 136
Easy Apple Dumplings 216
Easy Baked Turkey 140
Easy Bolognese 149
Easy Pineapple Pudding 220
Easy Taco Soup 47
Edith Oliver's Caramel Pie 173
Egg Custard Pie 174
Eggplant Casserole 95
Elvis Presley Cake 194
Enchiladas
    Chicken Enchiladas 134
    Enchilada Casserole 152

F

Family Pork Chops 163
Fantasy Fudge 226
FBC Greenville Chicken Casserole 131
4 Ingredient Butterscotch Cake 183
Fresh Apple Cake 194
Fried Green Tomatoes with Bacon Vinaigrette
        and Warm Frisee 113
Fried Pies 178
Fruit *See also specific fruit*
    Abbie's Fruit Cake 208
    Angel Lush with Pineapple 229
    Fried Pies 178
    Fruit Dip 24
    Fruit Pizza 209
    Fruit Salad 60
    Pistachio Fruit Salad 65
    Simple Fruit Salad 61
    Turkey, Rice, Fruit Salad 78
Fudge, Fantasy 226

G

Garden Fresh Pasta Salad 75
Gelatin
    Apricot Salad 64
    Coca-Cola Salad 66
    Mother's Strawberry Cake 190
    Mrs. Bailey's Strawberry Cake 191
    Orange Salad 64

Glazed Pineapple Kielbasa Bites 41
Grandmother Merle's Banana Pudding 219
Granny's Crunch 228
Grapes
    Broccoli Salad 69
    Chicken Salad 79
    Fruit Pizza 209
    Red Seedless Grape Salad 62
Greek Pasta Salad 74, 75
Green Bean Casserole 97
Grits
    Brunch Cheese Grits 116
    Cheese Grits with Rotel Tomatoes 116
Grover's Barbecue Sauce 162
Guacamole, A Lotta 17
Gumbo
    Gumbo 57
    Seafood Gumbo 57

H

Ham
    Best Ham Sandwiches 37
    Hot Ham Sandwiches 37
    Potato Chowder 53
    Redneck Hors d'oeuvres 30
Hash Brown Casserole 110
Hershey Bar Cake 187
HoBo Dinner 151
Holiday Dressing 118
Homecoming Chicken Dressing 117
Homemade Ice Cream 231
Homemade Mac & Cheese 114
Honey
    Honey and Spiced Glazed Chicken 128
    Honey Bars 215
    "No Sugar Added" Pecan Pie 168
Honey Hush Pie 169
Hot and Spicy Black-Eyed Peas 99
Hot Chicken Salad 79
Hot Ham Sandwiches 37
Hot Seafood Dip 26

I

Ice Cream
  Homemade Ice Cream 231
  Strawberry Ice Cream 230
  Turtle Delight 224
Indulgence 213
Italian Beef 159
Italian Bread Salad 82
Italian Spaghetti 149
Italian Steak 156

J

Jalapeño Bites 39
Jewish Pound Cake 207
Juanita's Pound Cake 203

K

Kate's Potato Chip Chicken 130
Kathy's Pecan Pie 168

L

Lasagna
  Lasagna 142, 143
  Slow Cooker Lasagna 142
  White Chicken Lasagna 141
Lasagna Grilled Cheese 144
Laura's Chicken 129
LBJ Dip 20
Lemon
  Apricot Salad 64
  Lemonade Pie 175
  Lemon Cream Cheese Pound Cake 202
  Lemon Delight 231
  Lemon Ice Box Cake 198
  Scallopine di Pollo 121
Lemonade Pie 175
Loaded Chicken Soup 48

M

Macaroni *See also Pasta*
  Baked Macaroni Casserole 115
  Cheese and Macaroni Casserole 114
  Homemade Mac & Cheese 114
  Macaroni Salad 77
  3 Cheese Mac 'n Cheese 115
Macaroni Salad 77
Mandarin Chicken Salad 81
Marinated Baked Chicken 127
Marinated Green Beans 98
Marinated Pork Chops with Herb Salsa 162
Meatballs
  Lasagna Grilled Cheese 144
  Swedish Meatballs 145
  Tangy Meatballs 144
Meatloaf
  Meatloaf 145, 147
  Mini Meatloaves 146
  Old-Fashioned Meatloaf 146
Mexican Dip 15
Mexican Fiesta Dip 15
Mexican Pinwheels 29
Microwave Party Mix 44
Mini Meatloaves 146
Moist 'n Creamy Coconut Cake 199
Mom's Potato Pancakes 109
Mother's Hot Dip 14
Mother's Strawberry Cake 190
Mrs. Bailey's Strawberry Cake 191
Ms. Maggie Black's Hash Brown Casserole 111
Muffins
  Banana Nut Bread 232
  Cheddar and Sausage Mini Muffins 36
Muscadine Cake 188
Mushrooms
  Broccoli Rice Casserole 100
  Cheese and Macaroni Casserole 114
  Chicken Rotel Dip 19
  Laura's Chicken 129
  Scallopine di Pollo 121
  Stuffed Mushrooms 38
  Swiss Bliss 156
  Upside Down Pizza 155
  White Chicken Lasagna 141

N

New-Fashioned Banana Pudding 219
New Yorkers 225
No Crust Egg Custard 222
Noodles *See Pasta*
"No Sugar Added" Pecan Pie 168
Nuts *See also Almonds, Peanuts, Pecans, Walnuts*
  Apple Bread 233
  Blueberry Cream Cheese Pie 176
  Broccoli Salad 69
  Chocolate Cake 186
  Chocolate Nut Cluster Candy 227
  Fresh Apple Cake 194
  Honey Hush Pie 169
  Jewish Pound Cake 207
  Lemon Delight 231
  Microwave Party Mix 44
  Orange Slice Cake 200
  Roasted Asparagus with Pine Nuts 100
  Strawberry Cake 190
  Sweet Potato Casserole 87
  Sweet Trash 44
  Vanilla Wafer Cake 193
  Velvet Nut Candy 226
  White Wine Cake 189

O

Oatmeal Cookies 210
Oats
  Oatmeal Cookies 210
  Old-Fashioned Meatloaf 146
Okra
  Gumbo 57
  Spicy Fried Okra 105
Old-Fashioned Meatloaf 146
Old-Fashioned Pound Cake 201
Old Southern Pound Cake 205
Old Time Chocolate Cake 186

Olives
  Chicken Fajita Potatoes 134
  Greek Pasta Salad 74, 75
  Italian Bread Salad 82
  Mexican Fiesta Dip 15
  Mexican Pinwheels 29
  Pasta Salad 77
  Smoked Oyster Dip 26
  Taco Salad 84
One Pan Potatoes & Pepper Steak 154
Onion Dip 22
Ooey Gooey Butter Cake 183
Oranges
  Apricot Salad 64
  Fruit Dip 24
  Fruit Salad 60
  Mandarin Chicken Salad 81
  Orange Salad 64
  Orange Slice Cake 200
  Simple Fruit Salad 61
Oven-Fried Chicken 125
Oyster Dip, Smoked 26

P

Pancakes, Mom's Potato 109
Party Cheese Ball 32
Pasta
  3 Cheese Mac 'n Cheese 115
  Baked Macaroni Casserole 115
  Beef Tips and Rice 159
  Cajun Shrimp Pasta Salad 76
  Cheese and Macaroni Casserole 114
  Chicken Casserole 132
  Chicken Noodle Soup 49
  Chicken Spaghetti Casserole 130
  Chinese Slaw 71
  Easy Bolognese 149
  Garden Fresh Pasta Salad 75
  Greek Pasta Salad 74, 75
  Homemade Mac & Cheese 114
  Italian Spaghetti 149
  Lasagna 142, 143
  Macaroni Salad 77
  Pasta Salad 77

Scallopine di Pollo 121
Shrimp Salad 77
Slow Cooker Lasagna 142
Spinach Tomato Tortellini 148
Tricia's Crawfish Mexicala 165
White Chicken Lasagna 141
Peaches
  Blueberry Salad 63
  Fruit Salad 60
  Peach Cobbler 179
Peanut Butter
  Chocolate Nut Cluster Candy 227
  New Yorkers 225
  Peanut Butter Bacon Pie 172
Peanuts
  Chocolate Nut Cluster Candy 227
  Sweet Trash 44
Pears
  Abbie's Fruit Cake 208
  Roquefort Pear Salad 61
Peas
  Brother Jerry's Veggie Beef Soup 46
  Chicken Pot Pie 138
  Hot and Spicy Black-Eyed Peas 99
Pecans
  Abbie's Fruit Cake 208
  Banana Nut Bread 232
  Bread Pudding 218
  Broccoli Salad 67, 68, 69
  Brownies 212
  Caramel Apple Cake 184
  Caramel Pound Cake 205
  Cheese Ball 31, 32
  Cheese Cookies 42
  Cheese Ring 33
  Chocolate Chess Pie 171
  Chocolate Chip Dessert Cheese Ball 227
  Coca-Cola Salad 66
  Elvis Presley Cake 194
  Fantasy Fudge 226
  Granny's Crunch 228
  Hershey Bar Cake 187
  Indulgence 213
  Kathy's Pecan Pie 168
  Mrs. Bailey's Strawberry Cake 191

"No Sugar Added" Pecan Pie 168
Party Cheese Ball 32
Pecan Bites 223
Pecan Pie Cake 185
Pecan Pie Trifle 223
Pineapple Cheese Ball 30
Pistachio Fruit Salad 65
Polynesian Dip 24
Poppy Seed Chicken Salad 80
Red Seedless Grape Salad 62
Ritz Cracker Snacks 43
Roquefort Pear Salad 61
Simple Fruit Salad 61
Strawberry Supreme 230
Sweet Potato Casserole 86
Sweet Trash 44
Sylvia's Cornbread Cake 189
Texas Millionaires 224
Turtle Delight 224
VBS Tea Cakes 211
Pepperoni
  Hot and Spicy Black-Eyed Peas 99
  Italian Bread Salad 82
Pies
  Blueberry Cream Cheese Pie 176
  Chess Pie 171
  Chicken Pie 138
  Chicken Pot Pie 138
  Chocolate Chess Pie 171
  Chocolate Pie with Meringue 170
  Coconut Pie 173
  Cornmeal Pie 174
  Crawfish Pie 165
  Edith Oliver's Caramel Pie 173
  Egg Custard Pie 174
  Fried Pies 178
  Honey Hush Pie 169
  Kathy's Pecan Pie 168
  Lemonade Pie 175
  "No Sugar Added" Pecan Pie 168
  Peanut Butter Bacon Pie 172
  Pineapple Cheesecake Pie 177
  Sweet Potato Pie 169
  Tomato Pie 112

Pineapple
  Abbie's Fruit Cake 208
  Angel Lush with Pineapple 229
  Blueberry Salad 63
  Candied Yams 88
  Chicken Salad 79
  Coca-Cola Salad 66
  Easy Pineapple Pudding 220
  Elvis Presley Cake 194
  Fruit Salad 60
  Glazed Pineapple Kielbasa Bites 41
  Granny's Crunch 228
  Mandarin Chicken Salad 81
  Orange Salad 64
  Pineapple Cake 195
  Pineapple Casserole 221
  Pineapple Cheese Ball 30
  Pineapple Cheesecake Pie 177
  Pineapple Upside-Down Cake 196
  Pistachio Fruit Salad 65
  Polynesian Dip 24
  Scalloped Pineapple 229
  Simple Fruit Salad 61
Pink Dip 22
Pistachio Fruit Salad 65
Pizza
  Fruit Pizza 209
  Upside Down Pizza 155
Polynesian Dip 24
Poppy Seed Chicken 122, 123
Poppy Seed Chicken Salad 80
Pork *See also Bacon, Sausage*
  Barbecued Pork Chops 163
  Family Pork Chops 163
  Marinated Pork Chops with Herb
    Salsa 162
  Russian Pot Roast 161
  Scallopine di Pollo 121

Potatoes
  Beef Casserole 151
  Cheesy Potato Soup 51
  Cheesy Ranch Potatoes 108
  Chicken Fajita Potatoes 134
  Chili Topped Potatoes 153
  Corn Chowder 54
  Hash Brown Casserole 110
  HoBo Dinner 151
  Loaded Chicken Soup 48
  Mom's Potato Pancakes 109
  Ms. Maggie Black's Hash Brown Casserole 111
  One Pan Potatoes & Pepper Steak 154
  Potato Casserole 106, 107
  Potato Cheese Soup 51
  Potato Chowder 53
  Potato Doughnuts 234
  Potato Salad 67
  Potato Soup 52
  Pot Roast 160
  Ranch Potatoes 108
  Roasted New Potatoes with Herbs 111
  Scalloped Potatoes 107
  Slow Cooker Tater Tot Casserole 112
  Tater Tot Casserole 154
Pot Roast 160
Pound Cakes
  Caramel Pound Cake 205
  Chocolate Pound Cake 206
  Cream Cheese Pound Cake 202, 203
  Jewish Pound Cake 207
  Juanita's Pound Cake 203
  Lemon Cream Cheese Pound Cake 202
  Old-Fashioned Pound Cake 201
  Old Southern Pound Cake 205
  Pound Cake 207
  Sour Cream Pound Cake 204
Pretzels
  Microwave Party Mix 44
  Strawberry Pretzel Salad 62
  Sweet Trash 44

Pudding
  Angel Lush with Pineapple 229
  Bread Pudding 218
  Butterscotch Bundt Cake 182
  Chocolate Cake 186
  Corn Pudding 103
  Easy Pineapple Pudding 220
  4 Ingredient Butterscotch Cake 183
  Grandmother Merle's Banana Pudding 219
  Hershey Bar Cake 187
  Indulgence 213
  Jewish Pound Cake 207
  Muscadine Cake 188
  New-Fashioned Banana Pudding 219
  No Crust Egg Custard 222
  Pistachio Fruit Salad 65
  Rice Pudding with Cherries 220
  Strawberry Cake 190
  Strawberry Short Cake 193
  White Chocolate Bread Pudding 217
  White Wine Cake 189

Q

Quiche, Chicken & Spinach 139

Raisins
  Abbie's Fruit Cake 208
  Apple Carrot Raisin Salad 71
  Bread Pudding 218
  Broccoli Salad 67, 68, 69
  Candied Yams 88
  Cauliflower-Broccoli-Raisin Salad 72
  Mandarin Chicken Salad 81
  Oatmeal Cookies 210
  Sweet Trash 44
Ranch Potatoes 108
Redneck Hors d'oeuvres 30
Red Seedless Grape Salad 62

Rice
  Artichoke Chicken Casserole 120
  Beef Tips and Rice 159
  Broccoli Rice Casserole 100
  Cabbage Casserole 151
  Chicken Olé 135
  Chicken String Bean Casserole 133
  Crawfish with Rice 164
  Eggplant Casserole 95
  FBC Greenville Chicken Casserole 131
  Homecoming Chicken Dressing 117
  Hot and Spicy Black-Eyed Peas 99
  Mexican Dip 15
  Poppy Seed Chicken 124
  Rice Pudding with Cherries 220
  Shrimp Casserole 166
  Spicy Stuffed Peppers 118
  Texas Hash 153
  Tricia's Crawfish Mexicala 165
  Turkey, Rice, Fruit Salad 78
Ritz Cracker Snacks 43
Roasted Asparagus with Pine Nuts 100
Roasted Cauliflower White Cheddar Soup 50
Roasted New Potatoes with Herbs 111
Roasts
  Italian Beef 159
  One Pan Potatoes & Pepper Steak 154
  Pot Roast 160
  Russian Pot Roast 161
  Venison or Beef Roast 160
Roquefort Pear Salad 61
Russian Pot Roast 161

S

Salads
  Apple Carrot Raisin Salad 71
  Apricot Salad 64
  Blueberry Salad 63
  Broccoli Salad 67, 68, 69
  Cajun Shrimp Pasta Salad 76
  Cauliflower-Broccoli-Raisin Salad 72
  Chicken Salad 79
  Chinese Slaw 71
  Christmas Crunch Salad 70
  Coca-Cola Salad 66
  Cornbread Salad 73
  Corn Salad 73
  Dorito Salad 81
  Fruit Salad 60
  Garden Fresh Pasta Salad 75
  Greek Pasta Salad 74, 75
  Hot Chicken Salad 79
  Italian Bread Salad 82
  Macaroni Salad 77
  Mandarin Chicken Salad 81
  Orange Salad 64
  Pasta Salad 77
  Pistachio Fruit Salad 65
  Poppy Seed Chicken Salad 80
  Potato Salad 67
  Red Seedless Grape Salad 62
  Roquefort Pear Salad 61
  Seven Layer Salad 83
  Shrimp Salad 77
  Simple Fruit Salad 61
  Strawberry Pretzel Salad 62
  Strawberry Romaine Salad 82
  Taco Salad 84
  Taco Salad Catalina 84
  Tookie's Sauerkraut Salad 72
  Turkey, Rice, Fruit Salad 78
Salsa
  Chicken Fajita Potatoes 134
  Kate's Potato Chip Chicken 130
  Marinated Pork Chops with Herb Salsa 162
  Mexican Pinwheels 29
  Pink Dip 22
  Tostados 38

Sandwiches
  Best Ham Sandwiches 37
  Hot Ham Sandwiches 37
Saucy Cocktail Franks 40
Sauerkraut
  Swedish Meatballs 145
  Tookie's Sauerkraut Salad 72
Sausage
  Bacon-Wrapped Cocktails 40
  Cheddar and Sausage Mini Muffins 36
  Corn Chowder 55
  Crescent Sausage Squares 33
  Glazed Pineapple Kielbasa Bites 41
  Gumbo 57
  Lasagna 142
  LBJ Dip 20
  Saucy Cocktail Franks 40
  Sausage Balls 34, 35
  Sausage Loaf 35
  Spicy Stuffed Peppers 118
  Upside Down Pizza 155
Scalloped Pineapple 229
Scalloped Potatoes 107
Scallopine di Pollo 121
Seafood *See also Crabmeat, Crawfish, Shrimp*
  Gumbo 57
  Hot Seafood Dip 26
  Seafood Bisque 56
  Seafood Gumbo 57
  Smoked Oyster Dip 26
Seasoned Crackers 43
Sesame Snap Beans 98
Seven Layer Salad 83
Shrimp
  Cajun Shrimp Pasta Salad 76
  Gumbo 57
  Pasta Salad 77
  Seafood Bisque 56
  Seafood Gumbo 57
  Shrimp Casserole 166
  Shrimp & Corn Chowder 54
  Shrimp Dip 25
  Shrimp Salad 77
Simple Fruit Salad 61
Slaw, Chinese 71

Slow Cooker Chicken and Dressing 139
Slow Cooker Green Beans 97
Slow Cooker Lasagna 142
Slow Cooker Pulled Chicken 140
Slow Cooker Tater Tot Casserole 112
Slow Cookery Chili Cheese 20
Smoked Oyster Dip 26
Soups *See also Bisques, Chili, Chowders*
   Brother Jerry's Veggie Beef Soup 46
   Cheesy Potato Soup 51
   Chicken Noodle Soup 49
   Chicken Tortilla Soup 48
   Cream of Chicken Soup 49
   Easy Taco Soup 47
   Gumbo 57
   Loaded Chicken Soup 48
   Potato Cheese Soup 51
   Potato Soup 52
   Roasted Cauliflower White Cheddar
      Soup 50
   Seafood Gumbo 57
   Taco Soup 47
Sour Cream Chicken 127
Sour Cream Pound Cake 204
Spicy Fried Okra 105
Spicy Stuffed Peppers 118
Spinach
   Chicken & Spinach Quiche 139
   Spinach Dip 23
   Spinach Tomato Tortellini 148
   White Chicken Lasagna 141
Squash
   Squash Casserole 93
   Squash Delight Casserole 91
   Squash Dressing 90, 91, 92
Steak
   Beef Tips 158
   Italian Steak 156
   One Pan Potatoes & Pepper Steak 154
   Steak Stir-Fry 157
   Swiss Bliss 156
Steamed Cauliflower and Cheese Sauce 89
Stir-Fry, Steak 157

Strawberries
   Cheese Ring 33
   Fruit Pizza 209
   Fruit Salad 60
   Mother's Strawberry Cake 190
   Mrs. Bailey's Strawberry Cake 191
   Strawberry Cake 190, 192
   Strawberry Cake with Strawberry Cream
      Cheese Icing 192
   Strawberry Ice Cream 230
   Strawberry Pretzel Salad 62
   Strawberry Romaine Salad 82
   Strawberry Short Cake 193
   Strawberry Supreme 230
Stuffed Mushrooms 38
Swedish Meatballs 145
Sweet and Sour Cabbage 95
Sweet Potatoes
   Candied Yams 88
   Pot Roast 160
   Sweet Potato Casserole 86, 87
   Sweet Potato Pie 169
Sweet Trash 44
Swiss Bliss 156
Sylvia's Cornbread Cake 189

T

Taco
   Easy Taco Soup 47
   Taco Salad 84
   Taco Salad Catalina 84
   Taco Soup 47
Tangy Meatballs 144
Tastes Like Fresh Corn 103
Tater Tot Casserole 154
Tea Cakes, Aunt Jewel's 211
Tea Cakes, VBS 211
Texas Hash 153
Texas Millionaires 224
3 Cheese Mac 'n Cheese 115
Tomatoes with Bacon Vinaigrette and Warm
      Frisee, Fried Green 113
Tomato Pie 112
Tookie's Sauerkraut Salad 72

Tortellini, Spinach Tomato 148
Tortillas
  Chicken and Dumplin's 137
  Chicken Enchiladas 134
  Chicken Ranch Pinwheels 29
  Crab Roll Ups 28
  Easiest Chicken and Dumplings Ever, The 136
  Enchilada Casserole 152
  Mexican Pinwheels 29
  Tortilla Cobbler 181
Tostados 38
Tricia's Crawfish Mexicala 165
Trifle, Pecan Pie 223
Turkey
  Easy Baked Turkey 140
  Lasagna 142
  Slow Cooker Tater Tot Casserole 112
  Turkey, Rice, Fruit Salad 78
Turtle Delight 224

U

Upside Down Cake, Blackberry 197
Upside-Down Cake, Pineapple 196
Upside Down Pizza 155

V

Vanilla Wafer Cake 193
VBS Tea Cakes 211

Vegetables *See also specific vegetable*
  Brother Jerry's Veggie Beef Soup 46
  Chicken and Vegetable Casserole 133
  Vegetable Casserole 105
Velvet Nut Candy 226
Venison
  Old-Fashioned Meatloaf 146
  Venison or Beef Roast 160

W

Walnuts
  Banana Nut Bread 232
  Butterscotch Bundt Cake 182
  Fantasy Fudge 226
Water Chestnuts
  Artichoke Chicken Casserole 120
  Hot Chicken Salad 79
  Laura's Chicken 129
  Spinach Dip 23
  Squash Casserole 93
White Chicken Chili 58
White Chicken Lasagna 141
White Chili 58
White Chocolate Bread Pudding 217
White Wine Cake 189

Y

Yams, Candied 88
Yummy Baked Beans 96

Your Favorite Recipes

These pages are included to encourage you to record your favorite recipes... a recipe handed down through generations of your family, the recipe for that dish that is always the first to go at the church supper or potluck dinner, or a new favorite you want to save and pass down.

Recipe name: _____

From: _____

Ingredients: _____

_____

_____

_____

Directions: _____

_____

_____

_____

_____

_____

_____

_____

Recipe name:_____

From:_____

Ingredients: _____

_____

_____

_____

Directions: _____

_____

_____

_____

_____

_____

_____

_____

_____

_____

_____

Recipe name:_____

From:_____

Ingredients: _____

_____

_____

_____

Directions: _____

_____

_____

_____

_____

_____

_____

_____

_____

_____

_____

Recipe name:_____

From:_____

Ingredients: _____

_____

_____

_____

Directions: _____

_____

_____

_____

_____

_____

_____

_____

_____

_____

_____

Recipe name:_____

From:_____

Ingredients:_____

_____

_____

_____

Directions:_____

_____

_____

_____

_____

_____

_____

_____

_____

_____

_____

Recipe name:_____

From:_____

Ingredients:_____

_____

_____

_____

Directions:_____

_____

_____

_____

_____

_____

_____

_____

_____

_____

Recipe name: _____

From: _____

Ingredients: _____

_____

_____

_____

Directions: _____

_____

_____

_____

_____

_____

_____

_____

_____

_____

It's So Easy to Cook Food Your Family will Love

This cookbook series features easy-to-afford, easy-to-prepare recipes for feeding your family. *Kitchen Memories Cookbook* is a cookbook, memory book, and activity book—all in one—making it so easy to spend time with your family making fun kitchen memories of your own. *Family Favorite Recipes* is a collection of recipes handed down through three generations of outstanding cooks. You will find easy recipes using ingredients you probably already have on hand so you can feed your family fast…and deliciously.

EACH: $18.95 • 256 pages • 7x10 • paperbound • full-color

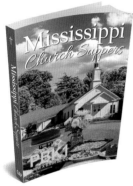

Mississippi Church Suppers Makes a Great Gift

It is available at many of the churches included in this book. If you can't find it locally, call 1-888-854-5954 or visit us on-line at www.GreatAmericanPublishers.com to order.

$21.95 • 288 pages • 7x10 • paperbound • full-color

Don't miss out on our upcoming titles—join our Cookbook Club and you'll be notified of each new edition.

www.GreatAmericanPublishers.com • toll-free 1-888-854-5954

- -